OUTPERFORMING THE MARKET
Everyone's Guide to High-Profit, Low-Risk Investing

John F. Merrill

McGraw-Hill

New York • San Francisco • Washington, D.C. • Auckland • Bogotá
Caracas • Lisbon • London • Madrid • Mexico City • Milan
Montreal • New Delhi • San Juan • Singapore
Sydney • Tokyo • Toronto

Library of Congress Cataloging-in-Publication Data

Merrill, John F.
  Outperforming the market: everyone's guide to high-profit, low-risk investing / John F. Merrill.
    p.   cm.
  Includes bibliographical references and index.
  ISBN 0-07-041979-5
  1. Portfolio management.   2. Investment analysis.   3. Stock exchanges.   I. Title
HG4529.5.M47 1998
332.6—DC21   98-13950
                                                                          CIP

McGraw-Hill

A Division of The McGraw-Hill Companies

Special thanks is given to the following for permission to use their material in the preparation of this book:

© Computed using data from *Stocks, Bonds, Bills & Inflation 1997 Yearbook*^{TM}, Ibbotson Associates, Chicago (annually updates work by Robert G. Ibbotson and Rex Sinquefield). Used with permission. All rights reserved.

Excerpts from *Wall $treet Week with Louis Rukeyser*, Maryland Public Television, Owings Mills, Maryland. Permission granted.

1 2 3 4 5 6 7 8 9 0 DOC/DOC 9 0 2 1 0 9 8 7

ISBN 0-07-041979-5

The sponsoring editor for this book was Stephen Isaacs, the editing supervisor was John M. Morriss, and the production supervisor was Suzanne W. B. Rapcavage.

Printed and bound by R. R. Donnelley & Sons Company.

This publication is designed to provide accurate and authoritative information in regard to the subject matter covered. It is sold with the understanding that the publisher is not engaged in rendering legal, accounting, or other professional service. If legal advice or other expert assistance is required, the services of a competent professional person should be sought.

—From a Declaration of Principles jointly adopted by a Committee of the American Bar Association and a Committee of Publishers.

McGraw-Hill books are available at special quantity discounts to use as premiums and sales promotions, or for use in corporate training programs. For more information, please write to the Director of Special Sales, McGraw-Hill, 11 West 19th Street, New York, NY 10011. Or contact your local bookstore.

This book is printed on recycled, acid-free paper containing a minimum of 50% recycled de-inked fiber.

Table of Contents

Acknowledgments

This book would not have been possible without a lot of encouragement and hard work by many people. My clients, associates and friends were all instrumental in different ways.

My associate, John Goott, was especially supportive of this effort early on and stayed steadfastly behind it all the way through. My right-hand for over 16 years, Debra Courson, provided the necessary backup to keep everything running smoothly at the office and therefore allow me the time to write. The most instrumental person has been Gwyn Welsh. She dedicated herself to this project for more than a year, providing countless hours of research, computer data evaluations and day-to-day organization of the manuscript. I also owe a great deal of the credit to Bridgett Akin for graphic design.

My beloved Patti, a dream come true, supplied inspiration and sustenance as needed. My two boys, Brian and Brady, were not only supportive, they also made life around the home conducive to this working sabbatical. My mother, Galva Merrill and my sister, Connie Snowden, were extremely encouraging, while providing good common sense.

Numerous friends and clients became personally involved in reviewing one or more chapters for content and clarity. Especially helpful were Bert Rosenbaum, Michael Yackira, Jonathan Kagan, Tom Pazera, Victor Lamanuzzi, Baker Mitchell, Chuck Bracht, Don Ward, Bruce Golubock, Fred Mitchell, John Creed, Ann Clinton, David Lampe, Bill Phillips, Milton Gray, Melinda Van Paasschen, Margaret Meaden, Ed Williamson, Eileen Black, Sharon Dodson and Mark Grenader.

John F. Merrill

Introduction

Information, Knowledge and Noise

Over the past decade, there has been a major shift in responsibility for your retirement from Big Business and Big Government to YOU. This change in responsibility has substantially increased the public's interest in investments. This has not been lost on the media.

Media coverage of the stock market, bonds, currencies, mutual funds, interest rates and all things financial has exploded in the past 5-10 years. Much of this is good. The media does an outstanding job of providing timely and authoritative information that may have only been circulated around Wall Street 15 years ago.

On the other hand, information is not the same as knowledge. It is important to distinguish between the two. Hundreds of pieces of new information may not impart one new bit of knowledge. Knowledge is *understanding* the information and knowing what to discard and what few pieces add value to what is currently understood. New information without a proper context can be less than useful. It is just noise.

As we receive the lion's share of our financial information from the media—print and broadcast—it is important to understand both the motives and goals behind financial reporting.

First and foremost, the financial media is no different than other media. Job number one is to maintain and increase readers and viewers. This forces their primary focus to be on *today*. It is in their interest to hook their audience on daily information (or weekly or monthly, depending on publishing or broadcasting dates). It is a huge challenge—to make each day's market activity seem meaningful.

Therefore, certain elements of the financial media have moved beyond the numbers and qualitative analysis to those aspects of human nature that will bring the audience back day-after-day, week-after-week. Herein lies the potential danger to your financial health.

Fear and Greed

One of the easiest ways to rope in an audience is by appealing to emotions. The market didn't rise—it *soared*! The market didn't decline—it *plunged*!

However, words alone would also get somewhat stale over time. To have the captivating effect desired, they must be tied to one of the two primal emotions of investors—fear or greed.

Greed is the harder of the two emotions to capture or stimulate by the traditional media. This particular emotion has been more broadly tapped by investment newsletters. Their allure is to let you in on something, to get the big bucks that only their subscribers get, to be privy to insights Wall Street would never want you to know, to take advantage of their closely guarded *black box* secret to financial success.

Hogwash. Study after study has proved that simple buy-and-hold strategies have greatly outperformed the investment newsletter industry over long periods of time (even more so after taxes and transaction costs).

Fear is the bigger emotional hook. This is the emotion that has proved to be far easier to tap for all of the financial media. Studies have shown that investors are twice as emotional about a 20% loss as they are about a 20% gain in their investments.

Therefore, much of the financial media has taken on a negative or pessimistic tone. "Technical trends are scary." "Fundamentals are overvalued." "The cycle is turning negative." "Public enthusiasm is speculative." "Downside risk is growing." "How much farther can these positive earnings continue?" Etc., etc., etc....

The Game

If emotions are the hook, then the market forecast is the game. The market forecast game is built around a dialog of bull and bear markets. Once set up, it seems axiomatic that the listener/reader would want to be **in** bull markets (greed) and **out** of bear markets (fear). Therefore, you need to keep up with their financial forecasts.

Actually, these are not the media's forecasts, but the forecasts of a parade of "experts." Most of the media prefers not to prepare its own analyses; that would not appear impartial. Worse, journalists and program hosts might be responsible for follow-up and evaluation of prior forecasts. So, most of the media brings in outside experts to provide market forecasts.

Most of these experts come from Wall Street brokerage firms. This works out well for both. The media needs experts in order to give credibility to the views expressed, so it is in the media's own interest to build up the reputations of its experts—even to *guru* status—so that their audiences feel privileged to get these insights and predictions. They rarely dwell on the expert's lousy market calls, choosing to sing the praises of his great ones instead. (Remember, a coin flip is right 50% of the time.) *Strict and thorough accountability would ruin the game—so it is ignored.*

An example will at least illustrate the point.

> One high profile Wall Street expert is the Chief Portfolio Strategist of a major Wall Street firm. He is often quoted in the press and interviewed on business news shows. He has been consistently *bearish* since 1991!
>
> In April 1991, for instance, this expert said that if the Dow Jones Industrial Average went above 3000, "it would be one of the great *sell* signals of all time."[1] Thousands of points higher, he was still bearish, still asked for his expert opinion and not too embarrassed to give it.

The next time you watch a business news show, notice that each expert must cooperate and play the game. "Are you a bull or a bear?" "Where will the market be in six months?" "What's your market forecast?"

In return, the expert and his firm get free advertising and the credibility of being referred to as an expert by a supposedly disinterested person. The expert's status is confirmed, his firm's prestige is enhanced, and perhaps the expert will get to tout some stocks for which his/her firm is interested in finding new buying power.

On a broader basis, all of Wall Street benefits from this game. Keep in mind that the real engine of Wall Street is *transactions*—buys and sells. The ongoing bull and bear game plays on greed and fear, which generates tickets (buys and sells). Wall Street is well aware that while long-term, buy-and-hold investors are not very profitable, *traders* are.

Therefore, the market forecast game is perfectly symbiotic. The media and Wall Street both win. It is the investor-turned-market-timer, trader or speculator who loses.

Wall Street will always be able to provide legions of very bright, articulate, well-educated, sincere experts who show complete confidence in their own forecasts, despite market history and their own past mistakes. At any point in time, some will be bullish and others will be bearish and both will be equally convincing.

Perhaps one day the Securities and Exchange Commission (SEC) will catch on to this game and enforce proper disclosure as it does with paid advertising. It would be nice to hear the following:

> *"The views expressed are the views of our guest and not that of this network. They may be unfounded, biased, self-serving and completely at odds with your long-term investment success. No due diligence on all past recommendations has been attempted."*

Or see this:

> *"Warning!! The following market analysis will likely be hazardous to your long-term investment strategy if acted upon. It is designed to motivate you to be a short-term trader (most of whom eventually fail) instead of a long-term investor (most of whom succeed)."*

You don't need daily, weekly or monthly market forecasts. They are a poor substitute for a long-term strategy, a well-designed portfolio and the patience and discipline to strictly apply them while avoiding the noise and excitement served up by the media.

This book will serve your long-term interests and be your ready antidote to the media's emotional noise.

Who Should Read This Book?

Outperforming the Market is written for long-term investors. It will have little value for market timers, active traders or speculators.

Based upon extensive new historical research, Outperforming the Market offers unique insights into the risks and rewards of all the major asset classes and, more importantly, complete portfolios of the most reliable of those asset classes. The objective is to provide you with all the tools and rationale for the structure of *your* best portfolio, the one most likely to provide the highest rate of return for your desired level of risk.

Outperforming the Market is intended for any investor who is interested in obtaining more knowledge of the investment process and particularly those seeking better long-term performance from their investments.

This book does not address the many related and important concepts that together provide a total financial plan. However, those financial planning issues which have a direct bearing on investment decisions are addressed. For example, this book shows how to calculate the maximum amount of income a retirement portfolio can provide under various market conditions and different inflation scenarios.

Although not written specifically for investment professionals, **financial planners, money managers and security brokers** will benefit greatly from the original research, dramatic portfolio illustrations and client-friendly analogies throughout the book.

Mutual Fund Focus

Mutual funds have been available to investors since the mid-1920s. In recent years, both individual and institutional investors have increasingly turned to mutual funds as their investment medium of choice.

This is partly the result of the many innovations in the buying, selling and holding of mutual funds. Mutual fund marketplaces first pioneered by Charles Schwab & Company, Inc. offer one custodial account for all funds. They typically offer fee-less and paperless trading, money market fund sweep privileges and electronic portfolio services, such as pricing, performance and tax accounting, all of which now allow mutual funds to be fully managed by individuals and institutions alike.

The end result: **managed portfolios of mutual funds.** Mutual funds are the stocks and bonds of today's portfolios.

For all these reasons, this book will use a mutual fund focus wherever relevant. It is believed that more readers will identify with the points and illustrations this way. However, most of the principles, concepts and illustrations are equally valid for portfolios of individual stocks and bonds.

Major Points Highlighted Throughout Text

The following symbols are placed in the margin next to major points in the text:

    Key Point

    Valuable New Research

Thoroughly Revised Version of *Beyond Stocks*

The author's first book on this subject is titled <u>Beyond Stocks</u>. <u>Outperforming the Market</u> updates all the financial numbers of the first book through the end of 1997. More importantly, this book presents the information in a user-friendly manner for the reader who has had little experience with investments.

Section I

Your
Wealth and Retirement
Portfolio

Overview
of Section I

Most investment professionals remain awed throughout their careers by the power of compounding returns. Maybe this is why Benjamin Franklin referred to it as the "eighth wonder of the world."

One aspect of compounding that never ceases to amaze is the magnified difference in wealth created by minuscule changes in rates of return over time. In this section, the impact of increasing rates of return will be taken one step further—to the bottom line. How does a change in the long-term rate of return of a portfolio increase or decrease the income the portfolio can provide during retirement?

This section also contains critical definitions of financial terms used throughout this book. These definitions are straightforward and easy to comprehend.

In addition, this section introduces the term used throughout this book to signify an investor's long-term investments—the **Wealth and Retirement Portfolio**. The importance of viewing all long-term investments as a single unit with singular performance is a critical step in developing a comprehensive approach to investing.

1

Seeing the Big Picture — Returns, Risk and *At Risk*

Many investors spend the majority of their time juggling their various investments in an attempt to gain a short-term advantage. Other investors are completely wrapped up in the attempt to avoid short-term market setbacks. All too often this preoccupation with individual investments or short-term risks ends up sidetracking investors from the big picture, their long-term retirement objectives. The best time spent on investments is that time taken to structure their entire portfolio. The sum is more important than the parts, and the long-term more important than today in reaching financial goals.

"A ship in port is safe, but that's not what ships are built for."
— Grace Murray Hopper, quoted by Roger von Oech, <u>A Kick in the Seat of the Pants</u>, Perennial Library: New York, 1986

The Sum is More Important than the Parts

In January of 1994, I had an appointment with a man I will call Mr. Smith. Mr. Smith, 55, had worked at Exxon for many years. A little more than two years before our meeting, Mr. Smith had elected early retirement. He received close to $500,000, which he rolled over into an IRA. He had been investing the money himself but was now interested in our money management services. He was currently acting as a consultant and did not plan to retire for about 10 years, at which time he would live off his portfolio.

After a few minutes of getting to know each other, he asked me how we had performed in 1993. I told him that our firm had a good year, and the average account was up over 20%.

He was silent for a moment, then he came back with, "I beat you guys. I made 26%!" Well, I was impressed, so I asked him what he had invested in. He responded with the names of two Fidelity funds. He was right, I knew they had done well.

"That's it?" I asked, a little incredulously. "You invested your half million dollar portfolio in two Fidelity funds?"

"Oh, heaven forbid!" he quickly responded. "I had about $15,000 in each."

"Okay," I queried. "Where did you invest the bulk of your portfolio to earn such a good return?"

"No, you don't understand," he said. "Those are my investments. The rest I keep in CDs so it won't be at risk….so it will be safe."

"King's X," I threw out. "The $500,000 is your investment portfolio. The 26% return on the small part of it you call your investments is of little importance. What is important is the total return of the entire portfolio. The size of your retirement income in 10 years is completely dependent on the return you achieve from the **total portfolio.**"

We spent a few minutes reviewing his rollover IRA papers and determined that his total return for 1993 on his investment portfolio was just a little over 6%! That was 1993's contribution to the financial quality of his retirement.

The Hodge-Podge Portfolio

Most investors acquire their individual investments over time in a somewhat seat-of-the-pants fashion. A certificate of deposit (CD) here, a mutual fund there, this municipal bond, that stock and so on.

Many such decisions are based upon what is **convenient** (local bank), what options are **available** (401(k)), what's **promoted** (broker-dealer) or what's **advertised** (mutual funds). Each institution disseminates financial data—but only about the securities held at that institution.

 Most investors are more or less like Mr. Smith. They don't look at their entire portfolio. Moreover, they don't <u>plan</u> their entire portfolio. As a result, they tend to follow and fret over the individual moves and short-term performance of each investment. This can easily cause excessive trading and bad decisions, or at the other end of the spectrum, a stagnant portfolio and no decisions at all.

The Big Picture

Do you know what your *entire* portfolio's return was last year...for the past five years...for the past ten years? Even most sophisticated investors do not have an accurate measurement of their total performance. And many investors who think they know how their portfolio is performing are seriously overestimating their overall results. A recent study showed that investors, on average, thought their portfolios were providing investment returns several percentage points greater than they actually were.

Do you know what your portfolio is currently worth? Do you have a computer program or ledger that contains a composite of all of your investments on one page? Do you update and evaluate it at least annually—as a portfolio, not a collection of individual investments? If you are like most individuals, you do not.

Your Wealth and Retirement Portfolio

The portfolio referred to here—and throughout the book—is your Wealth and Retirement Portfolio. This is your long-term portfolio, your wealth builder. This is the portfolio that may replace a substantial part of your income during retirement.

Your Wealth and Retirement Portfolio is made up of your "liquid investments," investments that are easily converted to cash, such as stocks, bonds, mutual funds, insurance cash values, certificates of deposit and mortgage notes.

It does not matter whether you own these investments directly or indirectly for portfolio management purposes. Directly owned investments are in your name or that of your spouse. Indirect ownership includes IRAs, company retirement and savings plans, trust accounts (of which you are a direct beneficiary) or any other portfolio assets that are earmarked for your future enjoyment and will be available for your retirement.

Your Wealth and Retirement Portfolio should *not* be broken into two periods—before retirement and after retirement. Economist Richard Thaler, a professor at the University of Chicago, pointed out in the September/October 1996 issue of Fee Advisor magazine, "People act like something magical happens on the day they retire, and it shrinks their (investment) time horizon to zero." Your investment time horizon should reach at least 30 years after retirement and perhaps well into the next generation of your heirs.

Defining Critical Terms

Before going any further, it is important that you have a quick reference to the precise meaning of certain critical terms as used throughout this book.

Definitions

RISK	Risk	Possibility of, or intensity of, a decline in market value
	Loss	A decline in value that is not recovered
	At Risk	The possibility of falling short of an investment objective
	Volatility	Large random swings in market value
	Fluctuation	Up and down movements in market values that are historically normal for a particular asset or set of assets
	Decline	Downturn in market value from a prior level
	Recovery	The period after a decline in which the market regains its former high value
REWARD	Advance	Upturn in market value from a prior level
	Return	Total Return - Includes all items of gain or loss, plus dividends and interest
	Riskless Rate of Return	The return from 30-day U.S. Treasury bills
	Reward	A measurement of the return above the riskless rate
	Performance	The risk and reward characteristics of an investment
ASSET CLASSES & POLICIES	Asset Class	Types of investments grouped together because they possess similar investment characteristics (see page 24 for a list of the major asset classes)
	Asset Class Families	Most asset classes can be grouped into three major families—stocks, bonds, cash
	Investment Policy	Establishes and maintains a specific weighting for each asset class family
	Asset Allocation Policy	Identifies the weighting for each individual asset class; the policy may require fixed weightings over time or call for a changing mix of asset classes
TIME	Short-Term	A period of less than 5 years
	Intermediate-Term	A period of between 5 and 15 years
	Long-Term	A period exceeding 15 years (easily encompassing most wealth building or retirement portfolios)

Definitions   (Continued)

MISCELLANEOUS	Wealth	Purchasing power
	SBBI	Stocks, Bonds, Bills & Inflation Yearbook, Ibbotson Associates, Chicago
	Market Capitalization (Cap)	The market cap of a particular stock is its total market value—the number of shares outstanding times the market price of each share
	Correlation	The degree with which the advances and declines of two separate investments parallel each other. Highly correlated assets tend to track each other's movements.

CHART 1-1

Just How Important are Rates of Return?

Let's return to my conversation with Mr. Smith, the retiree from Exxon. He wanted an idea of what level of retirement income he could expect from his portfolio. Using Chart A1-1 in the Appendix, we can estimate the income that his retirement portfolio will provide. A portion of this chart is shown in Chart 1-2.

As pointed out earlier, Mr. Smith's current portfolio experienced a rate of return of close to 6% the year prior to our discussion. If 6% were his average annual return for 40 years into the future (10 years until retirement plus 30 years after retirement), the chart indicates that Mr. Smith's retirement income in 10 years would be calculated as 6.6% of his current retirement portfolio. Applied to his $500,000 portfolio, this chart indicates that he would be able to take an annual income worth $33,000—in today's dollars—for 30 years ($500,000 x 6.6% = $33,000) after he retires fully in 10 years.

Note: Charts A1-1 through A1-6 in the Appendix will help calculate your retirement income from your current investments and from your 401(k) and/or other ongoing retirement contributions.

How Much Retirement Income Will Your Current Tax-Sheltered Account Provide?

Years to Retirement	*Average Annual Return on Your Investments*							
	5%	6%	7%	8%	9%	10%	11%	12%
10	5.2%	6.6%	8.1%	10.1%	12.4%	14.9%	18.0%	21.8%

(Inflation-Adjusted, Retirement Income as a Percentage of the Current Balance of Your Tax-Sheltered Retirement Account)

CHART 1-2
(from A1-1 in Appendix)

Note: In order to estimate future income from a portfolio, it is necessary to make certain assumptions:

- Inflation is assumed to be 3.0% per year (both before and after retirement).
- Retirement income will be adjusted annually by the increase in inflation.
- Retirement income will be paid out for 30 years before the investment principal is depleted.
- The long-term rate of return from a portfolio is constant both before and after retirement.

The point of this chart is to isolate one variable—the average annual rate of return on Mr. Smith's investments—and determine its impact on his retirement income. As we reviewed this chart together, **Mr. Smith was very surprised by the increase in his retirement income that just a one percent change in his average annual rate of return would make**.

For example, if Mr. Smith's portfolio were to provide an average return of 7%, his retirement income would increase to $40,500 per year in current dollars. An 8% portfolio return provides him $50,500 per year. *This is 50% more retirement income for a 2% increase in his portfolio rate of return.* A 9% return provides $62,000 per year, a 10% return provides $74,500 per year—more than *double* the retirement income of a 6% return!

The rewards of better investing are real and significant. Of course, Mr. Smith already knew he could take more risks in order to make higher returns than he had been making, but he had not understood the magnitude of change in his retirement income that comes from such small changes in his overall rate of return.

Which Financial Risk?

As presently constituted, Mr. Smith's portfolio might be thought of as very low risk. With a large investment in CDs, 94% of his portfolio is insulated from market declines. However, there is a different kind of risk to which this portfolio is more exposed. His portfolio appears to be *at risk* of not achieving the return necessary to support his present lifestyle during his retirement. Mr. Smith had suggested to me that his retirement needs would be about $50,000 per year (in today's buying power) at his retirement. For this objective, his current portfolio is highly *at risk* of falling far short of his needs.

Mr. Smith and I discussed changes to his current portfolio that would bring these two risks more into balance. If he could accept more short-term risk (intensity of portfolio declines), he could practically eliminate the risk of not meeting his long-term retirement income needs.

Mr. Smith was becoming motivated to seek a higher rate of return on his Wealth and Retirement Portfolio. Yet he well understood his sensitivity to risk. Both his fears and needs are disclosed by his concluding comments.

> "I want my portfolio as predictable as possible for the long term."

> "I want to keep my overall level of risk as low as possible — while still likely to achieve my retirement income objective."

> "I want to know the worst that can happen. How would another big bear market like 1973–'74 affect my portfolio and its ability to maintain my income throughout retirement?"

Notice that the goals are specific to Mr. Smith's personal needs. Success is measured in terms of reaching a stated long-term objective while minimizing risks along the way. This is so much more important than the elusive and fuzzy goals that most investors espouse, such as "maximizing my returns" or "beating the market." Either of these illusive goals may incur substantially more risk than an investor is willing to live with for a goal that is not meaningful to his or her own financial circumstances.

Conclusions

The key objectives of this chapter are:

- Put it all together. Assemble all of your long-term investments into one Wealth and Retirement Portfolio.

- Understand the significant difference that just a one percent difference in your average annual return will make in your available retirement income.

- Run your own race. Measure the performance of your Wealth and Retirement Portfolio (as one value) against your own established objective.

**You Only Have One Investment *Portfolio*
with Many Different Slices**

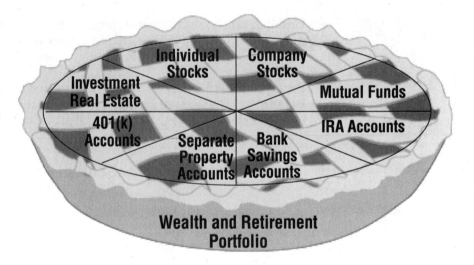

Bottom Line: It is the performance of the portfolio as a whole that really matters.

Section II

Financial Asset Classes

Overview of Section II

Are Investment Returns Predictable?

No. Investment returns cannot be forecast with precision either in the short run or long term. However, the range of returns that are highly probable becomes smaller and smaller as the time horizon increases. The chart below illustrates this point.

**The Longer Your Investment Horizon...
The Narrower the Range of Expected Returns**

Range of average annual returns over increasing holding periods

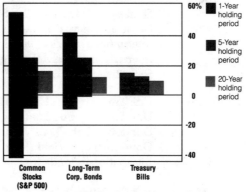

Source: © Computed using data from Stocks, Bonds, Bills & Inflation 1996 Yearbook™ with data updated January 1997, Ibbotson Associates, Chicago (annually updates work by Roger G. Ibbotson and Rex Sinquefield). Used with permission. All rights reserved.

One clear message of this chart is that investment returns become more predictable with time. A fundamental premise of this book is that investors with time horizons of 20 years or more should take full advantage of this tendency toward predictability in structuring their portfolios.

Asset Classes

Types of investments with similar characteristics are grouped together as asset classes. As a group, the securities within an asset class tend to react in the same way to economic or investment forces. It is critically important to understand the fundamentals of each of the alternative asset classes available to your portfolio, particularly the degree of risk taken in order to deliver its return. Your portfolio's mix of asset classes will be far more important in determining its performance than will be your selection of individual securities or mutual funds.[2]

In the broadest sense, there are three families of asset classes: common stocks, bonds and cash equivalents. The three asset class families are comprised of 13 separate asset classes that will be the focus of this section.

Asset Class Family	Asset Class
Stocks	Domestic Large Cap Stocks
	Domestic Mid/Small Cap Stocks
	Domestic Micro Cap Stocks
	International Stocks (Developed Country)
	International Stocks (Emerging Markets)
	Securitized Real Estate (REITs)
Bonds	U.S. Treasury Bonds - Intermediate Maturity
	U.S. Treasury Bonds - Long Maturity
	Domestic High-Quality Corporate Bonds
	Domestic High-Yield (Junk) Bonds
	International Bonds
Cash	U.S. Treasury Bills – 30-Day Maturity (equivalent to Money Market Accounts)
	Gold

Each asset class has provided the American investor with distinctly different long-term rewards and shorter term fluctuations. According to Mark Reipe, Vice President of Ibbotson Associates, "thirty years ago, nobody thought about small stocks versus large stocks, ...Your asset classes were stocks, bonds and cash. But as people collected more data, they found that those old categories masked a great deal of divergent performance." This section of the book will provide a discussion and evaluation of each of these liquid or tradable asset classes with the particular view of long-term inclusion in your Wealth and Retirement Portfolio.

2

The Impressive
Record of Domestic
Stocks

Domestic stocks, while volatile in the short-term, have been the most rewarding asset class family for U.S. investors over the long term. Events like the 1987 crash lead to the belief that the U.S. stock market is irrational, yet since 1802, long-term investors have enjoyed remarkably consistent long-term inflation-adjusted returns. U.S. equities are a critical component of the well-designed Wealth and Retirement Portfolio.

"The market itself really represents nothing more than a pendulum that swings back and forth through the median line of rationality. It spends very little time at the point of rationality and most of the time on one side or the other."
— Robert Kirby, Research Paper at the Institute of Chartered Financial Analysts (1976)

Long-Term Rationality

A basic characteristic of the stock market is that it is both rational and irrational at the very same time. The difference is simply the time period under the microscope.

Measured over long periods of time, the market value of common stocks exhibits very rational and rewarding behavior. Essentially, market values track corporate earnings (profits). For example, the earnings of the stocks that make up the S&P 500 Index were up 4,258% for the six decades ending 1995. The market value of shares of those companies were up 4,486% for those same sixty years. Good tracking, indeed.

Short-Term Irrationality

Comparing the performance of the stock market relative to the underlying earnings of its companies over much shorter time periods, however, may show little connection between the two. This is what makes the stock market so frustrating. Earnings often go up while stock prices go down and vice versa.

The short-term fluctuations of any company's stock price is in large part a result of market participants (investors) not knowing what the company's earnings will be looking ahead. Keep in mind that, while investors know today's earnings, they are investing based upon what they estimate will be the future earnings of the individual companies in which they choose to invest.

This estimating of corporate earnings is further complicated by interest rates. In theory, the value of a company's stock today is the discounted present value of all future earnings that could be paid out as dividends to the current owner. The discount rate is arbitrary, yet many, if not most market participants believe the best discount rate is the current interest rate for 30-year U.S. Treasury bonds. Therefore, stock prices also reflect changes in interest rates and *anticipated* changes in interest rates…more guesswork.

With all of its uncertainties, frustrations and erratic behavior, market participation draws on investors' emotions. At times, the ever-changing market psychology (the collective enthusiasm or pessimism of participants) goes to extremes. The outlook for future earnings (or interest rates) will reach heights or depths that become very detached from the more probable, mundane reality, meaning stock prices in the shorter term don't necessarily reflect the reality of their underlying earnings potential.

1987 Blow-off and Crash

An extreme example of the entire process was provided in one fairly recent calendar year—1987. January to August of 1987 experienced an outbreak of market "fever"—one of those occasional periods of over-exuberant market psychology. Market prices as measured by the S&P 500 Index bolted upward by over 23% in just that eight-month period. Meanwhile, corporate earnings were flat to down, and interest rates were rising rapidly (usually a depressant to stock market prices because higher rates cause a heftier discounting of future earnings).

The infamous crash of 1987 occurred in the three months of September through November when stock prices lost over 30% from their August highs.

Unfortunately, this is *not* a singular aberration. Such bull market exuberance followed by bear market depression has occurred many times over the market's long history. What was new, and very unnerving, was the one-day 22% decline in the Dow Jones Industrial Average market value in a single day!

The crash of 1987 has received a lot more attention than the exuberant upside blow-off that preceded it. In reality, the crash of 1987 was a correction of market psychology as much as it was a correction of market prices. Such corrections have a way of bringing market expectations back to earth.

It is interesting to view the full calendar year of 1987 as one piece of market history. For that 12 months, the S&P 500 index was up 5.2%. Reviewing changing stock prices for the year-as-whole, one might assume that the year was a yawner (not a goner) and that it had exhibited perfectly rational long-term behavior.

Long-Term Rewards

Despite episodes like 1987, domestic stocks have been a very rewarding asset class for U.S. shareholders over the long term. Stocks, Bonds, Bills & Inflation (SBBI), published annually by Ibbotson Associates, Chicago, Illinois, has become the financial industry's bible of historical information on domestic asset classes. According to SBBI, from the beginning of 1926 through the end of 1997, the average annual compounded return from the S&P 500 (and its predecessor index) has been 11.0%. Over that same period, inflation has averaged just 3.1% annually. Thus, U.S. stockholders have earned the remarkable real return of 7.9% per year since 1926. This is meaningful wealth creation...more than doubling the real value of a diversified portfolio of stocks every 10 years.

Better still, this appears to be the normal, long-term, real return for stocks. Jeremy Siegel, a professor at the University of Pennsylvania's Wharton School, completed an extensive study of the U.S. stock market back to the year 1801 in his book Stocks for the Long Run (1994). His major finding: stocks have delivered a relatively consistent 6½% to 7½% over inflation in virtually any long period of time.

The attraction of common stocks is the significant and consistent wealth creation they have historically provided. *Well, not quite.*

Going Forward

The true attraction of common stocks *today* is their prospect *going forward*. Will domestic stocks continue to provide long-term returns in the future that are in line with their consistent long-term returns of the past?

Obviously, there are no 100% guarantees, yet the future of the U.S. stock market is tied inevitably to the future of the U.S. economy. In the long run, they are basically one and the same. (The prospect of the global economy has had increasing influence on our domestic stock market, and this trend seems set to continue in the 21st century.)

Both the American economy and stock market have shown remarkable resilience and progress over the past 200 years. From an agrarian economy, through the industrial age, on into the services economy and now entering the information age, the American workplace has undergone many significant transformations. Yet with all the dislocations caused by these enormous changes—not to mention world wars, cultural revolutions and so forth—there has been amazingly consistent economic growth.

Why? **People and productivity.** The population of the U.S., like the balance of the world, has grown. Each person needs to be fed, clothed and sheltered. The total consumption of an expanding population is a strong impetus to growth in the economy.

Increasing productivity is what allows an economy to grow even faster than its population. For example, the phenomenal improvements in U.S. farming techniques is what allows 2% of the current U.S. population to provide all the agricultural products that it took almost 90% of the population to provide 200 years ago. New farm equipment, land management techniques, fertilizers and so forth have produced this seeming miracle.

Productivity encompasses all of the inventions, infrastructure, education and so forth that allows the average U.S. factory to put out 50 times as much goods per worker today as it did in 1900.[3] U.S. companies have done a truly commendable job of sharing that growth with both workers and shareholders.

Will the growth in the economy (and an ever higher stock market) continue? To believe otherwise is to believe that either population or productivity will not continue growing. Advancements in health and nutrition, as well as the wide global net of their dissemination, are but one reason to expect the population to keep enlarging.

As for productivity increases, it is difficult to make any credible case for a slowdown in new developments. As John Templeton and others have pointed out on many occasions, there are more scientists alive today than in all the balance of history *combined*. There is more money invested in non-military research and development today—by far—than in any other era. If anything, the world seems poised on the edge of major technological breakthroughs in areas like biotechnology, the Internet, education, robotics and on and on.

No one knows with any precision what the future will look like. But for investors who own a broad cross-section of U.S. stocks, crystal ball gazing is not necessary. To gain confidence that the long-term upward trend of the U.S. stock market will continue, one only needs to believe that the fundamentals of "people and productivity" are still in place.

This attribute of domestic common stocks makes them an ideal candidate for your Wealth and Retirement Portfolio. However, investing in stocks is by no means a free ride.

Drawback to Stocks

The drawback to common stocks is their susceptibility to large and frequent declines in market value.

These wide swings in market prices make stocks by themselves an inappropriate vehicle for most short-term funding goals. Money that will be needed in five years or less is taking on substantial risk of losing principal that cannot be recovered when invested solely in common stocks.

But most portfolios should include some portion of domestic stocks. What portion should be invested in stocks is discussed in Section III – "Asset Allocation Policies."

Market Capitalization

Domestic, publicly-traded stocks are separated into asset classes by "market capitalizations," the size of companies in total dollar value. The market capitalization (market cap) of a particular stock is simply its total market value—the number of shares outstanding times the market price of each share.

At year-end 1997, the largest U.S. company was General Electric with a market cap of close to $228 billion. The smallest publicly-traded company was well below $5 million.

The approximately 6,375 domestic, publicly-traded operating companies* on the New York Stock Exchange (NYSE), American Stock Exchange (AMEX) and the over-the-counter (OTC or NASDAQ) markets, are grouped by their market caps into three domestic stock asset classes: large cap, mid/small cap and micro cap.

Unfortunately, these terms are *not* uniformly applied to the same size firms by all Wall Street observers. This book will utilize the convention set forth by the Center for Research in Security Pricing at the University of Chicago (CRSP) and more or less followed by Ibbotson's SBBI. CRSP's methodology divides all stocks listed on the NYSE into ten deciles by the size of the underlying companies.

Deciles one and two, the largest 20% of all NYSE firms, are defined as large cap, and all listed securities on the AMEX or NASDAQ *of the same size* are included in this category. Deciles nine and ten, the smallest 20% of all NYSE firms, are defined as micro cap and all listed securities of the same size on the AMEX or NASDAQ are included. All of the stocks that fall in between, NYSE deciles three through eight and equivalent size firms on the AMEX and NASDAQ, are mid/small cap firms.

These definitions of market capitalization are somewhat different than those used by Morningstar Mutual Funds, among others. The primary reason for adopting CRSP definitions is the extensive research this allows back to 1926 (with CRSP or SBBI data) and the wide use of Ibbotson charts and data. (The small companies in Ibbotson's SBBI are the micro cap universe.)

---

* The term "operating companies" includes all corporations domiciled in the U.S. as compiled in the database of the Center for Research in Security Prices at the University of Chicago (CRSP). Excluded are American Depository Receipts (ADRs) of foreign-based corporations, Real Estate Investment Trusts (REITs), and Closed-End Investment Companies.

Asset Class	Range of Market Capitalizations	Approximate Number of Companies	Approximate Percentage of Total Stock Market Value
Large Cap*	Over $4 billion	435	74%
Mid/Small Cap	$260 million - $4 billion	2,260	23%
Micro Cap	Under $260 million	3,680	3%

* The S&P 500 is used within Ibbotson's SBBI as an index for large cap stocks.

CHART 2-1

As you can see on the accompanying Chart 2-1, Large Caps represent about 74% of the entire market value of all 6,375 stocks in the CRSP database even though they are represented by just 435 stocks. On the other end of the spectrum, Micro Cap stocks represent only about 3% of total market value, yet this group has 3,680 stocks.

If you want to own a domestic stock portfolio that matches the whole U.S. stock market—a market weight portfolio—you would not own an equal amount of each of the 6,375 stocks. Instead, your market weight portfolio would have 74% of its value in large cap stocks, 23% in mid/small cap stocks and 3% in micro cap stocks.

Size Effect

There is a straightforward reason why domestic stocks often are segregated in this way. The long-term returns from large cap stocks have been lower in aggregate than those from mid/small cap stocks, which in turn, have produced smaller returns than the returns from micro cap stocks (see Chart 2-2). This size effect has held true over time.

Over the past seven decades, micro cap stocks have consistently beaten their larger cap brethren when measured in 20-year stretches. As of the end of 1996, micro cap stocks outpaced large cap stocks in fully 49 of the 52 twenty-year periods beginning with 1926 (1926 through 1945, 1927 through 1946, ...).[4]

Given that micro cap stocks historically outperform larger cap issues, it would seem to make sense to concentrate on these companies. However, this conclusion is tempered somewhat by the following:

- The smaller the market capitalization, the larger the fluctuation in market prices. (The volatility in micro cap stocks is about 50% greater on average than that of large cap stocks.)

- Over periods of time even longer than a decade, the returns from smaller company stocks can severely lag the returns of their larger brethren (see Chart 2-3). The size effect will be explored in more detail in Chapter 4.

In addition, the returns reflected for Micro Cap stocks in Chart 2-2 may be hard to duplicate. James O'Shaughnessy, author of What Works on Wall Street, points out the severe lack of *liquidity* or ease of purchase and sale of micro cap issues. The implication is that micro cap stock returns reflected in historical data may not actually be possible in the real world. The supply of micro cap stocks is limited and their true cost may be understated. Transaction costs (spreads between the bid and ask price and commissions) may be quite a bit higher than those of larger cap issues.

This is undoubtedly a major factor behind Ibbotson Associates' decision at the end of 1981 to switch from using the complete micro cap data (as collected and published by CRSP) in its historical analysis to using the real world results of a dedicated micro cap mutual fund—DFA 9-10 Fund from Dimensional Fund Advisors, which typically invests in more than 2,500 micro cap stocks.

As part of the research analysis conducted for this book, the performance of the DFA 9-10 Fund (as reported in SBBI as Small Companies) was compared to the complete results of all micro cap stocks (as recorded by CRSP). It was anticipated that the performance of the DFA 9-10 Fund (which reflects all transaction costs and bid/ask spreads) would be substantially below that of the full micro cap index (calculated without the impact of transaction costs and spreads.)

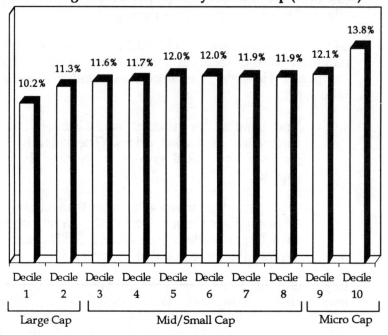

Average Annual Returns by Market Cap (1926-1997)

Source: Center for Research in Security Prices

CHART 2-2

The actual results were the exact opposite of what was expected. The DFA 9-10 fund outperformed the entire micro cap asset class — and by a wide margin. The micro cap universe of stocks as recorded by CRSP produced an annualized return of 12.9% between 1982-1997 while the DFA 9-10 Fund, which experienced the illiquidity pricing and costs of the real world, produced an annualized return of 14.9%.*

---

* Part of the explanation lies in the fact that the DFA 9-10 fund is not run like large cap index funds. A large cap index fund constantly monitors its target asset class and buys or sells stocks within the fund in order to closely replicate the asset class. The poor liquidity of micro cap stocks makes this precision impossible. Therefore, the managers of the DFA 9-10 fund mainly buy those micro caps that become available for purchase — typically when they are out of favor — and then hold the stocks as they would any other index fund.

U.S. Stock Performance – History of the Size Effect

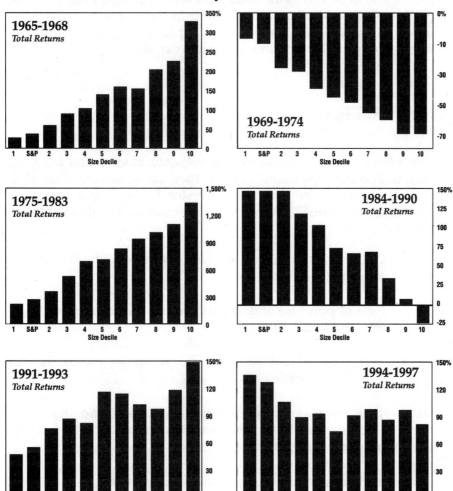

THE SIZE EFFECT CAN PERSIST IN EITHER DIRECTION FOR LONG PERIODS OF TIME.

Theses charts illustrate the total returns of Large Cap stocks (Deciles 1 & 2), Mid/Small Cap stocks (Deciles 3 to 8), and Micro Cap stocks (Deciles 9 & 10) from 1965 to 1997. This data was organized to illustrate the extreme variance in returns within "the market" over periods of time as long as 9 years.

Sources: Center for Research in Security Prices (CRSP)

CHART 2-3

The performance of the DFA 9-10 fund demonstrates that micro cap results are, in fact, achievable by the average mutual fund investor. (O'Shaughnessy's observation is true for large institutional investors who would undoubtedly experience great difficulty in moving large dollar amounts into micro cap stocks.)

Advantage USA: Big Picture

Thus far, we have only addressed domestic stocks. And for good reason. The old expression "you can't see the forest for the trees" is very apropos for the American investor today. There are many advantages to investing at home that are simply taken for granted, such as:

- Currency invisibility – no direct consideration of currency movements or costs

- Ease of purchase and sale (liquidity), particularly for large, mid and small cap issues

- Transparent and accurate accounting standards for company reporting

- True regulatory supervision (Securities and Exchange Commission) to prevent market manipulation and unfair insider trading practices

- Wide availability and easy access to markets

- *English* is the de facto business language of the world—but everything is in English here—nothing is lost in the translation and

- Relatively low transaction costs, no transaction taxes.

In addition, the U.S. economy is by far the largest in the world as Chart 2-4 so clearly demonstrates.

Top 20 Global Economies

Ranked by 1996 GDP, in billions of 1990 dollars

County	1996 GDP
U.S.	$6,462.9
Japan	3,291.7
Germany	1,811.6
France	1,281.0
Italy	1,165.6
U.K.	1,059.8
China	715.2
Canada	627.2
Spain	538.8
Brazil	515.3
South Korea	388.6
India	382.1
Australia	350.6
Netherlands	323.7
Mexico	267.6
Sweden	236.9
Taiwan	232.8
Switzerland	224.5
Belgium	209.4
Argentina	190.4

Source: DRI/McGraw-Hill

CHART 2-4

While these inherent advantages may diminish in the future, they are very real and significant in the 1990s and will remain so for many years to come.

Advantage USA: Culture

Beyond certain indisputable advantages of U.S. investment markets, there are also cultural advantages that bode especially well for American investment:

- **Incubation of new ideas** – America's fertile intellectual fields are the envy of the world, particularly the depth of our graduate and post-graduate programs.

- **Entrepreneurship** – The U.S. is unique in small business creation, as well as small business funding through venture capital, initial public offerings, small business loans, etc. Entrepreneurs from around the globe consider the U.S. the best place to launch an innovative new business. No other country in the world comes close to developing great growth companies like the U.S according to Ralph Wanger, Manager of the Acorn Fund.

- **Technological leadership** – The U.S. has a major or dominant position in almost every industry of the future including: computers, software, telecommunications, biotechnology "and the largest proportion of companies with world-class productivity advantages."[5] This technological edge may be expanding. The Wall Street Journal (September 26, 1996) reported that the Internet "is overwhelmingly U.S. centric, inundated with English language sites and U.S. generated content." This is the information technology platform of the future.

- **Relatively pro-business government** – Although far from perfect, the degree of government regulation of business in America is far less intrusive than our major trading partners. This is particularly important in areas of hiring and firing, subsidies and taxation.

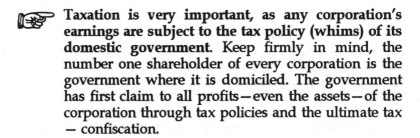 **Taxation is very important, as any corporation's earnings are subject to the tax policy (whims) of its domestic government.** Keep firmly in mind, the number one shareholder of every corporation is the government where it is domiciled. The government has first claim to all profits—even the assets—of the corporation through tax policies and the ultimate tax — confiscation.

- And finally, as Shelby Davis, portfolio manager of Davis New York Venture Fund and Selected American Shares, posed to an audience at Morningstar's June 1996 investment conference, "What other country in the world has people lined up to be let in?"

Advantage USA: Shareholder Value Imperative

Last, but not least, investing in U.S. companies has a major, under-appreciated advantage over companies virtually anywhere in the world—a management imperative to deliver increasing value to shareholders. Perhaps more than any other single factor, this imperative is why the U.S. stock market has outperformed its international brethren in the 1990s and is uniquely positioned to continue to outperform in the future. The tangible evidence of this benefit to stockholders in U.S. companies lies in:

- **Share buy-backs** to increase earnings-per-share

- **Downsizing** to create more efficient use of capital and labor

- **Return-on-equity** results that are close to double that of Europe and eight times that of Japan (summer 1997)

- **Management accession** policies that develop and grow management talent without regard to family ties

- **Third-party shareholders** that want (demand?) returns on their investment. In Japan or Europe, business partners and/or banks own majority stakes in business and, therefore, have other ways of being compensated than through increasing share value. In many emerging markets, family ties are often more important than the corporate officer/shareholder relationship. Here again, other compensation methods can supersede adding value for shareholders.

- **Aggressive management** that aids U.S. competitiveness; the threat of hostile takeovers (almost non-existent in Japan and Europe) allows for poor performing managers to be removed.

Conclusion

A recent study by the National Bureau of Research Fellow William Goetzmann and economist Philippe Jorion included the following excerpt in its conclusions:

> *"The United States is the exception in a global capital market frequently wracked by financial crisis, political upheaval, expropriation and war."*

> ...Looking at stock market data from 1921 to 1995 in 39 countries, the authors concluded that the U.S. was the big winner. Its "uninterrupted" real return rate was the best and most consistent of all and averaged 3.25% more per year than the real median growth of the other countries taken together.[6]

All three of the domestic stock asset classes—large cap, mid/small cap and micro cap stocks—offer long-term investors these advantages:

- Risks and rewards that have been meticulously recorded over seven decades

- Significant real returns over prevailing inflation over virtually any long-term period

- Big picture advantages in areas of access to the markets and reliability of securities regulation

- Cultural advantages that support entrepreneurship, new technology and pro-business regulation and

- A shareholder imperative by corporate managements to deliver increasing value.

While domestic stocks may be volatile and fluctuate irrationally in the short-term, U.S. equities have proved to be the best performing asset classes for the long term. They are a critical component of the well-designed Wealth and Retirement Portfolio.

3

Attractions and Drawbacks of Domestic Cash and Bonds

Cash and its equivalents, such as Certificates of Deposit (CDs) and Treasury bills, offer both interest rates that adjust quickly to inflation and a safe haven from fluctuation in principal values. Unfortunately, cash has also yielded consistently low real returns over any long-term period. Bonds typically pay higher yields than cash and have produced higher total returns over the long run. Yet bonds are prone to significant fluctuations in their principal value due to changing levels of interest rates and/or changes in the credit quality of a bond's issuer.

High-yield (junk) bonds offer the highest yields in the domestic market but come with several caveats connected with their erratic history.

"...Diversification is the nearest an investor or business manager can ever come to a free lunch."
— Peter Bernstein, Against the Gods,
New York: John Wiley & Sons, 1996

Cash Asset Class

Attractions

Money market accounts are a necessary component of virtually every portfolio. This is the account that transaction proceeds flow through for purchases, sales, contributions and withdrawals. Cash is an ideal vehicle for parking funds that could be needed in the near future.

While the daily moves in the stock market are often "fast and *curious*," the daily moves in cash equivalent securities ("cash") are monotonously "*low* but sure." One of the main attractions of cash is that you will not read the newspaper and see that the investment you made yesterday is down in value today.

Cash equivalent securities come in many popular forms: money market accounts, certificates of deposit (CDs), commercial paper (short-term notes issued by corporations) and U.S. Treasury bills (T-bills) guaranteed by the U.S. Government.

The return from cash is so nearly certain (little or no fluctuation in the value of principal—up or down) that investors typically accept a very small return over the prevailing inflation rate in exchange for this safety.

On the other hand, these short-term positives are overwhelmed by the long-term negatives of cash equivalents when viewed as a major component of your Wealth and Retirement Portfolio.

Drawbacks

Whereas cash is a necessary asset class to hold in some portion within a well-planned Wealth and Retirement Portfolio, it comes with some significant long-term drawbacks:

- Lack of stable or dependable income level,
- Little real return (over inflation) and
- Inferior long-term returns relative to stocks and bonds.

An extreme personal example of the first drawback happened in 1981. A fairly young, new retiree (late 50s) came into my office to discuss his financial plans. He had just received a pension distribution of approximately $300,000, which was all *invested* in a money market account at the then current rate of 16%. He told me he retired because he could "make it" on the $48,000 per year that his money market account would pay him. (He assumed the 16% rate on money market accounts would last forever!)

This man fell prey to what might be called "current trend tunnel vision"; the feeling that whatever has been happening in the financial markets for a couple of years or more will go on forever. Regrettably, he stuck with his plan, and when interest rates fell from this lofty but temporary perch, he had to find another job.

The other two drawbacks are analyzed in the next chapter.

Bond Asset Classes

A bond is very similar to the cash equivalent securities discussed above but with a longer period until maturity, the date when the principal value of the bond is due "in full." Bonds are segregated in three different ways:

- Domestic or foreign
- Taxable or tax free and
- High grade or high yield (junk).

Attractions

The attractions of bonds as a stand-alone asset class are:

- Stable, locked-in rate of income until maturity and
- Typically higher interest rates than cash equivalents.

These attributes of bonds make them an ideal choice for a significant portion of short-term and intermediate-term funding requirements (like college educations) and to match specific financial obligations of a longer-term nature (like known pension liabilities for retiring employees).

Bonds offer special diversification attributes when placed within a complete portfolio. These long-term features of bonds are discussed in Section III.

Drawbacks

The two drawbacks of bonds as a free-standing asset class are:

- No interest rate adjustments on bonds during long periods of rising rates, and

- Over long periods of time, the real returns from bonds have not compared favorably with the real returns of common stocks.

The first drawback was realized in spades by the bond buyers of the 1940s, 1950s and 1960s. They were never adequately compensated for the rising levels of both inflation and interest rates. An extreme example was the buyer of a 30-year U.S. Treasury bond in the 1940s and early 1950s. This investor was stuck with an interest rate under 3% for *three decades* in which inflation rose as high as 14% and interest rates on new Treasury bonds reached 15%. Selling those 3% bonds in the open market along the way would have incurred a huge loss in principal from the original cost.

The inflation-adjusted total return for U.S. Treasury bonds (with interest compounded) was just about zero ("0") from 1926 to 1981. No wealth accumulated whatsoever for 55 years. From 1926 through the end of 1997, the real return from the intermediate-term U.S. Treasury bond asset class averaged 2.2% per year. The real returns from bonds as compared to stocks will be further illustrated in the next chapter.

High Quality Bonds

SBBI has provided detailed information back to the beginning of 1926 for three domestic, high-quality bond asset classes:

- **Long-Term Government Bonds**   U.S. Treasury bonds 20-year constant maturity

- **Intermediate-Term Government Bonds**   U.S. Treasury bonds 5-year constant maturity

- **Long-Term Corporate Bonds**   High-grade bonds of domestic issuers with long-term maturities

Intermediate-term Government bonds offer much less volatility in returns than long-term Government bonds, yet have outperformed the long-term Treasury bonds for the full 1926-1997 period (5.3% versus 5.2%), according to SBBI. Receiving lower returns with higher volatility means getting the short-end of the stick in both risk and reward. Therefore, long-term U.S. Treasury bonds fall short of the attributes you want in your Wealth and Retirement Portfolio.

 Long-term corporate bonds are even more volatile than long-term U.S. Treasury bonds. However, high quality corporate bonds have at least produced a higher long-term rate of return (5.7%) than intermediate-term U.S. Treasury bonds. Yet corporate bonds must be evaluated more closely than Treasury bonds because of their **credit risk**, the risk that not all interest payments or all principal (at maturity) will be paid as due. In addition, the credit quality of the corporate bond issuer can change significantly over a bond's long life and have a direct effect on the price of the bond in the open market.

High-Yield Bonds

Unreliable History

Most of the available data on high-yield bonds is quite favorable. The problem is reliability. In this case, it is not reliability of the data. The problem lies in the changing and evolving nature of high-yield bonds themselves.

High-yield bonds are technically defined as those bonds that are rated below investment grade by credit rating agencies, such as

Moody's and Standard & Poor's. While this definition has been consistent, the bonds that fall within this definition have changed dramatically over the past two decades. There are three distinct periods in their evolution:

- Before the early 1980s
- Mid-1980s through 1990 (the Michael Milken era)
- 1991–Present

The high-yield bond market before the early 1980s was tiny in terms of market capitalization, but the total return on those high-yield bonds was quite favorable compared to U.S. Treasuries—even considering credit risks and defaults. These bonds produced a remarkably consistent default rate of approximately 2% annually but paid a much higher interest rate spread than 2% over U.S. Treasury bonds. Many of the issuers of high-yield bonds in that period were healthy—just small. Often their bonds were not rated because these small companies would not pay the fee required from Moody's or Standard & Poor's to receive a rating.

Michael Milken, a bond trader with Drexel, Burnham and Lambert, took notice of this apparent inefficiency in the high-yield bond market (high returns for *relatively* low risks). Furthermore, he fully recognized its marketing potential. Milken knew more investors would buy these bonds once they were made aware of their risk/reward characteristics.

The problem facing Milken was the tiny size of this market. There was not enough supply of these bonds to satisfy much new investor demand. His solution was to generate more high-yield bonds. And that he did. Most of the new high-yield bonds were created to fund the leveraged buy-outs that stormed Wall Street in the 1980s. Unfortunately, these bond issuers had little resemblance to those of the earlier period that had created the attractive track record. The new junk bond issues carried much higher debt ratios and thus were very sensitive to any change in their financial circumstances.

The day of reckoning came in 1989 when the pyramid of leveraged debt (high-yield bonds) began to unwind. Default rates skyrocketed. Worse still, many of these bonds suffered when their collateral was arbitrarily removed in the shuffling of corporate entities that ensued. The high-yield bond market virtually collapsed in 1990.

A new high-yield bond market emerged from the rubble beginning in early 1991. Characterized by super-high yields (demanded by investors) and uncertain collateral, it resembled a flea market more than a securities market.

Long-Term Value Uncertain

Today, the high-yield bond market has regained its equilibrium. Important changes have occurred in the industry. For one, liquidity has increased greatly since the '80s and early '90s. Junk-bond trader Michael Milken was the dominant dealer in high-yield securities, but one of the only ones making a market. Orders of $20 million were rare in those days, now they occur regularly.

Today there are hundreds of dealers, providing much more liquidity in a sector with $400 billion in debt outstanding. That's about one-fourth of the $1.5 trillion corporate debt market (1997).

The quality of new issues also has improved greatly. Issuers are bringing out more senior debt with first call on corporate assets than in the past.[7]

However, the history of high-yield bonds is too short and too erratic to instill confidence in their predictability going forward. High-quality indexes are only available beginning in 1985 and no high-yield bond index fund is readily available to the public. (In fact, it is somewhat difficult to isolate domestic high-yield bonds through the purchase of a high-yield mutual fund. Most such mutual funds regularly diversify into international, private placement and mortgage bond markets.) Lehman Brothers high-yield index does indicate interesting characteristics for the 1986-1997 time period: higher total returns than other domestic bond asset classes, low correlations with all other stock and bond asset classes and relatively mild risk. This is an asset class well worth watching for consistency over the years to come.

At this stage, however, high-yield bonds appear more appropriate for value investors, traders and other short-term investors to sort through than for those investors seeking a high degree of reliability and long-term predictability from the asset classes they choose for their Wealth and Retirement Portfolios.

Conclusion

Cash is a necessary part of virtually every Wealth and Retirement Portfolio. However, its short-term positives must be carefully weighed with its long-term deficiencies when constructing a portfolio design.

U.S. Treasury bonds of five years to maturity have demonstrated superior characteristics of higher returns and lower volatility when compared to U.S. Treasury bonds of much longer maturity.

High-quality corporate bonds have produced higher returns than those of 5-year U.S. Treasuries, although their relative risk level is an issue to be explored in the chapters that follow.

High-yield bonds are, as yet, too unreliable an asset class to include in long-term portfolios where predictability is desired.

Three of the asset classes discussed—cash, intermediate-term U.S. Treasury bonds and high-quality corporate bonds—appear to offer long-term investors attractive benefits for inclusion in their Wealth and Retirement Portfolio. These three asset classes will be further analyzed in the balance of this Section.

4

Domestic Stocks and Bonds: Real Returns in the Inflation Era (1960+)

Over the past 70 years, two major economic influences have significantly affected the nation's wealth: deflation and inflation. The first half of this period (1926-1959) may be deemed the Deflation Era. It began with a severe bout of deflation that affected financial markets for years thereafter. The second half (1960-1997) may be called the Inflation Era. This era experienced the build-up of a huge wave of inflation that, though reaching its peak in 1980, transfixed financial markets throughout the remaining years.

Comparing various asset-class returns in the Inflation and Deflation Eras offers a number of counter-intuitive observations that debunk common investment maxims while providing many insights into our future investment alternatives.

"Bank on the long-term trends, and ignore the tremors."
— J. Paul Getty

Chapters 2 and 3 discussed some of the attractions and drawbacks of the major domestic asset classes. These asset classes represent most of the portfolio investments widely owned by American investors until relatively recently.

They possess a long, rich history that has been meticulously documented back to 1926 in SBBI.[*] Other researchers have recorded the fluctuations and returns on these asset classes back considerably further. This documented financial history is of immeasurable value to U.S. investors.

In this chapter, the modern period of American financial markets will be dissected into two eras: the **Deflation Era** and the **Inflation Era**. The results of each era will be analyzed. As the Inflation Era has more relevance to your investing today, the returns and fluctuations of this era will be presented in detail in Chapter 5. To thoroughly understand these results, you need a full appreciation of the grip inflation holds on the financial markets.

Nominal and Real Returns

We live in a world of *nominal returns*, returns that are not adjusted for inflation. Your bank quotes interest rates this way, mutual funds advertise performance nominally, the U.S. government offers most Treasury bonds and T-bills at nominal rates and so forth.

 Yet *real returns*, those adjusted for inflation, are far more important to your Wealth and Retirement Portfolio. **There is no creation or addition to wealth without increased purchasing power.** And, in the same vein, the further in the future your proposed retirement is, the more the amount of your retirement income in nominal dollars becomes merely an abstraction. The purchasing power of those dollars is all that counts. (Even if you are currently retired, this is still a crucial distinction for your income for the remainder of your retirement.)

---

[*] Does not include High-Yield Bond index.

Inflation's Slow Burn

Inflation should be feared. Inflation is a particularly insidious financial disease. It attacks the corpus (principal) and the productive effort (yield or interest) of an investment at the same time. It is not only cumulative, it compounds like an interest-bearing account in reverse. After 30 years of retirement with inflation at 3%, you will need $250 to buy what $100 did when you retired. In other words, both your portfolio and retirement income must grow by 150% after taxes just to be even with inflation and purchase the goods and services it originally did.

Unfortunately, inflation is not reflected on either your bank or brokerage statements. It grows unseen like a cancerous tumor. A graphic analogy of how inflation exacts its price is that of the proverbial "frog on the stove." As you have probably heard, if you place a frog in a pot of water on the stove and turn on the burner so that the water slowly heats to a boil, the frog will stay in the pot— even with full opportunity to hop out—until he boils to death. The slow incremental burn never rings an alarm to get out until it is too late.

Deflation Era & Inflation Era

Focusing on inflation-adjusted or real returns has another important advantage. It allows for an apples-to-apples comparison of different periods of financial history...those with very different inflationary—even deflationary—conditions.

Ibbotson's SBBI documents what may be called the modern financial period (1926-1997). There are some significant advantages and insights to be gained by dividing this period into two roughly equal, yet very distinctive, financial eras:

- **The Deflation Era** (the Great Depression and its grip: 1926-1959) and

- **The Inflation Era** (the Great Inflation, its build-up and its lingering effects: 1960+).

Two Great Anomalies of the 20th Century

Sbbi data shows that inflation has averaged 3.1% for the entire modern period 1926-1997. This full period data hides the two great financial anomalies of the 20th century. The Great Depression's deflation of the 1930s and the great monetary inflation of the 1960s and 1970s.

In the first half of the 1930s, America suffered a severe deflationary shock. The price level *declined* between 6% and 10% each year in 1930, 1931 and 1932. Short-term interest rates fell from 4.7% in 1929 to 1% in 1932. After the deflation had run its course, interest rates continued to fall to a minuscule 0.2% annually on T-bills. Rates remained very low throughout the balance of the 1930s, the 1940s and well into the 1950s even though America never suffered deflation again and inflation returned to more normal levels of between one and three percent. *Interest rates were stuck at low levels as a skeptical public feared a return of the depression.*

Beginning in the 1960s but really taking off in the 1970s, America suffered a severe inflationary shock. The consumer price level rose at least 8.8% in every year except two from 1973 through 1981. Short-term interest rates on cash equivalents increased from 3.8% in 1972 to 14.7% in 1981. Rates on 5-year Treasury bonds rose from 6.8% to 14.0% over that same period.

Inflation came down quickly in 1982 and averaged a more normal 3.5% for the 1982-1997 period. *However, interest rates have remained stuck at historically high levels since 1982 as a skeptical public fears a return of inflation.* The heightened sensitivity to a return of inflation is likely to continue for many years to come.

Comparing the Two Eras

In comparing and contrasting the full modern financial period (1926-1997), the Deflation Era (1926-1959) and the Inflation Era (1960-1997), the following chart will be helpful.

	Average Annual Rates		
	Full Modern Period 1926-1997	Deflation Era 1926-1959	Inflation Era 1960-1997
Inflation	3.1%	1.5%	4.6%
Cash Returns (30-day T-bills)	3.8%	1.3%	6.1%
Real Returns (Inflation Adjusted)	0.7%	-0.2%	1.5%
Bond Returns (5-year Treasury bonds)	5.3%	2.8%	7.5%
Real Returns	2.2%	1.3%	2.9%
Stock Returns (S&P 500)	11.0%	10.3%	11.6%
Real Returns	7.9%	8.8%	7.0%

Source: © Computed using data from Stocks, Bonds, Bills & Inflation 1997
Yearbook™ with data updated January 1998, Ibbotson Associates, Chicago

CHART 4-1

Observations from the Comparison of Eras

- A general observation from this comparison is just how different the Deflation Era was from the Inflation Era with regard to inflation, interest rates and real returns in all three asset class families. The full period data (1926-1997) is simply an average of two distinctly different eras.

- The most counter-intuitive observation from this data is that the Deflation Era produced lower real returns for bond investors than the later Inflation Era. This is contrary to the conventional wisdom that inflation is bad for bonds.

- Large cap stocks (S&P 500) delivered consistent long-term nominal returns, 11.6% in the Inflation Era and 10.3% in the Deflation Era. However, the real returns from the two periods were at opposite ends of the range of real long-term returns discussed in Chapter 2. The Deflation Era, which included the Great Depression and World War II, produced significantly higher inflation-adjusted returns than the Inflation Era, 8.8% versus 7.0%. This also flies in the face of conventional wisdom regarding the two periods.

• Perhaps the most significant observation from this data is that the Inflation Era has been a relatively poor one for stocks and a magnificent one for bonds and cash. Yet, stocks still more than doubled the real returns of bonds and more than quadrupled the real returns from cash.

Detailed Period for Stock Analysis: 1960-1997

 Closely studying the stock market's returns and fluctuations during the Inflation Era provides an excellent backdrop for any investor or investment professional today. In many ways, it paints a worst-case scenario of what could unfold over any long-term period of stock ownership. In fact, the very *worst* 30-year period for stock ownership in the modern era is the 30 years beginning in 1960.

During this period, inflation skyrocketed, interest rates quintupled and price/earnings (P/E) multiples of stocks were sliced by two-thirds. If you can develop confidence in the stock market from the 1960-1997 period, you are well on your way to relying on the near certainties that unfold over long periods of market experience.

High (P/E) Ratios: Past and Present

Many investors felt that the U.S. stock market was fully valued or even overvalued in 1991...and each year thereafter. Their primary cause for concern has been the relatively high P/E ratios of the major market averages. These investors will want to take special note of the P/E ratios in 1960 and for the decade that followed. The late 1950s through the late 1960s is the only extended period of relatively high P/E ratios for the domestic stock market other than that which began in 1991 (see Chart 4-2). **As the performance of the 1960-1997 period attested, the U.S. stock market provided excellent returns even though it began with relatively high P/E ratios.**

Large Company Stocks: S&P 500
P/E Ratios - 1960-1997

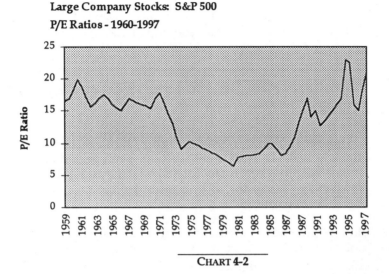

CHART 4-2

The Market Multiple (Review of a Basic Point)

What is the market multiple? Why is it important?

The best single expression of the current consensus outlook for the stock market is the market multiple. At any point in time, the U.S. stock market—as typically denoted by the S&P 500 Index—is selling at a multiple of the combined earnings of the companies that make up that index. [For example, if the S&P 500 index was currently at 830 and the combined per share earnings of the 500 companies in the index had added up to $46 for the past 12 months, the P/E ratio of the market is 830/46 = 18. The S&P 500 is selling for 18 times earnings or a market multiple of 18 in this instance.]

During this century, the market multiple for the U.S. stock market has normally ranged between 10 and 20 times earnings. The average has been about 15. The higher the current market multiple, the rosier the consensus view is about corporate earnings, inflation and interest rates ahead. But higher-than-average market multiples imply that the market has less room to rise based on the multiple itself going up further. It is less likely that investors are willing to pay still more per one dollar of earnings. It also implies that the market has more room to fall if the market multiple contracts. If investors are willing to pay less per dollar of earnings, it is indicative of a darker consensus view of corporate earnings, inflation and interest rates looking ahead.

Striking Similarities of Mid to Late 1990s and Late 1950s to Early 1960s

Another similarity (besides high P/E ratios) of the early 1960s and the late 1990s is even more striking. Each period was preceded by a major bull market in stocks: 1949-1960+ and 1982-1997+. Each bull market saw a tripling of P/E ratios from 6 or 7 times earnings to 18 to 22 times earnings.

In 1959, the new investment firm of Donaldson, Lufkin and Jenrette introduced their firm through a small publication titled Common Stocks and Common Sense. This is an excerpt from that booklet:

> *"The most significant change in the position of the 1959 investor vis-à-vis the 1949 investor is in the multiple of earnings reflected in common stock prices today. Today's 'Favorite Fifty' stocks are selling at price-earnings ratios which are 21 times estimated 1959 earnings. Ten years ago these same stocks could have been purchased at prices averaging 7.7 times 1949 earnings."*

Almost this exact statement could have been written at any time in the mid to late 1990s, substituting 1982 for 1949 and the current year for 1959.

Yet another similarity of the two periods, both bull markets were led by large cap stocks. Despite the long-term advantage of micro cap stocks, large cap stocks outperformed by 2.5% annually in the 1950s bull market and by 2.5% annually in the 1980s/90s bull market.

Conclusion

 The stock market investor of the late 1990s is in a very similar investment environment to the stock market investor of 1960. This makes January 1, 1960, an ideal date to begin a detailed analysis of the stock market that may provide guidance for today's investors. Studying the entire 1960-1997 period provides a wonderful insight into the long-term returns and the frequency and degree of any setbacks that are the most likely to unfold over the years ahead.

5

Comparing Risks and Rewards of Domestic Stocks and Bonds

The first three chapters of this section provided a discussion of the major domestic asset classes and how to evaluate them relative to inflation (or deflation). This chapter will introduce a methodology for evaluating and measuring the long-term risks and rewards that each domestic asset class has offered. It will answer the question, *"How much reward has each domestic asset class delivered for the risks incurred?"*

"Nothing has really changed on Wall Street over the years. In fact, much of what happens in the financial world today has been played over in history many times before and has been captured in the cycles and trends of financial charts created over time. Understanding the movements within these charts provides a clearer perspective of today's market and can aid you in your investment decisions tomorrow."

— Ken Fisher, <u>The Wall Street Waltz</u>,
Chicago: Contemporary Books, Inc., 1987

The Enigma of Risk

The long history of domestic asset classes reveals an important fact: *not one has ever sustained a permanent loss.* Eventually, every decline in value has been recovered. However, any decline in market value can be turned into a permanent loss. For example, many investors sold their equity mutual funds right after the 1987 crash. These investors were not properly prepared for the magnitude of that decline—even though it fell well within historic parameters.

 The purpose of understanding the risks within each asset class is to be both intellectually and emotionally prepared for the range and intensity of its inevitable market declines. A special part of this preparation is to come to grips with the entirely random nature of these market declines. **Neither the timing nor the intensity of the *next* decline can be predicted.**

Therefore, the better an investor is prepared for the entire range of expected declines in a particular asset class (based upon its longest period of documented history), the more likely his actions will serve his own best long-term interests. Either he will not invest in a particular asset class in the first place or he will stay the course during its inevitable declines.

The study of the risks within any particular asset class thus becomes the study of the severity, frequency and duration of its declines in market value.

The academic measurement of risk is called standard deviation,[*] which is not an investor-friendly tool. It falls short of providing a real appreciation for the risk in owning a particular investment. In fact, standard deviation is not a measurement of market declines per se, it is a measurement of the annual volatility or degree of variance an investment experiences in producing a particular average rate of return. Upside movements are as influential as downside movements in its calculation. Therefore, right from the beginning, standard deviation *fails* as a measurement of market *declines.*

---

[*] A complete discussion of standard deviation is given in the Appendix, page 259.

Standard deviation does provide an insight into the normalized distribution of *annual* returns, but it fails to prepare investors for the full range of the declines they will likely incur over a lifetime of investing. A more useful measurement of risk is required to fulfill the mission of preparing investors for the declines in market value they face.

Long-Term Risk: Bear Markets

Risk, the intensity of market declines, can be measured over a variety of time periods. As this book takes a long-term perspective, it will focus on those major market declines that occur infrequently (about once every five years). These substantial setbacks in market value, often referred to as bear markets, tend to be the major concern of most *investors* as opposed to the short-term ups and downs that preoccupy *traders*.

Actually, the history of asset classes shows that there are two types of bear markets. First, there are the normal cyclical bear markets that tend to be sharp and short-term. Then there are the very infrequent mega bear markets that tend to be much deeper and more prolonged. The mega bear markets induce more than concern from investors, they instill real fear. Fortunately, such mega bear markets may only occur once in an entire investment lifetime (within each asset class). For example, the S&P 500 has endured two such mega bear market declines since 1925, the Depression Era crash of 1929 - '32 and the Inflation Era's monetary crisis of 1973-1974.

Chart 5-1 illustrates the S&P 500's mega bear market and the average of its seven cyclical bear markets in the Inflation Era. A more detailed discussion of the Risk Profile begins on page 258.

Bear Markets	*Risk Profile*
Mega Bear Market Decline*	43% (temporary loss)
Average Cyclical Bear Market Decline*	19% (temporary loss)

* Measured from high month-end market value to subsequent low month-end valuation.

CHART 5-1

These bear market characteristics are of great value when comparing different asset classes.

Long-Term Rewards

Financial performance is a combination of risk and reward. Whereas risk is multifaceted, the reward from investing is fairly easy to identify. The reward of owning any asset class or portfolio is the rate of return it has delivered *above* that of the riskless 30-day U.S. Treasury bill.

 Every investor can purchase a 30-day U.S. Treasury bill (the cash asset class) and receive the riskless return it offers. The return from cash therefore sets the base from which reward is measured. Your reward from an investment is only that *extra* return (above the riskless return of cash) for which you must incur some amount of bear market risk. *In other words, your return is only meaningful in relationship to the risk taken to achieve it!*

Reward = Rate of Return on Asset Class *less* the Rate of Return on Cash (T-bills)

For example, the Reward from owning the S&P 500 for the 1960-1997 period is 5.5%. This is simply the 11.6% rate of return of the S&P 500 for this period *less* the 6.1% return offered by Treasury bills (Chart 5-2).

Reward - S&P 500
(1960-1997)

Return (Annualized)	=	11.6%
Riskless Return (T-bills)	=	-6.1%
REWARD		**5.5%**

CHART 5-2

Historical Risk/Reward Charts

As stated earlier, "the purpose of understanding the risks within each asset class is to be both intellectually and emotionally prepared for the range and intensity of its inevitable market declines." The best preparation is to see and feel the major declines in market value that each asset class has experienced over its history and then to envision living through those setbacks as if they were occurring in your own investment in the years ahead.

The Historical Risk/Reward chart allows you to do just that. On a single page, it walks you through the month-by-month history of the asset class, segregating the bear markets and the bull markets. Spending just a few minutes studying a Historical Risk/Reward chart will greatly add to your appreciation of the relationship between the risks and reward within that asset class.

Historical Risk/Reward Chart for the S&P 500

Chart 5-3 is a Historical Risk/Reward chart of the S&P 500 for the Inflation Era. One hundred thousand dollars ($100,000) invested in the S&P 500 on December 31, 1959, grew to $6,457,000 by December 31, 1997. The equivalent value of an investment in cash (30-day T-bills) was $948,800. The S&P 500 more than quintupled the accumulated return from cash.

The computation of the Reward of owning the S&P 500 is shown on the bottom left side of this chart, while its Risk Profile is shown on the bottom right side.

To achieve these superior results, an investor in the S&P 500 lived through periods of significant setbacks which are highlighted as the solid areas on the chart. These are the bear markets that long-term owners must take in stride.

As you can see, the magnitude of these bear market declines vary widely from a mild 10% setback to an ugly 43% decline. Also notice that bear markets in the S&P 500 were as short as one month and as long as 21 months. The lightly shaded sections following each bear market show how long it took to recover the temporary loss of that decline. These periods vary sharply too. The entire solid area plus the following lightly shaded area together indicate the total length of time an investor was *underwater* from a prior high in market value. The white areas denote major periods of net new advancement.

The combined lightly shaded areas (recovery periods) and the white areas (net new advancement) together represent the bull markets that follow the bear markets (solid areas). One bull market plus one bear market (in either order) is a **full market cycle**.

The percentage gain and the number of months over which the bull markets unfolded are reflected in the numbers on the chart. These also varied widely in degree and duration. The smallest full bull market was up 42% over only eight months. The largest is the 286% bull market of 1990-1997, which is also the longest of this period.

The up and down arrows show whether that particular month-end value was up or down from the prior month. Directly below the chart, the standard deviation for the S&P 500 (15.6 for the period of 1960-1997) is also shown.

The current value of an initial $100,000 portfolio (beginning January 1, 1960) is shown at the end of each bull market and at the bottom of each bear market. This provides you an excellent view of where your month-end brokerage statements were heading in each major advance and each major decline. Visualize your own S&P 500 investment going through similar advances—and particularly declines—in the future. The intent is to prepare you today for what is likely to unfold in some random sequence in the decades ahead.

As you can see, the history of the S&P 500 is one of continuous progress punctuated by periodic setbacks of varying intensity.

Historical Risk/Reward Charts of Major Domestic Asset Classes

Historical Risk/Reward charts for Large Cap Stocks, Mid/Small Cap Stocks, Micro Cap Stocks and U.S. Treasury Bonds (5-year) during the Inflation Era are presented in Charts 5-4 through 5-7.

Standard & Poor's 500

Growth of $100,000
(12/31/59 – 12/31/97)

Year	Jan	Feb	Mar	Apr	May	Jun	Jul	Aug	Sep	Oct	Nov	Dec	Annual Returns
1960	$100,000	↑	↓	↓	↑	+25% 26 mo.	↑	↓	↓	↑	↑		0.5%
1961	↑	↑	↑	↑	↑	↓	↑	↑	↓	↑	↑	↑	26.9
1962	↓	$125,400	<21%> 4 mo.			$99,100	↑	↑	↓	↑	↑	↑	-8.7
1963	↑	↓	↑	↑	↑	↓	↓	↑	↓	↑	↓	↑	22.8
1964	↑	↑	↑	↑	↑	+88% 46 mo.		↓	↑	↑	↑	↑	16.5
1965	↑	↑	↓	↓	↑	↓	↑	↑	↑	↓	↑	↑	12.5
1966	↑	↓	$186,000	<15%> 5 mo.					$158,900	↑	↑	→	-10.1
1967	↑	↑	↑	↑	↓	+47% 32 mo.		↓	↑	↓	↓	↓	24.0
1968	↓	↓	↑	↑	↑	↑	↓	↑	↑	↑	↓		11.1
1969	↓	↓	↑	↑	$234,100	<27%> 13 mo.							-8.5
1970						$170,800	↑	↑	↑	↓	↑	↑	4.0
1971	↑	↑	↑	↑	↓	↑	↓	↑	↓	↓	↑	↑	14.3
1972	↑	↑	↑	↑	+76% 30 mo.		↑	↑	↓	↑	↑	$300,000	19.0
1973			<43%> 21 mo.										-14.7
1974									$172,100	↑	↓	↓	-26.5
1975	↑	↑	↑	↑	↑	↑	↓	↑	↓	↑	↓	↑	37.2
1976	↑	↓	↑	↓	↓	↑	↓	↑	↑	↓	↓	↑	23.8
1977	↓	↓	↓	↑	↓	+124% 65 mo.		↓	→	↓	↑	↑	-7.2
1978	↓	↓	↑	↑	↑	↓	↑	↑	↓	↓	↑		6.6
1979	↑	↓	↑	↑	↓	↑	↑	↑	↑	↓	↑		18.4
1980	↑	$398,800	<10%> 1 mo.	↑	↑	↑	+42% 8 mo.		↑	↑	$512,300		32.4
1981													-4.9
1982			<17%> 20 mo.				$425,600	↑	↑	↑	↑	↑	21.4
1983	↑	↑	↑	↑	↓	↑	↓	↓	↑	↑	↓		22.5
1984	↓	↓	↑	↑	↓	↑	↑	↑	↑	↑	↓	↑	6.3
1985	↑	↑	↑	↓	↑	↑	+282% 61 mo.	↓	↑	↑	↑	↓	32.2
1986	↑	↑	↑	↓	↑	↑	↓	↑	↓	↑			18.5
1987	↑	↑	↑	↓	↑	↑	↑	$1,623,700	<30%> 3 mo.	$1,144,200	↑		5.2
1988	↑	↑	↓	↑	↑	↑	↑	↓	↑	↑	↓	↑	16.8
1989	↑	↓	↑	+71% 31 mo.		↑	↑	↓	↓	↑	↑		31.5
1990	↓	↑	↑	↓	$1,958,900	<15%> 5 mo.			$1,670,900	↑	↑		-3.2
1991	↑	↑	↑	↑	↑	↓	↑	↑	↓	↑	↓	↑	30.5
1992	↓	↑	↓	↑	↑	↓	↑	↓	↑	↑	↑	↑	7.7
1993	↑	↑	↑	↓	↑	+286% 86 mo.		↑	↓	↑	↓	↑	10.0
1994	↑	↓	↓	↑	↑	↓	↑	↑	↓	↑	↓	↑	1.3
1995	↑	↑	↑	↑	↑	↑	↑	↑	↑	↓	↑	↑	37.4
1996	↑	↑	↑	↑	↓	↑	↓	↑	↑	↑	↑	↓	23.1
1997	↑	↑	↓	↑	↑	↑	↑	↓	↑	↓	↑	$6,457,000	33.3%

Total Return: Includes reinvested dividends and capital gains   **Standard Deviation: 15.6**

Source: © Computed using data from Stocks, Bonds, Bills & Inflation 1997 Yearbook™ with data updated January 1998, Ibbotson Associates, Chicago

↑↓ Up or Down Month   ● Cyclical Declines   ● Recovery (to pre-decline level)   ○ Net New Advancement

REWARD*

Total Return (1960-1997)	11.6%
Riskless Return (T-bills)	< 6.1%>
AVERAGE ANNUAL REWARD OF STANDARD & POOR'S 500	**5.5%**

*Annualized

RISK PROFILE

Mega Bear Market Decline	<43%>
Average Bear Market Decline	<19%>

CHART 5-3

Large Cap Stocks
Growth of $100,000
(12/31/59 – 12/31/97)

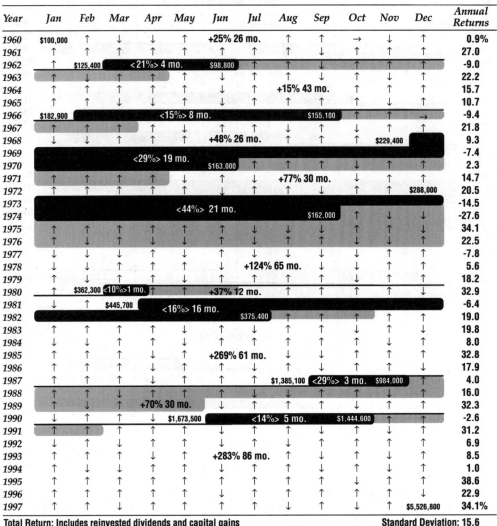

Year	Jan	Feb	Mar	Apr	May	Jun	Jul	Aug	Sep	Oct	Nov	Dec	Annual Returns
1960	$100,000	↑	↓	↓	↑	+25% 26 mo.		↑	↑	→	↓	↑	0.9%
1961	↑	↑	↑	↑	↑	↑	↑	↑	↓	↑	↑	↑	27.0
1962	↑	$125,400	<21%> 4 mo.			$98,800	↑	↑	↓	↑	↑	↑	-9.0
1963	↑	↓	↑	↑	↑	↓	↑	↑	↓	↑	↓	↑	22.2
1964	↑	↑	↑	↑	↑	↓	+15% 43 mo.			↑	↑	↑	15.7
1965	↑	↑	↓	↓	↑	↓	↑	↑	↑	↑	↓	↑	10.7
1966	$182,900	<15%> 8 mo.							$155,100	↑	↑	→	-9.4
1967	↑	↑	↑	↑	↓	↑	↓	↓	↑	↓	↑	↑	21.8
1968	↓	↓	↑	↑	↑	+48% 26 mo.		↑	↑	↑	$229,400		9.3
1969	<29%> 19 mo.												-7.4
1970						$163,000	↑	↑	↑	↓	↑	↑	2.3
1971	↑	↑	↑	↑	↓	↑	↓	+77% 30 mo.		↓	↑	↑	14.7
1972	↑	↑	↑	↑	↑	↓	↑	↓	↓	↑	↑	$288,000	20.5
1973	<44%> 21 mo.												-14.5
1974									$162,000	↑	↓	↓	-27.6
1975	↑	↑	↑	↑	↑	↑	↓	↓	↓	↑	↑	↓	34.1
1976	↑	↓	↑	↓	↑	↑	↓	↑	↑	↓	↑	↑	22.5
1977	↓	↓	↓	↑	↓	↑	↓	↓	↓	↑	↑	↑	-7.8
1978	↓	↓	↑	↑	↑	↓	+124% 65 mo.		↓	↓	↑	↑	5.6
1979	↑	↓	↑	↑	↓	↑	↑	↑	↑	↓	↑	↑	18.2
1980	↑	$362,300	<10%>1 mo.	↑	↑	+37% 12 mo.		↑	↑	↑	↑	↓	32.9
1981	↓	↑	$445,700	<16%> 16 mo.									-6.4
1982							$375,400	↑	↑		↑	↑	19.0
1983	↑	↑	↑	↑	↓	↑	↓	↑	↑	↓	↑	↓	19.8
1984	↓	↓	↑	↑	↓	↑	↑	↑	↑	↑	↓	↑	8.0
1985	↑	↑	↑	↓	↑	+269% 61 mo.		↓	↓	↑	↑	↑	32.8
1986	↑	↑	↑	↓	↑	↑	↓	↑	↑	↑	↑	↓	17.9
1987	↑	↑	↑	↓	↑	↑	↑	$1,385,100	<29%> 3 mo.	$984,000	↑		4.0
1988	↑	↑	↓	↑	↑	↓	↓	↓	↑	↑	↑	↑	16.0
1989	↑	↓	↑	+70% 30 mo.		↓	↑	↑	↑	↓	↑	↑	32.3
1990	↓	↑	↑	↓	$1,673,500	<14%> 5 mo.				$1,444,600	↑	↑	-2.6
1991	↑	↑	↑	↑	↓	↑	↓	↓	↑	↓	↑	↑	31.2
1992	↓	↑	↓	↑	↑	↓	↑	↓	↑	↑	↑	↑	6.9
1993	↑	↑	↑	↓	↑	+283% 86 mo.		↑	↓	↑	↓	↑	8.5
1994	↑	↓	↓	↑	↑	↓	↑	↑	↓	↑	↓	↑	1.0
1995	↑	↑	↑	↑	↑	↑	↑	↑	↑	↓	↑	↑	38.6
1996	↑	↑	↑	↑	↑	↓	↑	↑	↑	↑	↑	↓	22.9
1997	↑	↑	↓	↑	↑	↑	↑	↓	↑	↓	↑	$5,526,800	34.1%

Total Return: Includes reinvested dividends and capital gains   **Standard Deviation: 15.6**

Source: Center for Research in Security Prices (CRSP) University of Chicago

↑ ↓ *Up or Down Month*   ⬛ *Cyclical Declines*   ⬤ *Recovery (to pre-decline level)*   ⬭ *Net New Advancement*

REWARD*		RISK PROFILE	
Total Return (1960-1997)	11.1%	Mega Bear Market Decline	<44%>
Riskless Return (T-bills)	< 6.1%>	Average Bear Market Decline	<19%>
AVERAGE ANNUAL REWARD OF LARGE CAP STOCKS	**5.0%**		

*Annualized

CHART 5-4

Mid/Small Cap Stocks
Growth of $100,000
(12/31/59 – 12/31/97)

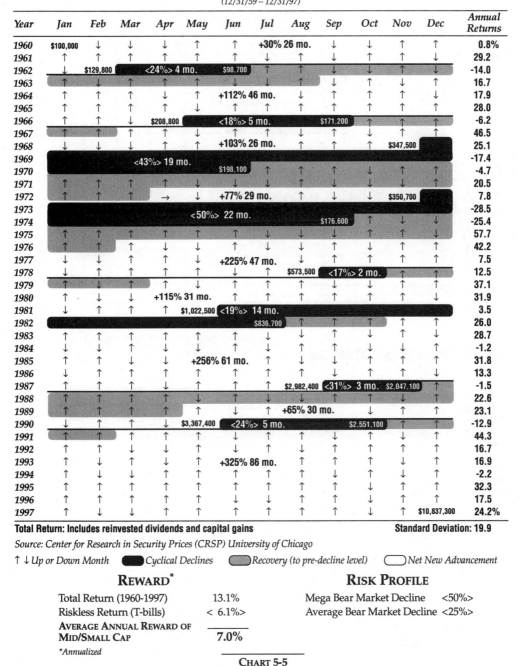

Year	Jan	Feb	Mar	Apr	May	Jun	Jul	Aug	Sep	Oct	Nov	Dec	Annual Returns
1960	$100,000	↓	↓	↓	↑	↑	+30% 26 mo.		↓	↓	↑	↑	0.8%
1961	↑	↑	↑	↑	↑	↑	↓	↑	↓	↑	↑	↓	29.2
1962	↓	$129,800	<24%> 4 mo.			$98,700	↑	↑	↓	↓	↑	↓	-14.0
1963	↑	↓	↑	↑	↑	↓	↓	↑	↓	↑	↓	↑	16.7
1964	↑	↑	↑	↓	↑	+112% 46 mo.		↓	↑	↑	↑	↓	17.9
1965	↑	↑	↑	↑	↓	↑	↑	↑	↑	↑	↑	↑	28.0
1966	↑	↑	↓	$208,800	<18%> 5 mo.				$171,200	↑	↑	↑	-6.2
1967	↑	↑	↑	↑	↓	↑	↑	↓	↑	↓	↑	↑	46.5
1968	↓	↓	↓	↑	↑	+103% 26 mo.		↑	↑	↑	$347,500		25.1
1969			<43%> 19 mo.										-17.4
1970					$198,100		↑	↑	↑	↓	↑		-4.7
1971	↑	↑	↑	↑	↓	↓	↓	↑	↓	↓	↓	↑	20.5
1972	↑	↑	↑	→	↓	+77% 29 mo.		↑	↓	↓	$350,700		7.8
1973				<50%> 22 mo.									-28.5
1974									$176,600	↑	↓	↓	-25.4
1975	↑	↑	↑	↑	↑	↑	↓	↓	↓	↑	↑		57.7
1976	↑	↑	↑	↓	↓	↑	↓	↓	↑	↓	↑	↑	42.2
1977	↓	↓	↑	↑	↓	+225% 47 mo.		↓	↑	↑	↑	↑	7.5
1978	↓	↑	↑	↑	↑	↓	↑	$573,500	<17%> 2 mo.		↑	↑	12.5
1979	↑	↓	↑	↑	↓	↑	↑	↑	↑	↓	↑	↑	37.1
1980	↑	↓	↓	+115% 31 mo.	↑	↑	↑	↑	↑	↑	↑	↓	31.9
1981	↓	↑	↑	↑	$1,022,500	<19%> 14 mo.							3.5
1982							$836,700	↑	↑	↑	↑	↑	26.0
1983	↑	↑	↑	↑	↑	↓	↓	↓	↓	↓	↑	↓	28.7
1984	↓	↓	↑	↓	↓	↑	↓	↑	↑	↓	↓	↑	-1.2
1985	↑	↑	↓	↓	+256% 61 mo.		↑	↓	↓	↑	↑	↑	31.8
1986	↓	↑	↑	↑	↑	↑	↑	↑	↓	↑	↑	↓	13.3
1987	↑	↑	↑	↓	↑	↑	↑	$2,982,400	<31%> 3 mo. $2,047,100		↑		-1.5
1988	↑	↑	↑	↑	↓	↑	↓	↓	↑	↑	↓	↑	22.6
1989	↑	↑	↑	↑	↑	↓	↑	+65% 30 mo.	↓	↓	↑	↑	23.1
1990	↓	↑	↑	↓	$3,367,400	<24%> 5 mo.				$2,551,100	↑	↑	-12.9
1991	↑	↑	↑	↑	↑	↓	↑	↑	↓	↑	↓	↑	44.3
1992	↑	↑	↓	↓	↑	↓	↑	↓	↑	↑	↑	↑	16.7
1993	↑	↓	↑	↓	↑	+325% 86 mo.		↑	↑	↑	↓	↑	16.9
1994	↑	↓	↓	↑	↑	↑	↑	↑	↓	↑	↓	↑	-2.2
1995	↑	↑	↑	↑	↑	↑	↑	↑	↑	↓	↑	↑	32.3
1996	↑	↑	↑	↑	↑	↓	↓	↑	↑	↓	↑	↑	17.5
1997	↑	↓	↓	↑	↑	↑	↑	↑	↑	↓	↑	$10,837,300	24.2%

Total Return: Includes reinvested dividends and capital gains   **Standard Deviation: 19.9**

Source: Center for Research in Security Prices (CRSP) University of Chicago

↑ ↓ Up or Down Month   ■ Cyclical Declines   ▬ Recovery (to pre-decline level)   ◯ Net New Advancement

REWARD*

Total Return (1960-1997)	13.1%
Riskless Return (T-bills)	< 6.1%>
AVERAGE ANNUAL REWARD OF MID/SMALL CAP	7.0%

*Annualized

RISK PROFILE

Mega Bear Market Decline	<50%>
Average Bear Market Decline	<25%>

CHART 5-5

Micro Cap Stocks
Growth of $100,000
(12/31/59 – 12/31/97)

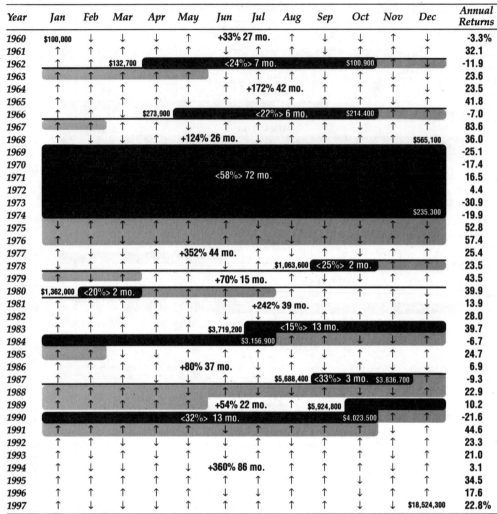

Year	Jan	Feb	Mar	Apr	May	Jun	Jul	Aug	Sep	Oct	Nov	Dec	Annual Returns
1960	$100,000	↓	↓	↓	↑	+33% 27 mo.		↑	↓	↓	↑	↓	-3.3%
1961	↑	↑	↑	↑	↑	↓	↑	↑	↓	↑	↑	↑	32.1
1962	↑	↑	$132,700	<24%> 7 mo.						$100,900	↑	↓	-11.9
1963	↑	↑	↑	↑	↑	↓	↑	↑	↓	↑	↓	↓	23.6
1964	↑	↑	↑	↑	↑	↑	+172% 42 mo.	↑	↑	↑	↑	↓	23.5
1965	↑	↑	↑	↑	↓	↑	↑	↑	↑	↑	↓	↑	41.8
1966	↑	↑	↓	$273,900	<22%> 6 mo.					$214,400	↑	↑	-7.0
1967	↑	↑	↑	↑	↓	↑	↑	↑	↑	↓	↑	↑	83.6
1968	↑	↓	↓	↑	+124% 26 mo.		↓	↑	↑	↑	↑	$565,100	36.0
1969													-25.1
1970													-17.4
1971					<58%> 72 mo.								16.5
1972													4.4
1973													-30.9
1974												$235,300	-19.9
1975	↓	↑	↑	↑	↑	↑	↓	↓	↓	↓	↑	↑	52.8
1976	↑	↑	↓	↓	↓	↑	↑	↓	↑	↑	↑	↑	57.4
1977	↑	↓	↓	↑	+352% 44 mo.		↑	↓	↑	↓	↑	↑	25.4
1978	↓	↑	↑	↑	↑	↓	↑	$1,063,600	<25%> 2 mo.		↑	↑	23.5
1979	↑	↓	↑	↑	↑	+70% 15 mo.		↑	↓	↓	↑	↑	43.5
1980	$1,362,000	<20%> 2 mo.	↑	↑	↑	↑	↑	↑	↑	↑	↑	↓	39.9
1981	↑	↑	↑	↑	↑	↑	+242% 39 mo.		↑	↑	↑	↓	13.9
1982	↓	↓	↓	↑	↓	↑		↑	↑	↑	↑	↑	28.0
1983	↑	↑	↑	↑	↑	$3,719,200	<15%> 13 mo.						39.7
1984							$3,156,900	↑	↑	↓	↓	↑	-6.7
1985	↑	↑	↓	↓	↑	↑	↑	↓	↓	↑	↑	↑	24.7
1986	↑	↑	↑	↑	+80% 37 mo.		↓	↑	↑	↓	↓		6.9
1987	↑	↑	↑	↓	↓	↑	↑	$5,688,400	<33%> 3 mo.	$3,836,700	↑		-9.3
1988	↑	↑	↑	↑	↓	↑	↓	↓	↑	↓	↓	↑	22.9
1989	↑	↑	↑	↑	↑	+54% 22 mo.		↑	$5,924,800				10.2
1990			<32%> 13 mo.							$4,023,500	↑	↑	-21.6
1991	↑	↑	↑	↑	↑	↓	↑	↑	↑	↑	↑	↑	44.6
1992	↑	↑	↓	↓	↓	↓	↓	↓	↑	↓	↑	↑	23.3
1993	↑	↓	↑	↓	↑	↓	↑	↑	↑	↑	↓	↑	21.0
1994	↑	↓	↓	↑	↓	+360% 86 mo.		↑	↑	↑	↑		3.1
1995	↑	↑	↑	↑	↑	↑	↑	↑	↑	↓	↑	↑	34.5
1996	↑	↑	↑	↑	↑	↓	↓	↑	↑	↓	↑	↑	17.6
1997	↑	↓	↓	↓	↑	↑	↑	↑	↑	↓	↓	$18,524,300	22.8%

Total Return: Includes reinvested dividends and capital gains   **Standard Deviation: 24.9**

Source: © Computed using data from Stocks, Bonds, Bills & Inflation 1997 Yearbook™ *with data updated January 1998, Ibbotson Associates, Chicago*

↑ ↓ *Up or Down Month*   ⬛ *Cyclical Declines*   ⬤ *Recovery (to pre-decline level)*   ⬭ *Net New Advancement*

REWARD*		**RISK PROFILE**	
Total Return (1960-1997)	14.7%	Mega Bear Market Decline	<58%>
Riskless Return (T-bills)	< 6.1%>	Average Bear Market Decline	<24%>
AVERAGE ANNUAL REWARD OF MICRO CAP STOCKS	**8.6%**		

*Annualized

CHART 5-6

5-Year Government Bonds
Growth of $100,000
(12/31/59 – 12/31/97)

Year	Jan	Feb	Mar	Apr	May	Jun	Jul	Aug	Sep	Oct	Nov	Dec	Annual Returns
1960	$100,000↑	↑	↑	↓	↑	↑	↑	↓	↑	↑	↓	↑	11.8%
1961	↓	↑	↑	↑	↓	↓	↑	↑	↑	↑	↓	↑	1.8
1962	↓	↑	↑	↑	↑	↓	↑	↑	↑	↑	↑	↑	5.6
1963	↑	↑	↑	↑	↑	→	↑	↑	↑	↑	↑	→	1.6
1964	↑	↑	↑	↑	↑	+45% 106 mo.		↑	↑	↑	↓	↑	4.1
1965	↑	↑	↑	↑	↑	↑	↑	↓	→	↑	↑		1.0
1966	→	↓	↑	↓	↑	↓	↓	↓	↑	↑	↑	↑	4.7
1967	↑	↓	↑	↓	↑	↓	↑	↓	↑	↓	↑	↑	1.0
1968	↑	↑	↓	↓	↑	↑	↑	↑	↑	$144,600			4.5
1969	<3%> 11 mo.								$139,700	↑	↓	↓	-0.7
1970	↑	↑	↑	↓	+25% 18 mo.		↑	↑	↑	↑	↑		16.8
1971	↑	↑	$174,300	<5%> 3 mo.		$165,600	↓	↑	↑	↑	↑	↑	8.7
1972	↑	↑	↑	↑	↑	↑	↑	↑	↑	+19% 32 mo.	↑		5.2
1973	↓	↓	↑	↑	↑	↓	↓	↑	↑	↑	↑		4.6
1974	↑	$197,700	<4%> 2 mo.		↑	↓	↓	↓	↑	↑	↑	↑	5.7
1975	↑	↑	↓	↓	↑	↑	↓	↓	↑	↑	↑		7.8
1976	↑	↑	↑	↑	↓	+47% 62 mo.		↑	↑	↑	↑	↑	12.9
1977	↓	↑	↑	↑	↑	↑	↑	↑	↑	↓	↑		1.4
1978	↑	↑	↑	→	↓	↑	↑	↑	↓	↑			3.5
1979	↑	↑	↑	↑	↑	$280,400		<9%>8 mo.					4.1
1980	$255,400	+19% 3 mo.		$304,300			<9%> 14 mo.						3.9
1981						$278,500	↑	↑	↑	↑	↑	↓	9.5
1982	↑	↑	↑	↑	↑	↑	↑	↑	↑	↑	↑	↑	29.1
1983	↑	↑	↑	↓	+59% 30 mo.		↑	↑	↑	↑	↑		7.4
1984	$444,000	<4%> 4 mo.		$428,500		↑	↑	↑	↑	↑	↑		14.0
1985	↑	↓	↓	↑	↑	↓	+64% 33 mo.		↑	↓	↑		20.3
1986	↑	↑	↑	↓	↑	↑	↓	↑	↑				15.1
1987	↑	$700,600	<3%>7 mo.				$676,600	↑	↑	↑			2.9
1988	↑	↑	↓	↓	↓	↑	↓	↓	↑	↑	↓	↓	6.1
1989	↑	↓	↑	↑	↑	↑	↑	↓	↓	↑	↑	↑	13.3
1990	↓	↑	↑	↓	↑	↑	↑	↓	↑	↑	↑		9.7
1991	↑	↑	↑	↓	+93% 76 mo.		↑	↑	↑	↑	↑		15.5
1992	↓	↑	↓	↑	↑	↑	↑	↑	↑	↓	↓	↑	7.2
1993	↑	↑	↑	↑	↓	↑	↑	↑	↑	↓	↑		11.2
1994	$1,305,000	<7%>10 mo.								$1,215,000	↑		-5.1
1995	↑	↑	↑	↑	↑	↓	↑	↑	↑	↑	↑		16.8
1996	↑	↓	↓	↓	↓	+30% 37 mo.	↓	↑	↑	↑	↓		2.1
1997	↑	↑	↓	↑	↑	↑	↑	↓	↑	↑	↓	$1,579,000	8.4%

Total Return: Includes reinvested interest   **Standard Deviation: 6.6**

Source: © Computed using data from Stocks, Bonds, Bills & Inflation 1997 Yearbook™ with data updated January 1998, Ibbotson Associates, Chicago

↑ ↓ *Up or Down Month*   ⬤ *Cyclical Declines*   ⬭ *Recovery (to pre-decline level)*   ⬭ *Net New Advancement*

REWARD*		**RISK PROFILE**	
Total Return (1960-1997)	7.5%	Mega Bear Market Decline	<9%>
Riskless Return (T-bills)	<6.1%>	Average Bear Market Decline	<5%>
AVERAGE ANNUAL REWARD OF 5-YEAR GOVERNMENT BONDS	**1.4%**		

*Annualized

CHART 5-7

Domestic Asset Classes in the Inflation Era

Chart 5-8 summarizes the risks and rewards of the major domestic asset classes. As can be seen, cash is truly the riskless, rewardless asset class. After inflation and taxes, money invested in cash is dead money — just treading water. *Real wealth stands still in cash* (T-bills, CD's, money market accounts).

Domestic Asset Classes – Risks and Rewards (1960-1997)

	Cash (30-Day T-Bills)	Bonds (5-Year Treasuries)	Bonds (Long-Term Corporate)
REWARD			
Return (Annualized)	6.1%	7.5%	7.6%
Riskless Return (T-bills)	-6.1%	-6.1%	-6.1%
REWARD	0%	1.4%	1.5%
RISK PROFILE			
Mega Bear Market	0	<9%>	<22%>
Average Bear Market	0	<5%>	<10%>

	Total U.S. Stock Market	S&P 500 Stocks	Mid/Small Cap Stocks	Micro Cap Stocks
REWARD				
Return (Annualized)	11.5%	11.6%	13.1%	14.7%
Riskless Return (T-bills)	-6.1%	-6.1%	-6.1%	-6.1%
REWARD	5.4%	5.5%	7.0%	8.6%
RISK PROFILE				
Mega Bear Market	<45%>	<43%>	<50%>	<58%>
Average Bear Market	<20%>	<19%>	<25%>	<24%>

Sources: © *Computed using data from* Stocks, Bonds, Bills & Inflation 1997 Yearbook™ *with data updated January 1998, Ibbotson Associates, Chicago; Center for Research in Security Prices (CRSP) University of Chicago*

CHART 5-8

In the family of domestic, high-quality bond asset classes, there is but one long-term winner: 5-year U.S. Treasury bonds. In Chapter 3, long-term U.S. Government bonds were found lacking. In more than 70 years, long-term U.S. Government bonds did not match the returns of the less volatile 5-year Treasuries. Now, long-term corporate bonds can also be safely eliminated from consideration for your Wealth and Retirement Portfolio. As shown in Chart 5-8, intermediate-term Treasury bonds substantially outperformed their corporate counterparts in each measurement of risk in the Inflation Era while providing an almost identical reward.

Domestic stocks do not offer such a lopsided comparison. True to the findings of the "size effect" discussed in Chapter 2, the large cap stocks' reward of 5.5% was outdone by the mid/small cap stocks' reward of 7.0%, which was topped by the outstanding reward of 8.6% from micro cap stocks. As each asset class's risk profile displays, however, the extra reward was earned with extra risk.

 It is interesting to note that, whereas the S&P 500 is a "large company index," it is an excellent gauge of the entire U.S. market. In fact, this is Standard and Poor's goal according to their own description of the index.[8] The S&P 500 has produced somewhat less risk than the Total U.S. Stock Market while delivering a slightly greater reward. No wonder the S&P 500 is so hard to beat when investing in large-cap-oriented mutual funds.

A Powerful Predictor

Long-term investors who have armed themselves with Historical Risk/Reward charts have a powerful advantage—they know what types of risks and rewards they are most likely to incur in the years ahead. The choice as to which asset classes to own is intentional. They understand the major risks of ownership.

 A Historical Risk/Reward chart is like a peek into the future of that asset class. All of the declines shown on its chart will likely unfold again—only in some unforeseen and random sequence. The good news is that the reward, too, is likely to repeat over the long haul.

Conclusion

The Historical Risk Reward charts introduced in this chapter are designed to give you a thorough understanding of both the risks and rewards that each domestic asset class has offered in the Inflation Era.

The clear winner in the bond family is 5-year U.S. Treasury bonds. Long-term quality corporate bonds produced about the same reward as the Treasuries but with a considerably higher risk profile. On the other hand, domestic stocks provided no clear-cut winner among the three asset classes—large cap, mid/small cap and micro cap. The smaller the size of the companies grouped into an asset class, the larger the rewards and the higher the risks (deeper bear markets).

6

Added Complexities of International Investments

Investing internationally entails some thorny issues which must be carefully considered. To begin with, a thorough analysis of international stock and bond asset classes is hampered by the lack of long-term quality data. Then the complications of currency gains and losses must be added to the normal investment criteria. These factors add a degree of uncertainty in evaluating international asset classes.

Nevertheless, investing in foreign securities offers a special type of diversification, so it is important to investigate its unique risks and rewards and then compare this approach with investing in U.S.-based global companies.

"International investing involves a whole set of risks
that investors are not necessarily compensated for."
— John Bogle, Chairman, Vanguard Funds

Innocents Abroad

Long known for our parochial, stay-at-home investing habits, Americans in the 1990s burst onto the scene of international investing. One major catalyst was the crash of 1987. Many financial observers noticed that the major international stock indexes did not suffer nearly the decline of the major U.S. stock indexes during the crash.

A second factor was the tearing down of the Berlin Wall and the crumbling of Communism. The world and all of its stock markets began to appear less menacing, less risky than before. A third impetus to diversifying into international stocks has been the wide circulation of an elliptical curve (developed in the mid-1990s) that showed how Americans could get higher returns with less risk by adding international stocks to their current portfolios (see Chart 6-3 on page 82).

As so often happens, the reality of international investing in the 1990s has not lived up to the expectation. Direct international investing has both unique attributes and thorny problems which need to be understood and evaluated by the American investor.

International Stocks: Similar But Different

Virtually all of the discussion of domestic stock markets in the first part of Chapter 2 is applicable to international stock markets in that they share these characteristics:

- Long-term rationality, short-term irrationality

- Long-term rewards far in excess of their domestic cash and bond markets and

- Size effect: smaller companies have produced superior long-term returns relative to their home-based large companies.

In addition, data available on the two major international markets (England and Germany) for the modern period for security analysis (1926-1997) indicates similar—if somewhat lower—performance for international stocks.[9] This result is echoed by the Jorion-Goetzmann study referred to in Chapter 2. Since the early 1920s, their research revealed that international stock markets lagged behind the U.S. market by just 0.28% per year—when each market was weighted by the size of its national economy.

This might imply that there is a universality to stock performance in major markets that cuts across country borders, that business is business in whatever language it is conducted and that the owners of common shares are treated equally in every culture.

There are two reasons why this conclusion is not 100% justified. The first is the limitation of available data and the second is the effect of currencies.

The Lack of Data

CRSP has provided meticulously compiled information on every publicly traded security of operating companies in America back to 1926. (Some of this information is accessed through reference guides like Ibbotson's SBBI.) This allows for in-depth research of every aspect of the risk and rewards of stock ownership in America.

Unfortunately, no such detailed long-term database is available for other countries. Therefore, conclusions built on the evaluation of international stocks are less reliable than with domestic stocks.

 Detailed analysis of international stocks begins with 1970, which means that virtually all of the truly in-depth studies of international stocks as an asset class for American investors are conducted in the historically "new era" of *floating* currencies discussed next.

The Importance of Currencies

International trade and commerce has been conducted for as long as history itself has been recorded. Businessmen want to trade, and no country can produce all the raw materials and finished goods it needs and wants within its own borders. One impediment to international trade has always been the establishment of a common unit of value that both sides could rely upon.

For most of history, gold has served the purpose of a common commodity of equal acceptance in all countries. Any country could participate in world trade if it would declare at what rate its currency was fully convertible to one ounce of pure gold. A gold standard was more or less in effect from the beginning of the modern period of security analysis 1926 through 1971 when President Nixon closed the "gold window" by declaring the U.S. dollar no longer convertible to gold.

From that year forward, the currencies of the world have *floated* against one another with no common anchor for business to rely upon. A change in a foreign currency's value will have the same impact on an American's investment abroad as it does on his/her travel abroad—a direct and immediate impact on cost and value.

The Currency Effect

A U.S. investor considering direct investment in international mutual funds will have two elements to her returns and two elements to her risks. She will have all the risks and rewards of underlying international stocks and additionally have the risks and rewards brought about by the changes in currency values as the foreign market's currencies are converted back into U.S. dollars.

The primary index of international stocks for U.S. investors is Morgan Stanley's EAFE Index (Europe, Australia and Far East). Chart 6-1 illustrates the performance of both the EAFE Index—*in U.S. dollars*—and the S&P 500 Index from the beginning of 1970 through the end of 1997.

For the entire period, the S&P 500 index delivered a 13.0% annualized total return, while the EAFE index produced a 12.4% annualized return for the American investor.

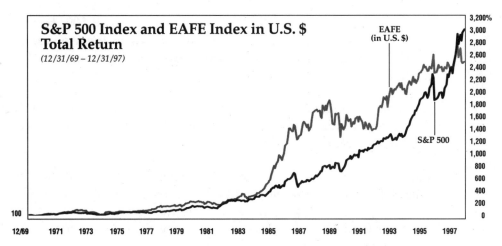

Source: Morgan Stanley Capital International; Standard & Poor's

CHART 6-1

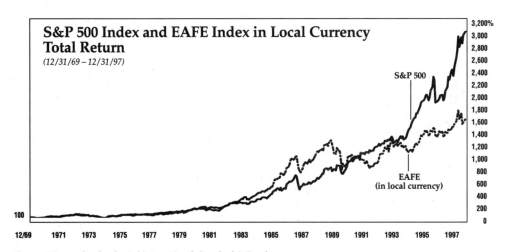

Source: Morgan Stanley Capital International; Standard & Poor's

CHART 6-2

Chart 6-2 also compares the EAFE Index to the S&P 500, but this chart compares *only* the returns from the stocks themselves; the EAFE Index is shown in local currencies—*not* converted into U.S. dollars.

As Chart 6-2 illustrates, the portfolio of international stocks (in local currencies) substantially underperformed the S&P 500 stock index producing a return of just 10.8% annualized for the period.

International stocks substantially underperformed U.S. stocks, but international currencies substantially outperformed the U.S. dollar. You lost ground on your *investment* in international stocks—but if your portfolio did not hedge your currency risk—you made money on your *currency speculation*!

This result shows up in the performance of international mutual funds. For example, George Murnaghan, a vice president at T. Rowe Price International Fund, reported that this fund had an annualized gain of 14.7% on average for the 15½ years ending in December 1996. Currency gains contributed about 1.3% per year and the underlying securities 13.4%. (The Wall Street Journal, February 11, 1997)

 With perfect hindsight, the big winner of this period maintained a 100% U.S. stock portfolio (to achieve the better stock returns) and purchased futures contracts on the international currencies, which outperformed the U.S. dollar during the post-gold-standard period.

Brief History of U.S. Dollar (Post World War II)

Before going further, a brief look at why the gold standard fell apart will be helpful in understanding the miserable performance of the U.S. dollar since 1971. The post-World War II gold standard was arrived at by establishing the price of gold to $35 per ounce in U.S. dollars and then pegging other countries' currencies to the U.S. dollar. The U.S. dollar would become the reserve currency of the world, de facto gold.

This was the Bretton Woods Agreement that provided the post-WW II world with a stable means of exchange to allow for the massive reconstruction that was desperately needed. Unfortunately, the inflation pressures that would normally be reflected in the price of gold were shifted to the U.S. dollar—because of gold's fixed price (by government decree).

For its part, the U.S. exacerbated the problem in the 1960s by financing both the Vietnam War and the Great Society social programs with printing press dollars, not taxes. Other countries recognized that U.S. gold reserves were increasingly inadequate to maintain convertibility to gold at $35 per ounce because of the expanding supply of U.S. dollars. These countries began shipping inflated U.S. dollars back to the U.S. to redeem them in gold. It was the dramatic call on its gold supply and the inability to maintain the conversion that finally forced the closing of the gold window by President Nixon.

In other words, by 1971, the U.S. dollar was vastly overvalued at $35 per ounce of gold. If the member nations to the Bretton Woods could have agreed upon a devaluation of the U.S. dollar, allowing for the convertibility at some higher number like $70 per ounce or more, then perhaps the fixed system of exchange could have survived. (Of course, a method of controlling the U.S. printing press would also have been needed, but this means giving up complete sovereignty with regard to internal monetary policy.)

This is an oversimplified view of the maze of post-World War II events, policies and actions that influenced world currencies. What this history provides is a context for understanding the long devaluation of the U.S. dollar that occurred after 1971 relative to the currencies of our main trading partners. From 1971 through 1997, the U.S. dollar lost approximately 60% of its value versus the Japanese yen, Swiss franc and German mark. (At its low point in April 1995, the U.S. dollar had lost a full 75% of its value versus these currencies.)

No Free Lunch

Many proponents of international investing ignore or downplay the role of currencies. As mentioned at the beginning of this chapter, they package international stocks as a *free lunch* for Americans—higher returns with lower risks. Chart 6-3 is a common illustration they use to support their argument.

 This chart shows that adding international stocks to a U.S. stock portfolio both lowered volatility and increased returns. When projecting the *future* risks and rewards of international stocks, this chart sends the wrong message. It is based on a unique period of world history in which currencies were removed from the gold standard and the U.S. dollar undertook a long unwinding of excessive valuation. The so-called free lunch was from the weakening U.S. dollar (or strengthening foreign currencies), *not* from international stocks.

In just three years after the dissemination of this chart (1995-1997), a large part of the so-called free lunch was given back! During these three years, the strength of the U.S. dollar *reduced* the returns from international securities to a U.S. investor. If the U.S. dollar finally reached an equilibrium level with other major currencies in the mid-1990s, then the "currency effect" will cease to have a significant impact on long-term returns from foreign markets.

Hypothetical U.S./International Equity Diversification Chart

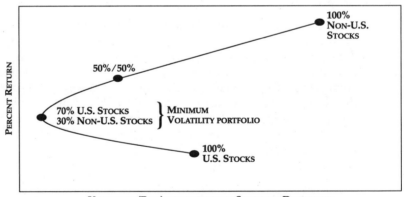

CHART 6-3

In addition, separating the performance of a country's stock market and currency may be misleading. Many economists believe that a devaluation of a country's currency will often make the businesses within that country more competitive internationally and thus benefit local share prices. **This means that you cannot simply strip away the currency effect to get at the real performance of the underlying stocks — one directly impacts the other!**

The Advantage of International Stocks

There is one very powerful advantage to investing in foreign equities: diversification. According to Jeremy Siegel's <u>Stocks for the Long Run</u> (1994), "Diversification will increase investor's expected compound returns while reducing risk even if expected returns on foreign equities do not exceed those of U.S. stocks."

Siegel elaborated on the diversifying impact of foreign stocks in a conversation with the author. He concluded that the long-term expected returns from unhedged foreign equities are about the same or slightly lower than from U.S. stocks.

As he expects the returns from foreign equities to remain uncorrelated with U.S. equities, combining U.S. and international stocks will be particularly worthwhile in reducing the volatility of a U.S.-only stock portfolio. In his view, "global investment is best viewed as an extension of domestic diversification." (The impact of foreign stocks within a portfolio will be demonstrated in Chapter 10.)

Emerging Markets

Emerging markets are a new and credible asset class within international investing. Emerging markets are those countries with stock markets that are not considered mature or developed. They may be roughly grouped into four geographic areas: Far East, Latin America, Central Europe/Russia, and Africa.

Can a fundamental case be made for dedicating a portion of a U.S. investor's stock portfolio to these stocks? The basic draw of investing in emerging markets boils down to this, *that's where the growth is*! Fueled by cheap labor and varying country or regional-specific advantages, the economies of many emerging countries are growing much faster than the 2–3% growth pace of developed economies like the U.S. With such high growth in these economies, their companies and stock markets must outperform those of the more sluggishly growing developed countries, right?

Wrong! According to Morgan Stanley, returns from emerging markets have lagged those of both the U.S. and non-U.S. developed equity markets by more than 5% per year in the 21 years ending 1996—*before* the turbulence of 1997! This is definitely not what most investors perceive to be the case.

There is yet another angle to the "growth story" as the following excerpt from the "outlook" column of the November 3, 1997, <u>Wall Street Journal</u> clearly illustrates.

> *Now, with financial bubbles bursting across the region, Asia is finding that its high-octane growth concealed sloppy banking practices, fueled dependence on foreign capital, inspired massive boondoggles, allowed rampant cronyism and widened the gap between the privileged and the masses. Expectations of ever-higher growth spawned enormous overcapacity....*

Stock returns do not necessarily follow economic growth in developed countries either. In roughly the same 21-year period cited above, the British stock market greatly outperformed that of Japan, yet the English economy grew at barely half the rate of the Japanese.[10]

 The lure of emerging markets appears to be not only the "growth story" but also the nature of their boom and bust cycles. When emerging markets boom, they explode to the upside. The dizzyingly high returns so easy to achieve during these periods are hard to ignore. From mid-1992 through the end of 1993 was such a period. **However, in this case, as with most such experiences, after the boom comes the bust. The bottom line is that this asset class has proved both unrewarding and highly volatile to long-term investors.**

Global Investing from the Safety of Home

Investing internationally has become synonymous with investing in foreign-based corporations. It is not the only way to invest overseas, and may not be the best way.

When renowned investor Warren Buffett made his one and only decision to invest in an offshore company (Guiness, English beverage company), *he* made the decision to invest internationally. On the other hand, when he made the most significant investment decision of his career (Coca Cola, U.S. beverage company), Buffett in effect yielded to Coke's management the decision to invest internationally.

Actually, both Coca Cola and Guiness are *global companies*. Guiness transacts a significant share of its business in America. And Coca Cola may call America home, yet consider these calendar year 1995 statistics on Coke:

- 71% of revenues were from outside the U.S.

- 80% of profits were from outside the U.S.

- 67% of new capital investment was outside the U.S.

Coca Cola is a premier global growth company that would have peaked long ago if it was only a premier American growth company.

American multinational companies, like Coca Cola and hundreds of others, are the most thoroughly globalized companies in the world. They produce about twice as much outside their borders as European and Japanese multinationals.[11]

Such geographic diversification helps U.S. companies smooth out the ups and downs internally. This is particularly true of investing in emerging markets. U.S.-based global companies are well positioned to invest in these countries and take advantage of their strategic production advantages and their rising consumer spending. U.S. companies' investment abroad is having a significant impact on their bottom lines and consequently their stock prices.

The U.S. has led the world in competitiveness throughout the middle 1990s according to the World Competitiveness Yearbook, and the future promises to be more of the same. Published annually by the Lausanne, Switzerland-based Institute for Management Development, the study measures and compares the competitiveness of 46 countries. It defines competitiveness in terms of the mechanisms that help create wealth within a nation. The United States has strengthened its lead in the world, coming out on top in the areas of economic strength, new technology and financial services, and placing second in international trade.[12]

 Investing in the U.S. large company asset class *is* investing internationally with all of the major advantages of domestic investing intact.

Conclusion: Investing in International Stocks is Not Necessary for Top Notch Returns

For Americans, the transition from investing mainly at home to becoming full participants in the international markets has been relatively short and bittersweet.

The conventional wisdom of the 1990s is that a dedicated portion of almost every American's portfolio should be invested abroad. Two of America's most respected investors do not agree.

Both Warren Buffett, America's most successful investor, and Peter Lynch, the highly regarded mutual fund manager, are on record against such a dedicated allocation to overseas investments. In 1993, Lynch wrote, "Let me put my two cents in about foreign investing....From all my trips abroad, I've concluded that the U.S. still has the best companies and the best system for investing in them."[13] And Buffett admitted he would have no interest in purchasing a foreign company, primarily because communication between companies and their foreign shareholders tends to be much weaker than that between companies domiciled in the same country as their owners.[14]

Both of these great investment managers made exceptions. Lynch occasionally invested Fidelity Magellan's assets abroad when he perceived significant and incomparable investment opportunities there. Buffett made but one foreign investment in his entire 40-year career, Guiness, as previously cited.

Buffett and Lynch are not alone. Many of today's cream-of-the-crop investment professionals have never left or seldom left our shores in search of better opportunities. These include Foster Friess (Brandywine Fund), Shelby Davis (New York Venture Fund), Bill Ruane (Sequoia Fund), Bill Nasgovitz (Heartland Value Fund), Bob Rodriguez (FPA Capital Fund) and many, many others.

Of course, many successful investment professionals, from Sir John Templeton (Templeton Funds) to Michael Price (Mutual Series Funds), have been very successful blending U.S. and international stock investments.

 The bottom line is that it has not been *necessary* to invest in foreign equities in order to achieve outstanding performance, and it is likely that it will not become necessary any time soon for long-term investors. Nevertheless, introducing international stock mutual funds into a U.S. portfolio may lower volatility and produce somewhat higher risk-adjusted rewards. This will be further evaluated in Chapter 8 and in Section III.

International Cash and Bonds

The role of currencies is much more direct and immediate for the foreign holders of a country's money market or bond investments. Any depreciation of a country's currency will directly reduce the value of its bonds or cash equivalents in the hands of a foreign national without the potential for an offsetting benefit as illustrated in the discussion of foreign stocks. The reverse is also true. The appreciation of a country's currency is a direct benefit to the foreign holders of that country's bonds and cash.

Therefore, the long unwinding of the value of the U.S. dollar was a huge and direct—if irregular—benefit to American holders of international cash and bonds between 1971 and 1995. Will this continue? It seems unlikely. Perhaps the U.S. dollar's strength since April of 1995 signals a major change of fortune going forward.

In the mid-1990s, the economic conditions and relative competitive positions between the U.S. and Japan, Germany, France and Switzerland have changed considerably from 1971. It is Europe and Japan that came to have relatively overvalued currencies (on a purchasing power parity basis), higher government debt and deficits as a percentage of their GNP (domestic economies), more intrusive governments, larger welfare and unfunded social security commitments, easier monetary policy and higher unit labor costs.

In addition, Lowell Bryan and Diana Farrell in Market Unbound: Unleashing Global Capitalism (1996) argue that global integration of bond markets is substantially completed. In other words, the bond yield in every country is approximately equal when adjusted for their individual inflation rates and country-specific risks.

This is evident from how closely world bond yields now tend to track U.S. bond interest rates. After 25 years of slightly negative correlation, U.S. and global interest rates have been 79% correlated since 1993.[15]

More importantly, all of the major trends in international markets such as...

- more currencies directly or indirectly tied to the U.S. dollar,

- integration of monetary policies by developed nations,

- global village of multi-national companies and

- exceptional cross-border trading and currency flows

...suggest that the high correlation in world bond returns will persist for some time. Given this leveling of relative yields worldwide, and considering currency risks associated with international investing, international bonds are not well positioned to enhance a portfolio's long-term returns. As Bryan and Farrell suggest, a dollar-based investor who is investing in bonds to reduce overall risks should stick to U.S. Treasury bonds.

7

Tangible Investments: Gold and REITs

The performance of precious metals tends to be extremely volatile while providing long-term returns that typically just match inflation. The other tangible investment considered in this chapter, real estate investment trusts (REITs), offers a combination of risk and reward that can be a valuable addition to your Wealth and Retirement Portfolio. REITs, however, come with a caveat with regard to their documented history, and different REIT indexes are miles apart.

"All that glisters is not gold."
— William Shakespeare, <u>The Merchant of Venice</u>

Common stocks, bonds and cash equivalents are by far the most widely held financial investments by Americans, either directly or through mutual funds.

There is, however, one other group of asset classes that are often included in portfolios. These are the tangible asset classes. The two most widely available for Wealth and Retirement Portfolios that are easily bought and sold are:

- Precious metals and
- REITs (Real Estate Investment Trusts)

Precious Metals

Gold and silver are speculations, not investments. Investments are income-producing. Speculations produce no income and therefore must rely on real or perceived changes in the relationship between supply and demand to effect a change in price.

Speculative commodities tend to make sharp moves up and down in the short run, yet often just match prevailing inflation over long periods of time. Gold is no exception.

In the Inflation Era (1960-1997), gold produced an average annualized return of approximately 5.8%. This result is well below the returns of bonds and stocks and even lower than that of cash equivalents!

The reality is that even this return for gold was artificially produced. From the end of 1935 to the beginning of 1960, the inflation rate averaged 3.2% per year. Yet gold's price could not adjust to inflation as it was held constant at $35 per ounce by government decree. Had gold's price been allowed free-market pricing, it is likely that its price would have been closer to $77 per ounce at the beginning of 1960. From that price in 1960, the average annual appreciation rate for gold until the end of 1997 would be close to the inflation rate for the same period. This is entirely consistent with gold's long history as an inflation hedge—or store of stable value.

"Consider three ounces of silver: The first is a four-drachma piece from Greece, from about 425 BC. The second, a U.S. silver dollar, dated 1898. The third, a U.S. Eagle silver coin, dated 1989.

"Each of these contains about one ounce of silver. Historians tell us that the one ounce of silver in 400 BC was about a week's wage for a skilled worker. About 100 years ago, a dollar, or its equivalent ounce of silver, was a day's wage. ('Another day, another dollar' is a slogan that survives from that era.) Today, a teenager working at a fast-food outlet can earn enough to buy an ounce of silver in an hour or two.

"So, in terms of the value of labor, an ounce of silver has lost about 95% of its value over the past 2,400 years. Had our Greek worker hoarded his week's pay in silver and hidden it, he'd be very disappointed if he were reincarnated and dug it up today!

"But suppose he had invested his week's pay in financial assets and earned a 3% annual return. Suppose that a week's pay in today's dollars is worth about $400. Since money doubles every 24 years at 3%, and since there have been one hundred 24-year periods since 400 BC, our worker (assuming he could avoid inheritance taxes and other forms of government confiscation) would have an account worth $400 times two to the 100th power. That's an 8 with 103 zeros after it."[16]

— Charles Carignan in Barron's

 Precious metals are a poor asset class choice for your Wealth and Retirement Portfolio. Their long-term returns are only expected to match inflation, at best, yet their volatility is very high. According to studies by the Wall Street firm of Morgan Stanley, since 1971 gold has generated less than a fourth of the returns small company stocks have, while experiencing as much or more fluctuation in market value.

REITs

Real estate investment trusts (REITs, pronounced "reets") are securitized real estate—listed securities that pool investors' money in all forms of real estate development, operations and lending. Typically the properties held by REITs are commercial real estate such as shopping centers and office buildings.

A REIT is like a mutual fund of real estate properties, typically offering investors a diversified portfolio with professional management. REITs are a form of common stock and therefore trade on stock exchanges. They offer "liquidity" to an otherwise illiquid real estate market.

Created by legislation passed in 1960, a REIT is essentially a corporation with special tax treatment. As investment companies, they can avoid income tax by distributing out 95% of their taxable income to their shareholders as do mutual funds. Most REITs generate substantial depreciation, so their cash flow is much higher than the taxable income they distribute. This allows many REITs to grow their asset base via new construction or new purchases over time. Still, it is the high yields from the distribution of their taxable income that is an essential feature of this asset class.

REITs have produced a checkered history in somewhat the same fashion as high-yield bonds. In their early years, REITs became a desirable source of capital for new realty development. A burst of enthusiasm in the late 1960s and early 1970s sent the microscopic base of REIT stocks soaring. In the early 1970s, the real estate market went through a devastating crash that went from one geographical area to another and one property type to the next. As real estate is typically highly leveraged—and REIT developments in the 1970s were no exception—the entire REIT industry was hit hard. Those most significantly impacted were those REITs referred to as mortgage REITs, which primarily lend money for commercial real estate development.

Chastened by this experience, most investors have focused on equity REITs which *own* the properties in the portfolio, although mortgage REITs and other specialized varieties continue to operate.

The National Association of Real Estate Investment Trusts (NAREIT) publishes several REIT indexes. From 1972 through 1997, the NAREIT equity index has outperformed the S&P 500 index. Incredibly, this performance was also delivered with less volatility than that of the stock market. However, the NAREIT index for all REITs (including mortgage and specialized REITs) has delivered substantially poorer performance. Therefore, only equity REITs will be evaluated for possible inclusion in your Wealth and Retirement Portfolio.

Note: The equity REIT performance is subject to qualification. In the REIT indexes published by NAREIT, "Only those REITs listed for the entire period are used in the Total Return calculation." In other words, delisted, bankrupt or merged REITs disappear from the index *without* accounting for their performance in the last month of their existence. How much impact this has had on performance is impossible to calculate.

The Rapid Growth of Equity REITs

The amount of publicly traded real estate is growing rapidly. The REIT asset class is quite small, totaling only about $132 billion at the end of 1997, yet it has grown substantially from a mere $9 billion base at the end of 1991. As the market has grown, so has the liquidity. About $250 million in REITs trade each day, more than 10 times as much as in 1992.

For years, large pension plans have allocated a portion of their investment portfolios to real estate. Increasingly, these pension plans are turning to REITs to fill out this allocation. This not only fuels demand for REITs but also helps stabilize the market as large pension plans tend to be patient, long-term holders of their investment assets.

The Maturing Public Real Estate Industry

From inception until the early 1990s, most equity REITs were little more than securitized ownership of specific properties. After a severe downturn in 1989 and 1990, the REIT has reinvented itself. Today, most are bigger, stronger and deeper than earlier models. The new model is that of a fully integrated real estate company. These companies have developed talented organizations that can acquire, manage, lease and develop commercial real estate.

The new model has opportunities to add value and increase cash flow from each activity within the organization. As the industry grows, it is also consolidating around ever bigger entities. Larger REITs are taking advantage of economies of scale and lower cost of capital.

The future of REITs looks quite promising. The real estate market in America alone is huge, being not too much smaller than the stock market. Yet it is still largely in private hands. Over time, a large portion of commercial real estate may find its way into public REITs. This is good for investors, too.

Publicly traded real estate securities offer ordinary investors access to real estate investment on terms that are typically more economical and favorable than direct property investment partnerships. When evaluating publicly traded real estate securities for inclusion in portfolios with the most predictable characteristics, however, the checkered history of REITs and their relatively new operating model needs to be taken into consideration. Model portfolios in Section III will be developed both with and without representation of equity REITs.

8

Comparing Risks and Rewards of Major Asset Classes

The risks and rewards of major *domestic* asset classes for the period 1960-1997 were presented in Chapter 5. These domestic asset classes enjoy a meticulously maintained monthly database that goes back to 1926. International stocks and bonds, equity REITs and U.S. high-yield bonds do not enjoy such a long historical database. Detailed indexes on these asset classes begin around 1970.

In this chapter, we compare the risks and rewards of the 13 major asset classes (except high-yield and international bonds) for the past quarter century (1972-1997). This comparison demonstrates clearly that some asset classes have performed better than others.

"At heart, America is a nation of careful gamblers. The contradictions in that description are rooted in our national character as a people who know instinctively that no gain is achieved without both risks and costs....The secret of our success, indeed the key to democracy itself, is in striking the balance between risk and rewards...."
— Senator Nancy Kassebaum (retired),
  The Wall Street Journal, December 26, 1996

In selecting the best investments to include in your Wealth and Retirement Portfolio, the various asset classes must be compared on an apples-to-apples basis.

All of the asset classes to be evaluated (except U.S. high-yield bonds and international bonds) have index-quality data back to January 1, 1972, (Chart 8-1). Therefore, January 1, 1972, through December 31, 1997, is the longest period for which all of these asset classes can be fairly compared during the same market conditions. This 26-year period of market history was rich in variation—major bull and bear markets, rising and falling inflation, high and low interest rates and stagnant and growing periods for the world economy. This is, therefore, an excellent quarter century to use as the basis of comparison.

Asset Class	Index Source	Beginning Date
Large Cap Stocks	CRSP	1/1/26
Mid/Small Cap Stocks	CRSP	1/1/26
Micro Cap Stocks	CRSP/DFA	1/1/26
Intermediate Bonds (5-year U.S. Treasuries)	Ibbotson	1/1/26
Long-Term Bonds (Long-Term Investment Grade Corporate)	Ibbotson	1/1/26
Cash (30-day U.S. T-bills)	Ibbotson	1/1/26
International Stocks (EAFE)	Morgan Stanley	1/1/70
International Bonds	Salomon Brothers	1/1/86
Equity REITs	NAREIT	1/1/72
Gold	Federal Register	1/1/72
U.S. High-Yield Bonds	Merrill Lynch	1/1/85

CHART 8-1

Index-quality data has been produced for international bonds and high-yield bonds for a relatively short period of time. Periods of less than 20 years are not thought to be statistically relevant for long-term planning purposes, and periods under 15 years are not even considered long-term for evaluation of asset classes. So, these asset classes would not yet be considered reliable for long-term portfolio planning.

Moreover, they have failed to make the cut for more fundamental reasons discussed previously, such as the currency effect on international bonds and the checkered history of high-yield bonds.

Historical Risk/Rewards

A Historical Risk/Reward chart covering the period 1972-1997 is presented for each of the following asset classes (Charts 8-2 through 8-9).

- Total U.S. Stock Market

- S&P 500 Index (Domestic Large Cap equivalent)

- Domestic Mid/Small Cap Stocks

- Domestic Micro Cap Stocks

- 5-Year U.S. Treasury Bonds

- International Stocks (in U.S. Dollars)

- Equity REITs

- Gold

The risks and rewards of these asset classes are summarized in Chart 8-10 and Chart 8-11.

Total Domestic Stock Market
Growth of $100,000
(12/31/71 – 12/31/97)

Year	Jan	Feb	Mar	Apr	May	Jun	Jul	Aug	Sep	Oct	Nov	Dec	Annual Returns
1972	$100,000	↑	↑	↑	↑	+17% 12 mo.		↑	↓	↑	↑	$116,900	16.9%
1973					<45%> 21 mo.								-18.1
1974									$64,000	↑	↓	↓	-27.2
1975	↑	↑	↑	↑	↑	↑	↑	↓	↓	↑	↑	↓	38.7
1976	↑	↑	↑	↓	↑	↑	↓	↓	↓	↓	↑	↑	26.7
1977	↓	↓	↓	↑	↓	+158% 65 mo.		↓	↑	↓	↑	↑	-4.2
1978	↓	↓	↑	↑	↑	↓	↑	↑	↓	↓	↑	↑	7.5
1979	↑	↓	↑	↑	↓	↑	↑	↑	↑	↓	↑	↑	23.0
1980	↑	$141,000	<11%> 1 mo.	↑	↑	↑	↑	+44% 12 mo.		↑	↑	↓	32.7
1981	↓	↑	$210,200										-3.7
1982			<16%> 16 mo.				$177,200	↑	↑	↑	↑	↑	20.8
1983	↑	↑	↑	↑	↑	↑	↓	↑	↑	↓	↑	↓	22.0
1984	↓	↑	↑	↑	↓	↑	↓	↑	↑	↑	↑	↑	4.3
1985	↑	↑	↓	+257% 61 mo.		↑	↓	↑	↓	↑	↑	↑	32.2
1986	↑	↑	↑	↓	↑	↑	↓	↑	↓	↑	↑	↓	16.1
1987	↑	↑	↑	↓	↑	↑	↑	$632,000	<30%> 3 mo.	$444,000	↑		1.8
1988	↑	↑	↓	↑	↑	↓	↓	↓	↑	↑	↓	↑	18.0
1989	↑	↓	↑	↑	↑	+68% 30 mo.		↑	↓	↑	↑	↑	28.9
1990	↑	↑	↑	↓	$743,600	<17%> 5 mo.				$618,500	↑	↑	-5.9
1991	↑	↑	↑	↑	↑	↓	↑	↑	↓	↑	↓	↑	34.7
1992	↓	↑	↓	↑	↑	↓	↑	↓	↑	↑	↑	↑	9.8
1993	↑	↑	↑	↓	↑	+294% 86 mo.		↑	↑	↑	↓	↑	11.1
1994	↑	↓	↓	↑	↑	↓	↑	↑	↓	↑	↓	↑	-0.1
1995	↑	↑	↑	↑	↑	↑	↑	↑	↑	↓	↑	↑	36.8
1996	↑	↑	↑	↑	↑	↓	↓	↑	↑	↓	↑	↓	21.3
1997	↑	↓	↓	↑	↑	↑	↑	↓	↑	↓	↑	$2,437,200	31.3%

Total Return: Includes reinvested dividends and capital gains   **Standard Deviation: 17.0**

Source: Center for Research in Security Prices (CRSP) University of Chicago

↑ ↓ *Up or Down Month*   ⬛ *Cyclical Declines*   ⬤ *Recovery (to pre-decline level)*   ⬭ *Net New Advancement*

REWARD*

Total Return (1972-1997)	13.1%
Riskless Return (T-bills)	< 6.9%>

AVERAGE ANNUAL REWARD OF
TOTAL DOMESTIC STOCK MARKET **6.2%**

*Annualized

RISK PROFILE

Mega Bear Market Decline	<45%>
Average Bear Market Decline	<18%>

CHART 8-2

For information on larger or updated versions of these charts, call 800-772-0072.

Historical Risk/Reward Chart

Standard and Poor's 500
Growth of $100,000
(12/31/71 – 12/31/97)

Year	Jan	Feb	Mar	Apr	May	Jun	Jul	Aug	Sep	Oct	Nov	Dec	Annual Returns
1972	$100,000	↑	↑	↑	↑	+19% 12 mo.		↑	↓	↑	↑	$119,000	19.0%
1973				<43%> 21 mo.									-14.7
1974									$68,300	↑	↓	↓	-26.5
1975	↑	↑	↑	↑	↑	↑	↓	↓	↓	↑	↑	↓	37.2
1976	↑	↓	↑	↓	↓	↑	↓	↑	↑	↓	↓	↑	23.8
1977	↓	↓	↓	↑	↓	↓	+124% 65 mo.		→	↓	↑	↑	-7.2
1978	↓	↓	↑	↑	↑	↓	↑	↑	↓	↓	↑	↑	6.6
1979	↑	↓	↑	↑	↓	↑	↑	↓	↑	↓	↑	↑	18.4
1980	↑	$158,200	<10%> 1 mo.	↑	↑	↑	+42% 8 mo.		↑	↑	$203,200		32.4
1981													-4.9
1982			<17%> 20 mo.				$168,800	↑	↑	↑	↑	↑	21.4
1983	↑	↑	↑	↑	↓	↑	↓	↑	↓	↑	↑	↓	22.5
1984	↓	↓	↑	↑	↓	↓	↓	↑	↑	↑	↓	↑	6.3
1985	↑	↑	↑	↓	↑	+282% 61 mo.		↓	↓	↑	↑	↑	32.2
1986	↑	↑	↑	↓	↑	↑	↓	↑	↓	↑	↑	↓	18.5
1987	↑	↑	↑	↓	↑	↑	↑	$644,000	<30%> 3 mo.		$453,800	↑	5.2
1988	↑	↑	↓	↑	↑	↑	↓	↓	↑	↑	↓	↑	16.8
1989	↑	↓	↑	↑	↑	+71% 30 mo.		↑	↓	↓	↑	↑	31.5
1990	↓	↑	↑	↓	$777,000	<15%> 5 mo.			$662,700		↑	↑	-3.2
1991	↑	↑	↑	↑	↑	↓	↑	↑	↓	↑	↓	↑	30.5
1992	↓	↑	↓	↑	↑	↓	↑	↑	↑	↑	↑	↑	7.7
1993	↑	↑	↑	↓	↑	↑	↓	↑	↓	↑	↓	↑	10.0
1994	↑	↓	↓	↑	↑	+286% 86 mo.		↑	↓	↑	↓	↑	1.3
1995	↑	↑	↑	↑	↑	↑	↑	↑	↑	↓	↑	↑	37.4
1996	↑	↑	↑	↑	↑	↑	↓	↑	↑	↑	↑	↓	23.1
1997	↑	↑	↓	↑	↑	↑	↑	↓	↑	↓	↑	$2,559,600	33.3%

Total Return: Includes reinvested dividends and capital gains **Standard Deviation: 16.5**

Source: © Computed using data from Stocks, Bonds, Bills & Inflation 1997 Yearbook™ with data updated January 1998, Ibbotson Associates, Chicago

↑ ↓ *Up or Down Month* ⬛ *Cyclical Declines* ⬤ *Recovery (to pre-decline level)* ⬭ *Net New Advancement*

REWARD*

Total Return (1972-1997)	13.3%
Riskless Return (T-bills)	< 6.9%>
AVERAGE ANNUAL REWARD OF STANDARD AND POOR'S 500	**6.4%**

Annualized

RISK PROFILE

Mega Bear Market Decline	<43%>
Average Bear Market Decline	<18%>

CHART 8-3

Historical Risk/Reward Chart

Mid/Small Cap Stocks
Growth of $100,000
(12/31/71 – 12/31/97)

Year	Jan	Feb	Mar	Apr	May	Jun	Jul	Aug	Sep	Oct	Nov	Dec	Annual Returns
1972	$100,000	↑	↑	→	↓	+9% 11 mo.		↑	↓	↓	$108,900		7.8%
1973						<50%> 22 mo.							-28.5
1974									$54,900	↑	↓	↓	-25.4
1975	↑	↑	↑	↑	↑	↑	↓	↓	↓	↑	↑	↓	57.7
1976	↑	↑	↑	↓	↓	↑	↓	↓	↑	↓	↑	↑	42.2
1977	↓	↓	↑	↑	+225% 47 mo.		↓	↓	↑	↓	↑	↑	7.5
1978	↓	↑	↑	↑	↑	↓	↑	$178,100	<17%> 2 mo.		↑	↑	12.5
1979	↑	↓	↑	↑	↓	↑	↑	↑	↓	↓	↑	↑	37.1
1980	↑	↓	↓	↑	↑	↑	↑	+115% 31 mo.		↑	↑	↓	31.9
1981	↑	↑	↑	↑	$317,600	<19%> 14 mo.							3.5
1982							$259,800	↑	↑	↑	↑	↑	26.0
1983	↑	↑	↑	↑	↑	↑	↓	↓	↑	↓	↑	↓	28.7
1984	↓	↓	↑	↓	↓	↑	↓	↑	↑	↓	↓	↑	-1.2
1985	↑	↑	↓	↓	+265% 61 mo.		↑	↓	↓	↑	↑	↑	31.8
1986	↑	↑	↑	↑	↑	↑	↓	↑	↓	↑	↑	↓	13.3
1987	↑	↑	↑	↓	↑	↑	↑	$926,300	<31%> 3 mo.	$635,800	↑		-1.5
1988	↑	↑	↑	↑	↓	↑	↓	↓	↑	↑	↓	↑	22.6
1989	↑	↑	↑	↑	↑	↑	+65% 30 mo.		↓	↓	↑	↑	23.1
1990	↓	↑	↑	↓	$1,045,800	<24%> 5 mo.				$792,300	↑	↑	-12.9
1991	↑	↑	↑	↑	↑	↓	↑	↑	↓	↑	↓	↑	44.3
1992	↑	↑	↓	↑	↑	↓	↑	↓	↑	↑	↑	↑	16.7
1993	↑	↓	↑	↓	↑	↑	↑	↑	↑	↑	↓	↑	16.9
1994	↑	↓	↓	↑	↓	+325% 86 mo.		↑	↓	↑	↓	↑	-2.2
1995	↑	↑	↑	↑	↑	↑	↑	↑	↑	↓	↑	↑	32.3
1996	↑	↑	↑	↑	↑	↓	↓	↑	↑	↓	↓	↑	17.5
1997	↑	↓	↓	↑	↑	↑	↑	↑	↑	↓	↑	$3,365,700	24.2%

Total Return: Includes reinvested dividends and capital gains   **Standard Deviation: 20.2**

Source: Center for Research in Security Prices (CRSP) University of Chicago
↑ ↓ *Up or Down Month*   ⬤ *Cyclical Declines*   ⬤ *Recovery (to pre-decline level)*   ⬭ *Net New Advancement*

REWARD*		RISK PROFILE	
Total Return (1972-1997)	14.5%	Mega Bear Market Decline	<50%>
Riskless Return (T-bills)	< 6.9%>	Average Bear Market Decline	<23%>
AVERAGE ANNUAL REWARD OF MID/SMALL CAP STOCKS	7.6%		

*Annualized

CHART 8-4

For information on larger or updated versions of these charts, call 800-772-0072.

Historical Risk/Reward Chart

Micro Cap Stocks
Growth of $100,000
(12/31/71 – 12/31/97)

Year	Jan	Feb	Mar	Apr	May	Jun	Jul	Aug	Sep	Oct	Nov	Dec	Annual Returns
1972	+15% 2 mo. $100,000 $114,600												4.4%
1973					<50%> 34 mo.								-30.9
1974												$57,800	-19.9
1975	↑	↑	↑	↑	↑	↑	↓	↓	↓	↓	↑	↓	52.8
1976	↑	↑	↓	↓	↓	↑	↑	↓	↑	↓	↓	↑	57.4
1977	↑	↑	↑	↑	↓	↑	+352% 44 mo.↓	↓	↓	↑	↑		25.4
1978	↓	↑	↑	↑	↑	↓	↑	$261,100	<25%> 2 mo.		↑	↑	23.5
1979	↑	↓	↑	↑	↑	+70% 15 mo.		↑	↓	↓	↑	↑	43.5
1980	$334,300	<20%> 2 mo.		↑	↑	↑	↑	↑	↑	↑	↑	↓	39.9
1981	↑	↑	↑	↑	↑	↑	↑	↓	↓	↑	↑	↓	13.9
1982	↓	↓	↓	↑	↓	↓	↓	↑	↑	↑	↑	↑	28.0
1983	↑	↑	↑	↑	↑	↑	↓	↓	↑	↓	↑	↓	39.7
1984	↓	↓	↑	↓	↓ +423% 89 mo.	↓		↑	↑	↓	↓	↑	-6.7
1985	↑	↑	↓	↓	↑	↑	↑	↓	↓	↑	↑	↑	24.7
1986	↑	↑	↑	↑	↑	↑	↓	↑	↓	↑	↓	↓	6.9
1987	↑	↑	↑	↓	↓	↑	↑	$1,396,300	<33%> 3 mo.	$941,800	↑		-9.3
1988	↑	↑	↑	↑	↓	↑	↓	↓	↓	↓	↓	↑	22.9
1989	↑	↑	↑	+54% 22 mo.		↓	↑	↑	$1,454,300				10.2
1990					<32%> 13 mo.					$987,600	↑	↑	-21.6
1991	↑	↑	↑	↑	↑	↑	↑	↑	↑	↑	↓	↑	44.6
1992	↑	↑	↓	↑	↓	↑	↑	↓	↑	↑	↑	↑	23.3
1993	↑	↓	↑	↓	↑	↓	↑	↑	↓	↑	↓	↑	21.0
1994	↑	↓	↓	↑	↓	+360% 86 mo.		↑	↑	↑	↓	↑	3.1
1995	↑	↑	↑	↑	↑	↓	↓	↑	↑	↓	↓	↓	34.5
1996	↑	↑	↑	↑	↑	↓	↓	↑	↑	↓	↓	↑	17.6
1997	↑	↓	↓	↓	↑	↑	↑	↑	↑	↓	↓	$4,547,200	22.8%

Total Return: Includes reinvested dividends and capital gains   **Standard Deviation: 22.4**

Source: © Computed using data from Stocks, Bonds, Bills & Inflation 1997 Yearbook™ *with data updated January 1998,* Ibbotson Associates, Chicago

↑ ↓ *Up or Down Month*   ⬛ *Cyclical Declines*   ⬛ *Recovery (to pre-decline level)*   ⬜ *Net New Advancement*

REWARD*

Total Return (1972-1997)	15.5%
Riskless Return (T-bills)	< 6.9%>
AVERAGE ANNUAL REWARD OF MICRO CAP STOCKS	8.6%

*Annualized

RISK PROFILE

Mega Bear Market Decline	<50%>
Average Bear Market Decline	<26%>

CHART 8-5

Historical Risk/Reward Chart

Government Bonds (5-Year Treasury)
Growth of $100,000
(12/31/71 – 12/31/97)

Year	Jan	Feb	Mar	Apr	May	Jun	Jul	Aug	Sep	Oct	Nov	Dec	Annual Returns
1972	$100,000	↑	↑	↑	↑	↑	↑	↑	↑	↑	↑	↑	5.2%
1973	↓	↓	↑	↑	↑	+11% 26 mo.		↑	↑	↑	↑	↑	4.6
1974	↑	$110,500	<4%> 2 mo.		↑	↓	↑	↓	↑	↑	↑	↑	5.7
1975	↑	↑	↓	↓	↑	↑	↓	↓	↑	↑	↓	↑	7.8
1976	↑	↑	↑	↑	↓	↑	↑	↑	↑	↑	↑	↑	12.9
1977	↓	↑	↓	↑	↑	+47% 62 mo.		↑	↑	↓	↑	↓	1.4
1978	↑	↑	↑	↑	→	↓	↑	↑	↑	↑	↑	↑	3.5
1979	↑	↓	↑	↑	↑	$156,600	<9%> 8 mo.						4.1
1980	$142,700		+19% 3 mo.		$170,000	<9%> 15 mo.							3.9
1981							$155,600		↑	↑	↑	↓	9.5
1982	↑	↑	↑	↑	↑	↓	↑	↑	↑	↑	↑	↑	29.1
1983	↑	↑	↓	↑	+59% 29 mo.		↓	↑	↑	↑	↑	↑	7.4
1984	$248,100	<4%> 4 mo.			$239,400	↑	↑	↑	↑	↑	↑	↑	14.0
1985	↑	↓	↑	↑	↑	↑	↓	↑	↑	↑	↑	↑	20.3
1986	↑	↑	↑	↑	↓	↑	↑	↑	↓	↑	↑	↓	15.1
1987	↑	↑	↓	↓	↓	↑	↑	↓	↓	↑	↑	→	2.9
1988	↑	↑	↓	↓	↓	↑	↓	↑	↑	↑	↓	↓	6.1
1989	↑	↓	↑	↑	↑	+205% 116 mo.		↓	↑	↑	↑	↑	13.2
1990	↓	↑	↑	↓	↑	↑	↑	↓	↑	↑	↑	↑	9.7
1991	↑	↑	↓	↑	↑	↑	↓	↑	↑	↑	↑	↑	15.5
1992	↓	↑	↓	↑	↑	↑	↑	↑	↑	↓	↓	↑	7.2
1993	↑	↑	↑	↑	↓	↑	↑	↑	↑	↑	↓	↑	11.2
1994	$729,500					<7%> 10 mo.					$678,900	↑	-5.1
1995	↑	↑	↑	↑	↑	↑	↓	↓	↑	↑	↑	↑	16.8
1996	↑	↓	↓	↓	↓	↓	+30% 37 mo.		↑	↓	↑	↓	2.1
1997	↑	↑	↓	↑	↑	↑	↑	↓	↑	↑	↓	$882,300	8.4%

Total Return: Includes reinvested interest　　　　　　　　**Standard Deviation: 6.9**

Source: © Computed using data from Stocks, Bonds, Bills & Inflation 1997 Yearbook™ with data updated January 1998, Ibbotson Associates, Chicago

↑ ↓ *Up or Down Month*　　⬛ *Cyclical Declines*　　⬤ *Recovery (to pre-decline level)*　　⬜ *Net New Advancement*

REWARD*		RISK PROFILE	
Total Return (1972-1997)	8.7%	Mega Bear Market Decline	<9%>
Riskless Return (T-bills)	<6.9%>	Average Bear Market Decline	<6%>
AVERAGE ANNUAL REWARD OF GOVERNMENT BONDS (5-YEAR TREASURY)	1.8%		

*Annualized

CHART 8-6

Historical Risk/Reward Chart

International Stocks – EAFE (U.S. $)
Growth of $100,000
(12/31/71 – 12/31/97)

Year	Jan	Feb	Mar	Apr	May	Jun	Jul	Aug	Sep	Oct	Nov	Dec	Annual Returns
1972	$100,000	↑	↑	↑	↑	+53% 15 mo.		↑	↓	↑	↑	↑	37.6%
1973	↑	↑	$152,600	<42%> 18 mo.									-14.2
1974									$89,200	↑	↑	↓	-22.1
1975	↑	↑	↓	↑	↓	↓	↓	↓	↓	↑	↑	↑	37.1
1976	↑	↓	↓	↓	↓	↑	↓	↑	↓	↓	↑	↑	3.7
1977	↓	↑	↑	↑	↓	↑	↓	↑	↓	↑	↓	↑	12.5
1978	↑	↑	↑	↑	↑	+201% 79 mo.		↑	↑	↑	↓	↑	34.3
1979	↑	↓	↑	↓	↓	↑	↑	↑	↑	↓	↑	↑	6.2
1980	↑	↓	↓	↑	↑	↑	↓	↑	↑	↑	↓	↑	24.4
1981	↓	↓	↑	$270,500	<19%> 17 mo.								-1.0
1982									$218,700	↑	↑	↑	-0.9
1983	↓	↑	↑	↑	↓	↑	↑	+68% 18 mo.	→		↑	↑	24.6
1984	↑	↑	$368,400	<13%> 4 mo.		$304,600	↑	↓	↑	↑	↑		7.8
1985	↑	↓	↑	↑	↑	↑	↑	↑	↑	↑	↑	↑	56.8
1986	↑	↑	↑	↑	↓	+327% 37 mo.		↑	↓	↓	↑	↑	69.9
1987	↑	↑	↑	↑	↑	↓	↓	$1,300,800	<15%> 2 mo.		↑	↑	24.9
1988	↑	↑	↑	↑	↓	↓	↑	↓	↑	↑	↑	↑	28.6
1989	↑	↑	↓	↑	+48% 26 mo.		↑	↓	↑	↓	↑	$1,632,500	10.8
1990	↑	<31%> 9 mo.							$1,133,200	↑	↓	↑	-23.2
1991	↑	↑	↓	↑	↓	↓	↑	↓	↑	↑	↓	↑	12.5
1992	↓	↓	↓	↑	↑	↓	↓	↑	↓	↓	↑	↑	-11.9
1993	↑	↑	↑	↑	↑	↓	↑	↑	↓	↑	↓	↑	32.9
1994	↑	↓	↓	↑	↓	+90% 87 mo.		↑	↓	↑	↓	↑	8.1
1995	↓	↓	↑	↑	↓	↓	↑	↓	↑	↓	↑	↑	11.6
1996	↑	↑	↑	↑	↓	↑	↓	↑	↑	↓	↑	↓	6.3
1997	↓	↑	↑	↑	↑	↑	↑	↓	↑	↓	↓	$2,155,900	1.8%

Total Return: Includes reinvested dividends and capital gains   **Standard Deviation: 21.9**

Source: Morgan Stanley Capital International

↑ ↓ *Up or Down Month*   ⬛ *Cyclical Declines*   ⬛ *Recovery (to pre-decline level)*   ⬤ *Net New Advancement*

REWARD*

Total Return (1972-1997)	12.5%
Riskless Return (T-bills)	< 6.9%>
AVERAGE ANNUAL REWARD OF INTERNATIONAL STOCKS	5.6%

*Annualized

RISK PROFILE

Mega Bear Market Decline	<42%>
Average Bear Market Decline	<20%>

CHART 8-7

For information on larger or updated versions of these charts, call 800-772-0072.

Historical Risk/Reward Chart

Equity REITs
Growth of $100,000
(12/31/71 – 12/31/97)

Year	Jan	Feb	Mar	Apr	May	Jun	Jul	Aug	Sep	Oct	Nov	Dec	Annual Returns
1972	$100,000	↑	↓	+14% 9 mo.		↑	↑	↓	$113,800				8.0%
1973					<37%> 27 mo.								-15.5
1974												$71,700	-21.4
1975	↑	↑	↑	↑	↑	↑	↓	↓	↓	↓	↑	↑	19.3
1976	↑	↑	↑	↓	↑	↑	↑	↑	↑	↑	↑	↓	49.9
1977	↑	↑	↑	↑	↑	+246% 56 mo.		↑	↑	→	↑	↑	20.5
1978	↓	↑	↑	↑	↓	↓	↑	↑	↓	↓	↑	↑	10.3
1979	↑	↑	↑	↑	↓	↓	↑	$248,300	<13%> 2 mo.		↑	↑	35.9
1980	↑	↑	↓	↓	↑	↑	↑	↑	↓	↑	↓	↓	24.4
1981	↑	↑	↑	↑	↓	↑	↓	↓	↓	↑	↑	↓	6.0
1982	↓	↓	↓	↑	↓	↓	↑	↑	↑	↑	↑	↑	21.6
1983	↑	↓	↑	↑	↑	+324% 93 mo.		↓	↓	↑	↑	↑	30.6
1984	↑	↑	↑	↓	↓	↓	↓	↑	↑	↑	↑	↑	20.9
1985	↑	↑	↑	↑	↑	↑	↑	↓	↓	↓	↑	↑	19.1
1986	↑	↑	↑	↓	↑	↑	↓	↑	↓	↑	↓	↑	19.2
1987	↑	↑	↑	↓	↓	↑	$919,600	<18%> 3 mo.		$754,900	↑	↑	-3.6
1988	↑	↑	↑	↑	↓	↑	↑	↓	↑	↓	↓	↑	13.5
1989	↑	↓	↑	↑	+37% 22 mo.		↑	$1,032,400	<24%> 14 mo.				8.8
1990										$785,900	↑	↓	-15.4
1991	↑	↑	↑	↑	↑	↓	↑	↓	↑	↓	↑	↑	35.7
1992	↑	↓	↓	↓	↑	+135% 36 mo.		↑	↑	↓	↑	↑	14.6
1993	↑	↑	↑	↓	↓	↑	↑	↑	↑	$1,853,500	<16%> 2 mo.		19.7
1994	↑	↑	↓	↑	↑	↓	↓	↑	↓	↓	↓	↑	3.2
1995	↓	↑	↓	↓	↑	↑	↑	↑	↑	↓	↑	↑	15.3
1996	↑	↑	↓	↑	↑	+92% 48 mo.		↑	↑	↑	↑	↑	35.3
1997	↑	↓	↑	↓	↑	↑	↑	↓	↑	↓	↑	$2,982,600	18.8%

Total Return: Includes reinvested dividends and capital gains   **Standard Deviation: 16.3**

Source: National Association of Real Estate Investment Trusts (NAREIT), 1972-1996; Vanguard REIT Index Fund (1997)

↑ ↓ *Up or Down Month*   ⬤ *Cyclical Declines*   ⬤ *Recovery (to pre-decline level)*   ◯ *Net New Advancement*

REWARD*

Total Return (1972-1997)	14.0%
Riskless Return (T-bills)	< 6.9%>
AVERAGE ANNUAL REWARD OF EQUITY REITs	7.1%

*Annualized

RISK PROFILE

Mega Bear Market Decline	<37%>
Average Bear Market Decline	<18%>

CHART 8-8

For information on larger or updated versions of these charts, call 800-772-0072.

Historical Risk/Reward Chart

Gold
Growth of $100,000
(12/31/71 – 12/31/97)

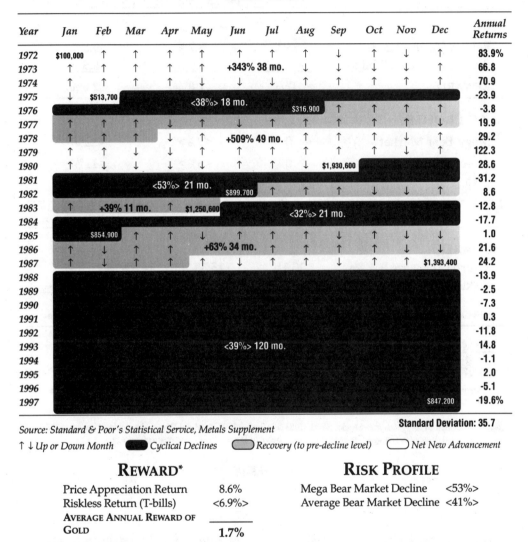

Year	Jan	Feb	Mar	Apr	May	Jun	Jul	Aug	Sep	Oct	Nov	Dec	Annual Returns
1972	$100,000	↑	↑	↑	↑	↑	↑	↑	↓	↑	↓	↑	83.9%
1973	↑	↑	↑	↑	↑	+343% 38 mo.	↓	↓	↓	↓	↑		66.8
1974	↑	↑	↑	↑	↓	↓	↓	↑	↑	↑	↑	↑	70.9
1975	↓	$513,700			<38%> 18 mo.								-23.9
1976							$316,900	↑	↑	↑	↑		-3.8
1977	↑	↑	↑	↓	↑	↓	↑	↑	↑	↑	↑	↓	19.9
1978	↑	↑	↑	↓	↑	+509% 49 mo.	↑	↑	↑	↑	↓	↑	29.2
1979	↑	↑	↓	↓	↑	↑	↑	↑	↑	↑	↓	↑	122.3
1980	↑	↓	↓	↓	↓	↑	↑	↓	$1,930,600				28.6
1981				<53%> 21 mo.									-31.2
1982					$899,700	↑	↑	↑	↑	↓	↓	↑	8.6
1983	↑	+39% 11 mo.		↑	$1,250,600		<32%> 21 mo.						-12.8
1984													-17.7
1985	$854,900	↑	↑	↓	↑	↑	↑	↓	↑	↓	↓		1.0
1986	↑	↓	↑	↑	+63% 34 mo.	↑	↑	↑	↑	↑	↓	↓	21.6
1987	↑	↓	↑	↑	↑	↓	↑	↑	↓	↑	↑	$1,393,400	24.2
1988													-13.9
1989													-2.5
1990													-7.3
1991													0.3
1992													-11.8
1993					<39%> 120 mo.								14.8
1994													-1.1
1995													2.0
1996													-5.1
1997												$847,200	-19.6%

Standard Deviation: 35.7

Source: Standard & Poor's Statistical Service, Metals Supplement

↑ ↓ Up or Down Month   ●Cyclical Declines   ●Recovery (to pre-decline level)   ○Net New Advancement

REWARD*		RISK PROFILE	
Price Appreciation Return	8.6%	Mega Bear Market Decline	<53%>
Riskless Return (T-bills)	<6.9%>	Average Bear Market Decline	<41%>
AVERAGE ANNUAL REWARD OF GOLD	**1.7%**		

*Annualized

Note: Gold has a unique attribute compared to all the other asset classes: it never has recovered to its 1980 valuation. To make gold's Historical Risk/Reward chart have similar characteristics to those of the other asset classes, the methodology was changed to allow for a decline to end at a subsequent low point even though there was no recovery to a new high in market value.

CHART 8-9

Domestic Asset Classes – Risks and Rewards (1972-1997)

	Cash (30-Day T-Bills)	Bonds (5-Year Treasuries)	Bonds (Long-Term Corporate)
REWARD			
Return (Annualized)	6.9%	8.7%	9.5%
Riskless Return (T-bills)	-6.9%	-6.9%	-6.9%
REWARD	0%	1.8%	2.6%
RISK PROFILE			
Mega Bear Market	0	<9%>	<22%>
Average Bear Market	0	<6%>	<11%>

	Total U.S. Stock Market	S&P 500 Stocks	Mid/Small Cap Stocks	Micro Cap Stocks
REWARD				
Return (Annualized)	13.1%	13.3%	14.5%	15.5%
Riskless Return (T-bills)	-6.9%	-6.9%	-6.9%	-6.9%
REWARD	6.2%	6.4%	7.6%	8.6%
RISK PROFILE				
Mega Bear Market	<45%>	<43%>	<50%>	<50%>
Average Bear Market	<18%>	<18%>	<23%>	<26%>

Sources: © Computed using data from Stocks, Bonds, Bills & Inflation 1997 Yearbook™ with data updated January 1998, Ibbotson Associates, Chicago; Center for Research in Security Prices (CRSP) University of Chicago

CHART 8-10

Among stock and bond asset classes, the relationship between long-term risk and long-term rewards is a close one—yet some asset classes have clearly delivered more reward for the risks taken.

	International Stocks (Local Currencies)	International Stocks (U.S. $)	Equity REITs	Gold
REWARD				
Return (Annualized)	11.0%	12.5%	14.0%	8.6%
Riskless Return (T-bills)	-6.9%	-6.9%	-6.9%	-6.9%
REWARD	4.1%	5.6%	7.1%	1.7%
RISK PROFILE				
Mega Bear Market	<40%>	<42%>	<37%>	<56%>
Average Bear Market	<20%>	<20%>	<18%>	<41%>

CHART 8-11

Evaluating the Asset Classes

A primary goal of this book is to develop the best portfolios built from history's top-performing asset classes. Charts 8-10 and 8-11 distill 26 years of head-to-head competition among these candidates for your Wealth and Retirement Portfolio. It shows the reward each provided and the risk endured to achieve that reward. The results are quite revealing. Chart 8-12 hands out "awards" to those asset classes exhibiting exceptional characteristics.

Asset Class "Awards" for the Quarter Century Ending December 1997

Most Rewarding:	Micro Caps blew away the competition
Least Risky:	5-Year Treasury Bonds, easily
Most Pitiful:	Gold served up stratospheric risks with a puny reward
Best Risk/Reward:	Equity REITs for posting better risk and reward characteristics than the total U.S. stock market
Biggest Surprise:	International stocks in their own currencies provided sub-par rewards

CHART 8-12

Domestic Stocks and Bonds

The domestic stock and bond asset classes were previously evaluated in detail over the Inflation Era (Chapter 5). They are included here in order to compare all asset classes over exactly the same time period with the same economic, political and market conditions.

International Stocks

Chapter 6 provided a detailed presentation of the problems in evaluating international stocks based on the 1970-1997 period even though this is the longest period of index-quality data. As you will recall, this period matches the "new era" of floating currencies fairly closely, and a prime characteristic of this period has been the unwinding of an overvalued U.S. dollar. This raises questions that are not possible to answer. For example, how would a long-term period of U.S. dollar stability—or strength—change the risks and rewards of international stock investing?

The longest period of index-quality data (1970-1997) indicates that international stocks in their own currencies have underperformed U.S. stocks. The reward they offered was significantly less than that of the total U.S. stock market, but their risks were fairly similar. Therefore, international stocks in their own currencies have not yet proved themselves as a valuable addition to long-term portfolios.

On the other hand, the rewards from international stocks for U.S. dollar based investors have been desirable for this period of analysis. They offered both slightly lower rewards and risks when compared to the total domestic stock market. Therefore, international stocks in U.S. dollars will be considered acceptable for inclusion in long-term portfolios. (As our enthusiasm is tempered by the uncertainties cited, our model portfolios will be built both with and without international stocks in Section III.)

 Referring back to the conclusions reached in Chapter 6, international stocks are not a *necessary* ingredient for profitable long-term portfolios, yet their less-than-perfect correlation with domestic stock markets should, in fact, reduce the overall risk within a portfolio. Both of these conclusions—and the concept of correlation—will be explored in more detail in Section III.

REITs

Equity REIT stocks offer a scenario very similar to that of international stocks. The reward from equity REITs also fits just between those of domestic large cap stocks and mid/small cap stocks while the risk from equity REITs was less than either. In addition, equity REITs have offered less than perfect correlation of returns (similar timing of advances and declines). Therefore, adding equity REITs to a portfolio should lower the overall risk within a long-term portfolio without reducing the expected long-term reward.

As with international stocks, there is a significant caveat to this conclusion. In the discussion of REITs in Chapter 7, it was pointed out that the equity REIT of today is far different than its 1970s and 1980s counterparts. This is an asset class of rising importance and integrity, yet still somewhat in its infancy. Therefore, the model portfolios in Section III will be assembled both with and without this asset class.

Gold

In Chapter 6, it was stated that gold is not an investment, it is a speculation. Its Historical Risk/Reward Chart 8-9 vividly demonstrates that gold is indeed in a class by itself. This precious metal generated fantastic risks, yet only produced a small reward. This asset class will obviously *not* be considered for your Wealth and Retirement Portfolio.

Note: Stocks of gold mining companies have far different characteristics than the metal. These stocks, like all operating companies, are included within the domestic asset classes based upon their market capitalizations.

Each Asset Class is Its Own "Market"

Market commentators often refer to "the market cycle" as if all asset classes were following the same ebb and flow. As you look through the Historical Risk/Reward charts for each asset class within this chapter, take special notice of **when** their bear markets occurred. You will quickly notice that *there is no general market cycle.* Each asset class marches to its own drummer; each asset class is in effect a market unto itself.

 Certainly periods like 1973-'74 and 1987 caught all of the common stock asset classes in their down draft, but not bonds or cash. And over the balance of the past quarter century, each asset class—even each equity asset class—advanced and declined in its own unique rhythm. Therefore, the performance of any investment such as a mutual fund, can only be fairly judged against the overall performance of the asset class within which it invests.

Conclusions

Section II began with the proposition that all of the major asset classes would be reviewed and analyzed as to their inherent risks and rewards using the best available *long-term* databases. With these evaluations completed, the following asset classes did not make the cut:

- Long-Term U.S. Treasury Bonds
- Long-Term U.S. Corporate Bonds
- High-Yield Bonds
- International Bonds
- Emerging Market Stocks
- Gold

In addition, two asset classes were sub-divided into two more narrowly defined asset class categories. One category of each asset class also failed to meet the desired criteria:

- Non-Equity REITs
- International Stocks in Local Currencies

This leaves the following asset classes as the most reliable long-term, dedicated asset class positions for your Wealth and Retirement Portfolio:

- 30-Day U.S. Treasury Bills
- 5-Year U.S. Treasury Bonds
- Domestic Large Cap Stocks or S&P 500
- Domestic Mid/Small Cap Stocks
- Domestic Micro Cap Stocks
- International Stocks in U.S. Dollars (with caveats noted)
- Equity REITs (with caveats noted)

These will be the asset classes used in Section III to build the most predictable portfolios.

Section III

Asset Allocation Policies

Overview of Section III

This section will take a thorough look at the impact of a portfolio's "asset allocation."

This term is used to denote the proportions of individual asset classes within a portfolio. The asset allocation of a well-diversified portfolio is the major determinant of its risks and rewards.

Maintaining fixed allocations to reliable asset classes is the most predictable policy for long-term portfolio planning. The historically best-performing asset allocations for each level of risk are introduced and thoroughly evaluated as far back as 1926.

Special attention was given to:

- How did each asset allocation policy perform during stressful market conditions such as the Great Depression?

- What range of returns did it offer during short and intermediate-term investment horizons?

- How much income could it provide for a long retirement without threatening to run out prematurely?

9

Creating Predictable Long-Term Portfolios

Substantially all of the investments within your Wealth and Retirement Portfolio can be placed in one of the 13 asset classes evaluated in Section II. The proportion that your portfolio holds of each asset class is referred to as its *asset allocation*.

Whether your asset allocation is "tactical" (ever changing) or "fixed" (proportions that are constant over time), it is a major contributor to your investment performance.

The appropriate fixed allocation policy offers the highest probability of achieving a targeted long-term rate of return and the least risk of falling short of your ultimate retirement objective.

> *"In investment management, the real opportunity to achieve superior results is not in scrambling to outperform the market, but in establishing and adhering to appropriate investment policies over the long term — policies that position the portfolio to benefit from riding the main long-term forces of the market."*
>
> — Charles D. Ellis, <u>Investment Policy</u>, Homewood, Illinois: Business One Irwin, 1985

Fundamental Principles

An asset allocation policy sets the proportions for each asset class held within a portfolio. Underlying the importance of such a policy are these fundamental principles:

- **Financial History is Rational and Repetitive (Over the Long-Term)** - The variation in returns from each asset class diminishes significantly with time. The longer an asset class (or combination of asset classes) is held, the more reliable its performance in relation to historical averages.

- **Primary Determinant of Performance** - The larger share of a portfolio's of long-term performance is determined by its asset allocation; the much smaller share is due to individual security selection.[17] (Ironically, many investors approach the investment process as if the exact opposite were true.)

- **Diversification** - A cross-section of securities within an asset class is required in order to deliver the return associated with that asset class and to minimize the risk of opportunity loss (substantial underperformance).

Asset Allocation Policy

An investment policy is satisfied by fixed allocations among the major asset class families: stocks, bonds and cash. The further breakdown into individual asset classes may be approached from either a tactical or fixed strategy.

A tactical asset allocation strategy attempts to continuously steer the stock portion of the investment policy into the currently most attractive individual stock asset classes (by some evaluation method).

A fixed asset allocation policy attempts to find a highly desirable "fixed mix" of asset classes that can be adhered to over time. This is a much more predictable approach. The fixed asset allocation strategy will be the focus of the remainder of this book. At a minimum, evaluating the risks and rewards of fixed allocation strategies over long time periods provides a unique opportunity to uncover outstanding "benchmark portfolios." These are portfolios that have provided superior performance *without* the aid of human (or computer) changes over time.

Example of a fixed asset allocation strategy:

Investment Policy	*Fixed Asset Allocation Policy*	
Stocks (50%)	20%	dedicated to domestic Large Cap mutual funds
	10%	dedicated to domestic Mid/Small Cap mutual funds
	5%	dedicated to domestic Micro Cap mutual funds
	10%	dedicated to International Stock mutual funds
	5%	dedicated to equity REIT mutual funds
Bonds (30%)	25%	dedicated to Intermediate U.S. Treasury Bond mutual funds
	5%	dedicated to High-Yield Bond mutual funds
Cash (20%)	20%	allocated to a general Money Market account
	100%	Total Portfolio

CHART 9-1

An asset allocation policy such as this one provides a highly predictable track for your Wealth and Retirement Portfolio. The lion's share of its ultimate performance will be determined by strict adherence to the policy—regardless of the mutual funds purchased for each asset class.[18]

The point cannot be overemphasized that the selection of asset classes and the proportions decided upon are the primary determinant of any portfolio's final performance. *This is by far the most significant set of decisions with regard to your Wealth and Retirement Portfolio and/or its benchmark.*

For those who choose to invest via a fixed asset allocation policy, their investment decisions become very focused. Mutual funds are only evaluated against other mutual funds within the same asset class. For example, a domestic micro cap fund is only evaluated against other micro cap funds to fulfill that requirement of the asset allocation. (Strategies for evaluating and selecting mutual funds are thoroughly analyzed in Section IV.)

It should be readily apparent that you would not choose a fixed asset allocation strategy unless you were completely committed to it. The balance of Section III is dedicated to the historically best performing fixed asset allocation policy for each level of risk.

10

The Best Performing Portfolios

The very best asset allocation policy is that combination of asset classes which will produce the highest long-term reward for a given level of risk.

Virtually every combination of the reliable asset classes (from Section II) has been evaluated in order to uncover the historically best-performing asset allocation policies. Based upon these studies, four Domestic Model Portfolios and four Global Model Portfolios are introduced.

The risk profiles of these model portfolios range from conservative to very aggressive. Each of these model portfolios offers the prospect of long-term predictability for your Wealth and Retirement Portfolio.

> *"Clients' expectations tend to err in an optimistic
> direction; they believe that higher returns are
> possible with less risk than is actually the case."*
> — Roger C. Gibson, Asset Allocation,
>   Homewood, Illinois: Business One Irwin,
>   1990

The Best Asset Allocation Strategy for You

The very best asset allocation policy for you is the one that has offered the highest rate of return within your own comfort level for risk—based on its long-term performance.

In order for you to isolate this ideal portfolio structure, you should know the following information about any asset allocation policy you may be considering for your Wealth and Retirement Portfolio:

- the maximum degree of decline it has suffered in a mega bear market

- the range of percentage declines it has incurred during normal cyclical bear markets

- the long-term *average return* it has delivered above that of 30-day Treasury bills

- the *range of returns* it has produced over various market conditions.

History is your best guide as to the risks and rewards that are inherent within complete portfolios just as it was with individual asset classes. Seeing is believing.

The historical risks and rewards for the most outstanding asset allocation policies (domestic-only and global) can now be introduced. These "model portfolios" should prove invaluable as you consider the best structure for your own portfolio or as a benchmark to measure your portfolio against.

Of course, you can still opt for the most common strategy—none at all. This is the hodge-podge portfolio discussed in Chapter 1 that never establishes nor adheres to a definite overall game plan and whose risks and rewards are all but unknown. Assuming you establish a fixed asset allocation policy, you will build a much higher level of predictability into your long-term planning.

Balanced Asset Allocation Policies & Correlation Benefits

The term "balanced" is an excellent descriptive term for portfolios made up of stocks, bonds and cash in that they bring together the growth from stocks, the higher income from bonds and the ready liquidity of cash equivalents.

As illustrated in Section II, the degrees of fluctuation are far different within these three U.S. asset class families. What may not have been so obvious, however, is that the *direction* of advances or declines within one asset class may not correlate with those of another. Bonds may *zig* when stocks *zag*. This was clearly evident in the stock market crash of October 1987. Bonds went up in value as stocks went down. Cash was, of course, stable in market value. Asset classes that do not move up and down together are said to be uncorrelated.

Look at Charts 10-1 and 10-2. Sitting side by side are the bull and bear markets of the total domestic stock market and long-term corporate bonds over the Inflation Era. As is clearly evident, stocks and bonds have gone in different directions more often than not.

By combining uncorrelated asset classes within your portfolio, you achieve the diversification necessary to smooth fluctuations and reduce overall risk. Academic research has proved that the more uncorrelated the returns from various asset classes, the less volatile will be the aggregate performance of a portfolio.

In addition, balanced asset allocations can lessen volatility for the same return. This is illustrated below by comparing the performance of the S&P 500 with that of a balanced portfolio (67% stocks, 28% bonds, 5% cash) for the period from 1960 to 1997.

	Inflation Era (1960-1997)		
	Return	*Worst Decline*	*Average Decline*
S&P 500	11.6%	43%	19%
Balanced Portfolio (page 131)	11.2%	30%	15%

 This is an excellent result—*a slightly reduced return with far lower risk!* Not all balanced portfolios are created equal, however. Each specific portfolio design delivers unique long-term rewards and shorter-term risks.

Total Domestic Stock Market
Growth of $100,000
(12/31/59 – 12/31/97)

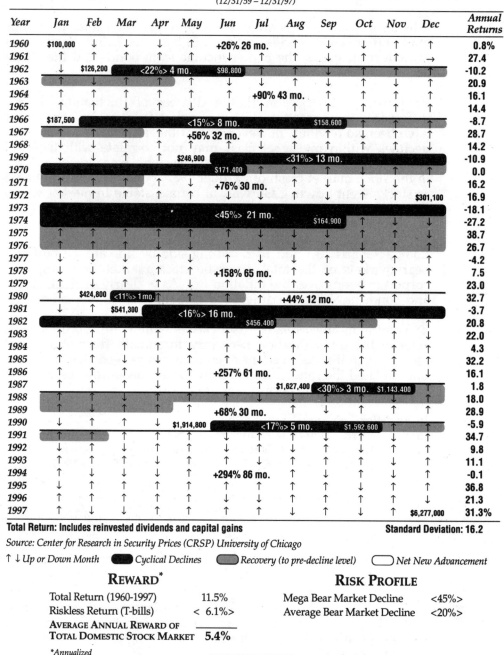

Year	Jan	Feb	Mar	Apr	May	Jun	Jul	Aug	Sep	Oct	Nov	Dec	Annual Returns
1960	$100,000	↓	↓	↑	+26% 26 mo.			↑	↓	↓	↑	↑	0.8%
1961	↑	↑	↑	↑	↑	↓	↑	↑	↓	↑	↑	→	27.4
1962	↓	$126,200	<22%> 4 mo.			$98,800	↑	↑	↓	↑	↑	↑	-10.2
1963	↑	↓	↑	↑	↑	↓	↓	↑	↓	↑	↓	↑	20.9
1964	↑	↑	↑	↑	↑	↑	+90% 43 mo.		↑	↑	↑	↑	16.1
1965	↑	↑	↓	↑	↓	↑	↑	↑	↑	↑	↑	↑	14.4
1966	$187,500		<15%> 8 mo.						$158,600	↑	↑	↑	-8.7
1967	↑	↑	↑	↑	+56% 32 mo.		↑	↓	↑	↑	↑	↑	28.7
1968	↓	↓	↑	↑	↑	↑	↓	↑	↑	↑	↑	↓	14.2
1969	↓	↓	↑	↑	$246,900		<31%> 13 mo.						-10.9
1970						$171,400	↑	↑	↑	↓	↑	↑	0.0
1971	↑	↑	↑	↑	↓	+76% 30 mo.		↑	↓	↓	↓	↑	16.2
1972	↑	↑	↑	↑	↑	↓	↑	↑	↓	↑	↑	$301,100	16.9
1973					*	<45%> 21 mo.							-18.1
1974									$164,900	↑	↓	↓	-27.2
1975	↑	↑	↑	↑	↑	↑	↓	↓	↓	↑	↑	↓	38.7
1976	↑	↑	↑	↓	↓	↑	↓	↓	↓	↓	↑	↑	26.7
1977	↓	↓	↓	↑	↓	↑	↓	↓	↓	↓	↑	↑	-4.2
1978	↓	↓	↑	↑	↑	+158% 65 mo.		↑	↓	↓	↑	↑	7.5
1979	↑	↓	↑	↑	↓	↑	↑	↑	↑	↓	↑	↑	23.0
1980	↑	$424,800	<11%> 1 mo.	↑	↑	↑	↑	+44% 12 mo.		↑	↑	↓	32.7
1981	↓	↑	$541,300	<16%> 16 mo.									-3.7
1982							$456,400	↑	↑	↑	↑	↑	20.8
1983	↑	↑	↑	↑	↑	↑	↓	↑	↑	↓	↑	↓	22.0
1984	↓	↑	↑	↑	↓	↑	↓	↑	↑	↑	↑	↑	4.3
1985	↑	↑	↓	↓	↑	↑	↑	↓	↓	↑	↑	↑	32.2
1986	↑	↑	↑	↓	↑	+257% 61 mo.		↑	↓	↑	↑	↓	16.1
1987	↑	↑	↑	↓	↑	↑	↑	$1,627,400	<30%> 3 mo.	$1,143,400			1.8
1988	↑	↑	↓	↑	↑	↑	↓	↓	↑	↑	↓	↑	18.0
1989	↑	↓	↑	↑	↑	+68% 30 mo.		↑	↓	↑	↑	↑	28.9
1990	↓	↑	↑	↓	$1,914,800	<17%> 5 mo.				$1,592,600	↑	↑	-5.9
1991	↑	↑	↑	↑	↑	↓	↑	↑	↓	↓	↓	↑	34.7
1992	↓	↑	↓	↑	↑	↓	↑	↓	↑	↓	↑	↑	9.8
1993	↑	↑	↑	↓	↑	↑	↓	↑	↑	↑	↓	↑	11.1
1994	↑	↓	↓	↓	↑	+294% 86 mo.		↑	↓	↑	↓	↑	-0.1
1995	↓	↑	↑	↑	↑	↑	↑	↑	↑	↓	↑	↑	36.8
1996	↑	↑	↑	↑	↑	↓	↓	↑	↑	↑	↑	↓	21.3
1997	↑	↓	↓	↑	↑	↑	↑	↓	↑	↓	↑	$6,277,000	31.3%

Total Return: Includes reinvested dividends and capital gains   **Standard Deviation: 16.2**

Source: Center for Research in Security Prices (CRSP) University of Chicago

↑ ↓ *Up or Down Month*   ⬛ *Cyclical Declines*   ⬛ *Recovery (to pre-decline level)*   ⬭ *Net New Advancement*

REWARD*

Total Return (1960-1997)	11.5%
Riskless Return (T-bills)	< 6.1%>
AVERAGE ANNUAL REWARD OF TOTAL DOMESTIC STOCK MARKET	**5.4%**

*Annualized

RISK PROFILE

Mega Bear Market Decline	<45%>
Average Bear Market Decline	<20%>

CHART 10-1

Long-Term Corporate Bonds

Growth of $100,000
(12/31/59 – 12/31/97)

Year	Jan	Feb	Mar	Apr	May	Jun	Jul	Aug	Sep	Oct	Nov	Dec	Annual Returns
1960	$100,000	↑	↑	↓	↓	↑	↑	↑	↓	↑	↓	↑	9.1%
1961	↑	↑	↓	↓	↑	↓	↑	↓	↑	↑	↑	↓	4.8
1962	↑	↑	↑	↑	→	↓	↓	↑	↑	↑	↑	↑	7.9
1963	↑	↑	↑	↓	↑	↑	↑	↑	↓	↑	↑	↓	2.2
1964	↑	↑	↓	↑	↑	+38% 104 mo.		↑	↑	↑	→	↑	4.8
1965	↑	↑	↑	↑	↓	→	↑	↓	↓	↑	↓	↓	-0.5
1966	↑	↓	↓	↑	↓	↓	↑	↓	↑	↑	↓	↑	0.2
1967	↑	↓	↑	↓	↓	↑	↑	↓	↑	↓	↓	↑	-5.0
1968	↑	↑	↓	↑	↑	↑	↑	$137,500	<14%> 16 mo.				2.6
1969												$118,100	-8.1
1970	↑	↑	↓	↓	↓	↑	↑	↑	↑	↓	↑	↑	18.4
1971	↑	↓	↑	↓	↓	↑	↓	↑	↓	↑	↑	↑	11.0
1972	↓	↑	↑	↑	↑	+42% 50 mo.		↑	↑	↑	↑	→	8.0
1973	↓	↑	↑	↑	↓	↓	↓	↑	↑	↓	↑	↓	1.1
1974	↓	$167,600		<12%> 6 mo.			$146,800	↑	↑	↑	↑		-3.1
1975	↑	↑	↓	↓	↑	↑	↓	↓	↓	↑	↑	↑	14.6
1976	↑	↑	↑	↓	↓	↑	↑	↑	↑	↑	↑	↑	18.6
1977	↓	↓	↑	↑	+63% 58 mo.		↓	↑	↓	↓	↑	↓	1.7
1978	↓	↓	↑	↓	↑	↑	↑	↑	↓	↓	↑	↓	-0.1
1979	↑	↓	↑	↓	↑	$239,600							-4.2
1980				<22%> 27 mo.									-2.8
1981									$186,000	↑	↑	↓	-1.2
1982	↓	↑	↑	↑	↑	+75% 19 mo.		↑	↑	↑	↑	↑	42.6
1983	↓	↑	↑	$324,900		<10%> 13 mo.							6.3
1984				$292,900	↑	↑	↑	↑	↑	↑	↑	↑	16.9
1985	↑	↓	↑	↑	↑	↑	↓	↑	↑	↑	↑	↑	30.1
1986	↑	↓	↑	↓	↓	+101% 33 mo.		↑	↓	↑	↑	↑	19.8
1987	↑	$588,900		<11%> 7 mo.				$526,100	↑	↑	↓		-0.3
1988	↓	↑	↓	↓	↓	↑	↑	↓	↑	↑	↓	↑	10.7
1989	↑	↓	↑	↑	↑	+40% 27 mo.		↓	↑	↑	↑	$735,500	16.2
1990	<4%> 4 mo.			$706,000	↑	↑	↑	↓	↑	↑	↑	↑	6.8
1991	↑	↑	↑	↑	↑	↓	+69% 45 mo.		↑	↑	↑	↑	19.9
1992	↓	↑	↓	↑	↑	↑	↑	↑	↓	↑	↑		9.4
1993	↑	↑	↑	↑	↑	↑	↑	↑	↑	↑	↓	↑	13.2
1994	$1,189,300		<9%> 9 mo.							$1,079,700	↑	↑	-5.8
1995	↑	↑	↑	↑	↑	+29% 14 mo.		↑	↑	↑	↑	↑	27.2
1996	<7%> 4 mo.			$1,308,500	↑	↑	↑	↑	↑	↑	↑	↓	1.4
1997	↓	↑	↓	↑	↑	+22% 20 mo.		↓	↑	↑	↑	$1,600,600	13.0%

Total Return: Includes reinvested interest   **Standard Deviation: 8.1**

Source: © Computed using data from Stocks, Bonds, Bills & Inflation 1997 Yearbook™ with data updated January 1998, Ibbotson Associates, Chicago

↑ ↓ *Up or Down Month*   ■ *Cyclical Declines*   ▬ *Recovery (to pre-decline level)*   ⬭ *Net New Advancement*

REWARD*		**RISK PROFILE**	
Total Return (1960-1997)	7.6%	Mega Bear Market Decline	<22%>
Riskless Return (T-bills)	<6.1%>	Average Bear Market Decline	<10%>
AVERAGE ANNUAL REWARD OF LONG-TERM CORPORATE BONDS	**1.5%**		

*Annualized

CHART 10-2

Risk does not feel the same to every investor!

Domestic-Only Model Portfolios

The domestic-only model portfolios are made up of the following asset classes: large cap stocks, mid/small cap stocks, micro cap stocks, 5-year Treasury bonds and cash (T-bills). One of the important findings from Section II of this book is that each of these five domestic asset classes has delivered a level of return that adequately compensates for its individual level of risk.

As importantly, the relationship between their risks and rewards has been shown to be *consistent and reliable* over various long-term periods of their financial history.

Using the historical monthly data for each asset class in the Inflation Era (1960-1997), practically every combination of these five asset classes was tested in order to uncover the fixed asset allocation policy that produced the highest reward for a given level of risk. (A detailed description of the guidelines used is on page 261 in the Appendix.)

A requirement for each model portfolio is that it be meaningful and realistic for the specific group of investors for whom it is intended. Put simply, this means that an asset allocation policy that refers to itself as "conservative" should have delivered a very low risk profile over its long history, yet still produced a reward that finances a much higher level of retirement income than a straight bond and/or cash portfolio. The terms "moderate" and "aggressive" should also meet similar tests when slotted into the full historic range of risks and rewards.

Based upon these objectives, the following four Domestic-Only Model Portfolios are now ready to be introduced: **Conservative Balanced, Moderate Balanced, Aggressive Balanced and 100% Stocks.** One of these model portfolios may be the best asset allocation policy for your Wealth and Retirement Portfolio. Each model portfolio has delivered a consistently high rate of return for its level of exposure to bear market declines.

Conservative Balanced Portfolio (Domestic Only)

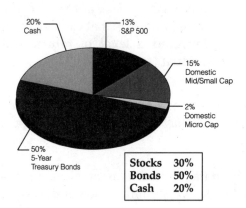

Stocks	30%
Bonds	50%
Cash	20%

Primary Objective: The asset allocation with the highest return that never incurred a decline in market value exceeding 10% (from any month-end high to a subsequent month-end low).

Performance Highlights: (1960-1997)

Rate of Return	9.1%
Riskless Rate (T-bills)	-6.1%
Reward	**3.0%**

Mega Bear Market Decline: 10%

Average Bear Market Decline: 7%

Moderate Balanced Portfolio (Domestic Only)

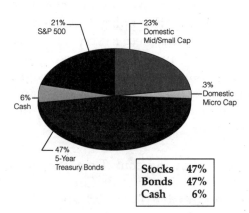

Stocks	47%
Bonds	47%
Cash	6%

Primary Objective: The asset allocation with the highest return that never incurred a decline in market value exceeding 20% (from any month-end high to a subsequent month-end low).

Performance Highlights: (1960-1997)

Rate of Return	10.2%
Riskless Rate (T-bills)	-6.1%
Reward	**4.1%**

Mega Bear Market Decline: 20%

Average Bear Market Decline: 11%

Aggressive Balanced Portfolio (Domestic Only)

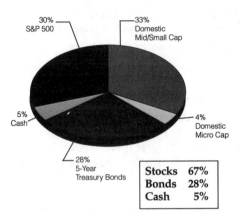

Stocks	67%
Bonds	28%
Cash	5%

Primary Objective: The asset allocation with the highest return that never incurred a decline in market value exceeding 30% (from any month-end high to a subsequent month-end low).

Performance Highlights: (1960-1997)

Rate of Return	11.2%
Riskless Rate (T-bills)	-6.1%
Reward	**5.1%**

Mega Bear Market Decline: 30%

Average Bear Market Decline: 15%

100% Stocks Portfolio (Domestic Only)

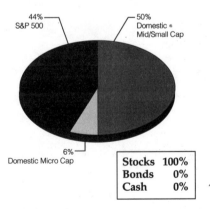

Stocks	100%
Bonds	0%
Cash	0%

Primary Objective: The asset allocation with the higest return without regard to risk, yet within the stated guidelines

Performance Highlights: (1960-1997)

Rate of Return	12.7%
Riskless Rate (T-bills)	-6.1%
Reward	**6.6%**

Mega Bear Market Decline: 46%

Average Bear Market Decline: 22%

Evaluating the Domestic Model Portfolios

Rewards. The table below shows the cumulative return achieved by each domestic model portfolio (and cash) during the Inflation Era from an initial investment of $100,000.

Domestic Model Portfolio Growth - $100,000 (1960-1997)

Cash	Conservative Balanced	Moderate Balanced	Aggressive Balanced	100% Stocks
$931,300	$2,734,900	$4,036,900	$5,697,700	$9,333,000

The return from a Conservative Balanced portfolio more than tripled the return from T-bills. This is three times the principal, which provides three times the retirement income. A Moderate Balanced portfolio nearly quintuples the return from cash, Aggressive provides seven times and 100% Stocks resulted in over ten times more principal and income-generating capacity.

The long-term rewards from adding more domestic stocks and 5-year Treasury bonds into your asset allocation policy have been very significant indeed! Chart 10-3 illustrates the total cumulative returns from the four domestic model portfolios from 1926 through 1997 after adjusting for inflation. This is an excellent view of their wealth creation histories.

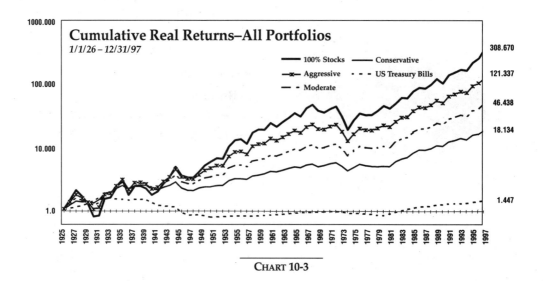

CHART 10-3

Another view of the performance of the Conservative Balanced portfolio is to compare it with that of a portfolio made up of only bonds, 5-year Treasury bonds in this example.

Performance Comparison: Conservative Balanced Model vs. Bonds - 1960-1997

	Reward	Worst Decline	Average Decline
Conservative Balanced (Domestic Only)	3.0%	10%	7%
5-Year Treasury Bonds	1.4%	9%	6%

The Conservative model more than doubled the reward from the bonds while not measurably increasing risk.

Risks. The domestic-only model portfolios provide widely different answers to the question, "What's the worst that can happen?" There is certainly a wide variance in the temporary suffering of those choosing a Conservative Balanced Portfolio (10% mega bear market decline), a Moderate Balanced Portfolio (20%), and Aggressive Balanced Portfolio (30%); and 100% Stocks Portfolio (46%).

 The differences between these four model portfolios were far less pronounced when comparing their respective *average* bear market declines of 7%, 11%, 15% and 22%. **In other words, among the model portfolios there is not nearly as significant a difference in normal bear market risk as would be suggested by their worst-case scenarios.**

By closely evaluating each domestic-only model portfolio, you are miles ahead of most investors in appreciating the inherent risks and rewards of the best asset allocation policies.

The following pages present a Historical Risk/Reward chart for each of the Domestic-Only Model Portfolios in the Inflation Era (Charts 10-4 through 10-7).

Note: All of the results of the portfolios presented in this chapter may be duplicated using the databases cited in Chart 8-1.

Conservative Balanced (Domestic) Portfolio (30-50-20)
30% Domestic 100% Stocks – 50% Bonds (5-Yr Treasury) – 20% T-bills
Growth of $100,000
(12/31/59 – 12/31/97)

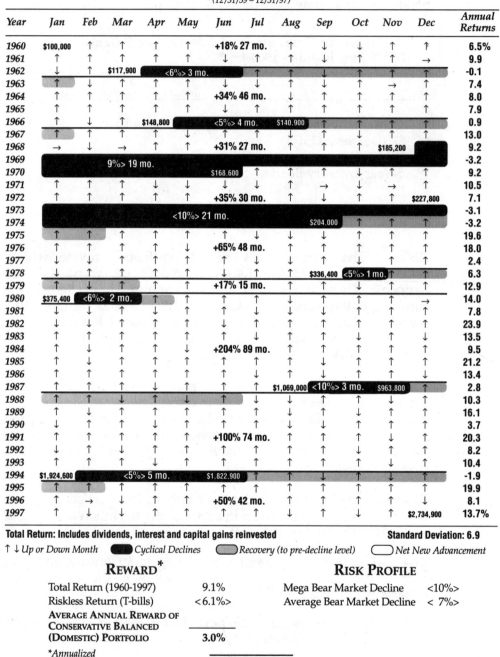

Year	Jan	Feb	Mar	Apr	May	Jun	Jul	Aug	Sep	Oct	Nov	Dec	Annual Returns
1960	$100,000	↑	↑	↑	↑	+18% 27 mo.	↑	↓	↓	↑	↑		6.5%
1961	↑	↑	↑	↑	↑	↓	↑	↑	↓	↑	↑	→	9.9
1962	↓	↑	$117,900	<6%> 3 mo.			↑	↑	↓	↑	↑	↑	-0.1
1963	↑	↓	↑	↑	↑	↓	↓	↑	↓	↑	→	↑	7.4
1964	↑	↑	↑	↑	↑	+34% 46 mo.	↓	↑	↑	↑	↑	↑	8.0
1965	↑	↑	↑	↑	↑	↓	↑	↑	↑	↑	↑	↑	7.9
1966	↑	↓	↑	$148,800	<5%> 4 mo.			$140,900	↑	↑	↑	↑	0.9
1967	↑	↑	↑	↑	↓	↑	↑	↓	↑	↓	↑	↑	13.0
1968	→	↓	→	↑	↑	+31% 27 mo.	↑	↑	↑	↑	$185,200		9.2
1969				9%> 19 mo.									-3.2
1970						$168,600	↑	↑	↑	↓	↑	↑	9.2
1971	↑	↑	↑	↓	↓	↓	↓	↑	→	↓	→	↑	10.5
1972	↑	↑	↑	↑	↑	+35% 30 mo.	↑	↓	↑	↑	↑	$227,800	7.1
1973				<10%> 21 mo.									-3.1
1974									$204,000	↑	↑	↑	-3.2
1975	↑	↑	↑	↑	↑	↑	↓	↓	↓	↑	↑	↑	19.6
1976	↑	↑	↑	↑	↓	+65% 48 mo.	↑	↑	↑	↑	↑	↑	18.0
1977	↓	↓	↑	↑	↑	↑	↓	↓	↑	↓	↑	↑	2.4
1978	↓	↑	↑	↑	↑	↓	↑	↑	$336,400	<5%> 1 mo. ↑		↑	6.3
1979	↑	↓	↑	↑	↑	+17% 15 mo.	↑	↑	↑	↓	↑	↑	12.9
1980	$375,400	<6%> 2 mo.		↑	↑	↑	↑	↓	↑	↑	↑	→	14.0
1981	↓	↓	↑	↓	↑	↑	↓	↓	↓	↑	↑	↑	7.8
1982	↓	↓	↑	↑	↓	↓	↑	↑	↑	↑	↑	↑	23.9
1983	↑	↑	↑	↑	↑	↑	↓	↑	↑	↓	↑	↓	13.5
1984	↑	↓	↑	↑	↓	+204% 89 mo.	↑	↑	↑	↑	↑	↑	9.5
1985	↑	↑	↑	↑	↑	↑	↑	↑	↑	↑	↑	↑	21.2
1986	↑	↑	↑	↑	↑	↑	↓	↑	↓	↑	↑	↓	13.4
1987	↑	↑	↑	↓	↑	↑	↑	$1,069,000	<10%> 3 mo.	$963,800	↑		2.8
1988	↑	↑	↓	↑	↓	↑	↓	↓	↑	↑	↓	↑	10.3
1989	↑	↓	↑	↑	↑	↑	↑	↓	↑	↓	↑	↑	16.1
1990	↓	↑	↑	↓	↑	↑	↑	↓	↓	↑	↑	↑	3.7
1991	↑	↑	↑	↑	↑	+100% 74 mo.	↑	↑	↑	↓	↑	↑	20.3
1992	↓	↑	↓	↑	↑	↑	↑	↑	↑	↑	↑	↑	8.2
1993	↑	↑	↑	↓	↑	↑	↑	↑	↑	↑	↓	↑	10.4
1994	$1,924,600	<5%> 5 mo.				$1,822,900	↑	↑	↓	↑	↓	↑	-1.9
1995	↑	↑	↑	↑	↑	↑	↑	↑	↑	↑	↑	↑	19.9
1996	↑	→	↓	↑	↑	+50% 42 mo.	↑	↑	↑	↑	↑	↓	8.1
1997	↑	↓	↓	↑	↑	↑	↑	↓	↑	↓	↑	$2,734,900	13.7%

Total Return: Includes dividends, interest and capital gains reinvested   **Standard Deviation: 6.9**

↑ ↓ *Up or Down Month*   ● *Cyclical Declines*   ◗ *Recovery (to pre-decline level)*   ○ *Net New Advancement*

REWARD*		RISK PROFILE	
Total Return (1960-1997)	9.1%	Mega Bear Market Decline	<10%>
Riskless Return (T-bills)	<6.1%>	Average Bear Market Decline	< 7%>
AVERAGE ANNUAL REWARD OF CONSERVATIVE BALANCED (DOMESTIC) PORTFOLIO	3.0%		

Annualized

CHART 10-4

Moderate Balanced (Domestic) Portfolio (47-47-6)

47% Domestic 100% Stocks – 47% Bonds (5-Yr Treasury) – 6% T-bills

Growth of $100,000
(12/31/59 – 12/31/97)

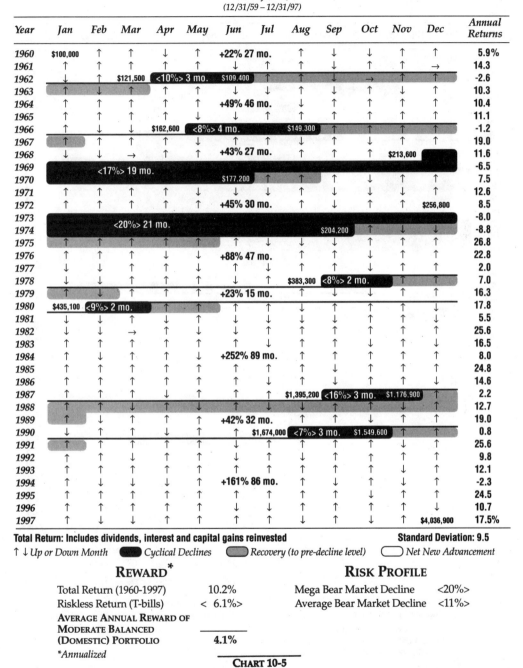

Year	Jan	Feb	Mar	Apr	May	Jun	Jul	Aug	Sep	Oct	Nov	Dec	Annual Returns
1960	$100,000	↑	↑	↓	↑	+22% 27 mo.		↑	↓	↓	↑	↑	5.9%
1961	↑	↑	↑	↑	↑	↓	↑	↑	↓	↑	↑	→	14.3
1962	↓	↑	$121,500	<10%> 3 mo.		$109,400	↑	↑	↓	→	↑	↑	-2.6
1963	↑	↓	↑			↓	↓	↑	↓	↑	↓	↑	10.3
1964	↑	↑	↑	↑	↑	+49% 46 mo.		↓	↑	↑	↑	↑	10.4
1965	↑	↑	↑	↑	↓	↓	↑	↑	↑	↑	↑		11.1
1966	↑	↓	↓	$162,600	<8%> 4 mo.		$149.300	↑	↑	↑	↑	↑	-1.2
1967	↑	↑	↑	↑	↓	↑	↑	↓	↓	↓	↑	↑	19.0
1968	↓	↓	→	↑	↑	+43% 27 mo.		↑	↑	↑	$213,600		11.6
1969	<17%> 19 mo.												-6.5
1970						$177,200	↑	↑	↑	↓	↑	↑	7.5
1971	↑	↑	↑	↑	↓	↓	↓	↑	↓	↓	↑		12.6
1972	↑	↑	↑	↑	↑	+45% 30 mo.		↑	↓	↑	↑	$256,800	8.5
1973	<20%> 21 mo.												-8.0
1974								$204.200	↑	↓	↓		-8.8
1975	↑	↑	↑	↑	↑	↑	↓	↓	↓	↑	↑		26.8
1976	↑	↑	↑	↓	↓	+88% 47 mo.		↑	↑	↓	↑	↑	22.8
1977	↓	↓	↑	↑	↓	↑	↓	↑	↑	↓	↑		2.0
1978	↓	↓	↑	↑	↑	↓	↑	$383,300	<8%> 2 mo.		↑	↑	7.0
1979	↑	↓	↑	↑	↑	+23% 15 mo.		↑	↓	↓	↑	↓	16.3
1980	$435,100	<9%> 2 mo.		↑	↑	↑	↑	↓	↑	↑	↑	↓	17.8
1981	↓	↓	↑	↓	↓	↓	↑	↑	↑	↑	↑	↓	5.5
1982	↓	↓	→	↑	↓	↓	↑	↑	↑	↑	↑	↑	25.6
1983	↑	↑	↑	↑	↑	↑	↓	↑	↑	↓	↑	↓	16.5
1984	↑	↓	↑	↑	↓	+252% 89 mo.		↑	↑	↑	↑	↑	8.0
1985	↑	↑	↑	↑	↑	↑	↑	↑	↓	↑	↑		24.8
1986	↑	↑	↑	↑	↑	↑	↓	↑	↓	↑	↓		14.6
1987	↑	↑	↑	↓	↑	↑	↑	$1,395,200	<16%> 3 mo.		$1,176,900	↑	2.2
1988	↑	↑	↑	↑	↓	↑	↓	↓	↑	↑	↓	↑	12.7
1989	↑	↓	↑	↑	↑	+42% 32 mo.		↑	↑	↑	↑		19.0
1990	↓	↑	↑	↓	↑	↑	$1,674,000	<7%> 3 mo.		$1,549,600	↑	↑	0.8
1991	↑	↑	↑	↑	↑	↓	↑	↑	↑	↑	↓	↑	25.6
1992	↑	↑	↓	↑	↑	↓	↑	↓	↑	↑	↑	↑	9.8
1993	↑	↑	↑	↑	↑	↑	↑	↑	↑	↑	↓	↑	12.1
1994	↑	↓	↓	↓	↑	+161% 86 mo.		↑	↓	↑	↓	↑	-2.3
1995	↑	↑	↑	↑	↑	↑	↑	↑	↑	↓	↑	↑	24.5
1996	↑	↑	↑	↑	↑	↓	↓	↑	↑	↑	↑	↓	10.7
1997	↑	↓	↓	↑	↑	↑	↑	↓	↑	↓	↑	$4,036,900	17.5%

Total Return: Includes dividends, interest and capital gains reinvested **Standard Deviation: 9.5**

↑ ↓ *Up or Down Month*   ⬛ *Cyclical Declines*   ⬤ *Recovery (to pre-decline level)*   ⬭ *Net New Advancement*

REWARD*

Total Return (1960-1997)	10.2%
Riskless Return (T-bills)	< 6.1%>
AVERAGE ANNUAL REWARD OF MODERATE BALANCED (DOMESTIC) PORTFOLIO	
	4.1%

Annualized

RISK PROFILE

Mega Bear Market Decline	<20%>
Average Bear Market Decline	<11%>

CHART 10-5

Aggressive Balanced (Domestic) Portfolio (67-28-5)
67% Domestic 100% Stocks – 28% Bonds (5-Yr Treasury) – 5% T-bills
Growth of $100,000
(12/31/59 – 12/31/97)

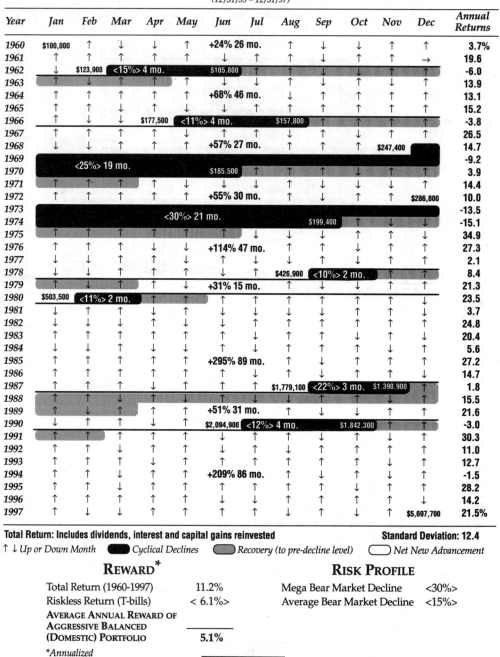

Year	Jan	Feb	Mar	Apr	May	Jun	Jul	Aug	Sep	Oct	Nov	Dec	Annual Returns
1960	$100,000	↑	↓	↓	↑	+24% 26 mo.		↑	↓	↓	↑	↑	3.7%
1961	↑	↑	↑	↑	↑	↓	↑	↑	↓	↑	↑	→	19.6
1962	↓	$123,900	<15%> 4 mo.			$105,800	↑	↑	↓	↓	↑	↑	-6.0
1963	↑	↓	↑	↑	↑	↓	↓	↑	↑	↑	↓	↑	13.9
1964	↑	↑	↑	↑	↑	+68% 46 mo.		↓	↑	↑	↑	↑	13.1
1965	↑	↑	↓	↑	↓	↓	↑	↑	↑	↑	↑	↑	15.2
1966	↑	↓	↓	$177,500	<11%> 4 mo.			$157,800	↑	↑	↑	↑	-3.8
1967	↑	↑	↑	↑	↑	↑	↑	↓	↑	↓	↑	↑	26.5
1968	↓	↓	↑	↑	↑	+57% 27 mo.		↑	↑	↑	$247,400		14.7
1969	<25%> 19 mo.												-9.2
1970						$185,500	↑	↑	↑	↓	↑	↑	3.9
1971	↑	↑	↑	↑	↓	↓	↑	↓	↓	↓	↑		14.4
1972	↑	↑	↑	↑	↑	+55% 30 mo.		↑	↓	↑	↑	$286,800	10.0
1973	<30%> 21 mo.												-13.5
1974								$199,400	↑	↓	↓		-15.1
1975	↑	↑	↑	↑	↑	↑	↓	↓	↓	↑	↓		34.9
1976	↑	↑	↑	↓	↓	+114% 47 mo.		↑	↑	↓	↑	↑	27.3
1977	↓	↓	↓	↑	↓	↓	↓	↓	↑	↓	↑	↑	2.1
1978	↓	↓	↑	↑	↑	↓	↑	$426,900	<10%> 2 mo.		↑	↑	8.4
1979	↑	↓	↑	↑	↓	+31% 15 mo.			↓	↓	↑	↑	21.3
1980	$503,500	<11%> 2 mo.		↑	↑	↑	↑	↑	↑	↑	↑	↓	23.5
1981	↓	↑	↑	↓	↓	↓	↓	↓	↓	↑	↑	↓	3.7
1982	↓	↓	↓	↑	↓	↓	↑	↑	↑	↑	↑	↑	24.8
1983	↑	↑	↑	↑	↑	↑	↓	↑	↑	↓	↑	↓	20.4
1984	↓	↓	↑	↓	↓	↑	↑	↑	↑	↑	↓	↑	5.6
1985	↑	↑	↑	↑	↑	+295% 89 mo.		↑	↓	↑	↑	↑	27.2
1986	↑	↑	↑	↑	↑	↑	↓	↑	↓	↑	↑	↓	14.7
1987	↑	↑	↑	↓	↑	↑	↑	$1,779,100	<22%> 3 mo.		$1,390,900	↑	1.8
1988	↑	↑	↓	↑	↓	↑	↓	↑	↑	↑	↓	↑	15.5
1989	↑	↓	↑	↑	↑	+51% 31 mo.		↑	↓	↓	↑	↑	21.6
1990	↓	↑	↑	↓	↑	$2,094,900	<12%> 4 mo.			$1,842,300	↑	↑	-3.0
1991	↑	↑	↑	↑	↑	↓	↑	↑	↓	↓	↓	↑	30.3
1992	↑	↑	↓	↑	↑	↓	↑	↓	↑	↑	↑	↑	11.0
1993	↑	↑	↑	↓	↑	↑	↑	↑	↑	↑	↓	↑	12.7
1994	↑	↑	↓	↑	↑	+209% 86 mo.		↑	↓	↑	↓	↓	-1.5
1995	↑	↑	↓	↑	↑	↑	↑	↑	↑	↓	↑	↑	28.2
1996	↑	↑	↑	↑	↑	↓	↓	↑	↑	↓	↑	↓	14.2
1997	↑	↓	↓	↑	↑	↑	↑	↓	↑	↓	↑	$5,697,700	21.5%

Total Return: Includes dividends, interest and capital gains reinvested   **Standard Deviation: 12.4**

↑↓ *Up or Down Month*   ⬤ *Cyclical Declines*   ⬤ *Recovery (to pre-decline level)*   ◯ *Net New Advancement*

REWARD*

Total Return (1960-1997)	11.2%
Riskless Return (T-bills)	< 6.1%>
AVERAGE ANNUAL REWARD OF AGGRESSIVE BALANCED (DOMESTIC) PORTFOLIO	5.1%

Annualized

RISK PROFILE

Mega Bear Market Decline	<30%>
Average Bear Market Decline	<15%>

CHART 10-6

Domestic 100% Stocks Portfolio (100-0-0)
100% Stocks (44% S&P 500/50% Mid/Small Cap/6% Micro Cap) – 0% Bonds – 0% T-bills
Growth of $100,000
(12/31/59 – 12/31/97)

Year	Jan	Feb	Mar	Apr	May	Jun	Jul	Aug	Sep	Oct	Nov	Dec	Annual Returns
1960	$100,000	↓	↓	↓	+28% 26 mo.		↓	↑	↓	↓	↑	↑	0.4%
1961	↑	↑	↑	↑	↑	↓	↑	↑	↓	↑	↑	↓	28.4
1962	↓	$128,000	<23%> 4 mo.			$99,000	↑	↑	↓	↓	↑	↑	-11.5
1963	↑	↓	↑	↑	↑	↓	↓	↑	↓	↑	↓	↑	19.8
1964	↑	↑	↑	↑	↑	+105% 46 mo.		↑	↑	↑	↑	↓	17.6
1965	↑	↑	↓	↑	↓	↓	↑	↑	↑	↑	↑	↑	22.0
1966	↑	↑	↓	$202,600	<17%> 5 mo.				$168,700	↑	↑	↑	-7.9
1967	↑	↑	↑	↑	↓	+73% 32 mo.		↑	↑	↓	↑	↑	38.8
1968	↓	↓	↑	↑	↑	↑	↓	↑	↑	↑	↑	$299,500	19.6
1969	<36%> 18 mo.												-13.9
1970						$192,300	↑	↑	↑	↓	↑	↑	-1.6
1971	↑	↑	↑	↑	↓	↓	+74% 30 mo.		↓	↓	↓	↑	17.5
1972	↑	↑	↑	↑	↑	↓	↓	↑	↓	↑	↑	$335,200	12.5
1973	<46%> 21 mo.												-22.5
1974									$182,000	↑	↓	↓	-25.5
1975	↑	↑	↑	↑	↑	↑	↓	↓	↓	↑	↑	↓	48.4
1976	↑	↑	↑	↓	↓	↑	↓	↓	↑	↓	↑	↑	35.0
1977	↓	↓	↓	↑	↓	+167% 47 mo.		↑	↓	↓	↑	↑	2.1
1978	↓	↓	↑	↑	↑	↓	↑	$485,700	<16%> 2 mo.	↑	↑	↑	10.5
1979	↑	↓	↑	↓	↑	↑	↑	↑	↓	↓	↑	↑	29.3
1980	↑	↓	↓	↑	↑	+86% 25 mo.		↑	↑	↑	$771,900		32.6
1981	<12%> 20 mo.												0.4
1982						$676,300	↑	↑	↑	↑	↑	↑	24.1
1983	↑	↑	↑	↑	↑	↑	↓	↓	↑	↓	↑	↓	26.6
1984	↓	↓	↑	↓	↓	↑	↓	↑	↑	↓	↓	↑	1.8
1985	↑	↑	↓	↓	↑	+219% 59 mo.		↑	↓	↑	↑	↑	31.5
1986	↑	↑	↑	↓	↑	↑	↓	↑	↓	↑	↑	↓	15.2
1987	↑	↑	↑	↑	↑	↑	↑	$2,465,600	<31%> 3 mo. $1,711,100		↑	1.0
1988	↑	↑	↓	↑	↓	↑	↓	↓	↑	↑	↓	↑	20.1
1989	↑	↓	↑	↑	↑	↓	+66% 30 mo.		↑	↓	↑	↑	26.0
1990	↓	↑	↑	↓	$2,844,700	<20%> 5 mo.				$2,272,700	↑	↑	-9.1
1991	↑	↑	↑	↑	↑	↓	↑	↑	↓	↑	↓	↑	38.3
1992	↑	↑	↑	↑	↑	↓	↑	↓	↑	↑	↑	↑	13.1
1993	↑	↓	↑	↓	↑	↑	↑	↑	↑	↑	↓	↑	14.1
1994	↑	↓	↓	↑	↑	+311% 86 mo.		↑	↓	↑	↓	↑	-0.3
1995	↑	↑	↑	↑	↑	↑	↑	↑	↑	↓	↑	↑	34.7
1996	↑	↑	↑	↑	↑	↓	↓	↑	↑	↑	↑	↓	19.9
1997	↑	↑	↑	↑	↑	↑	↑	↓	↑	↓	↑	$9,333,000	28.2%

Total Return: Includes reinvested dividends and capital gains   **Standard Deviation: 17.6**

↑ ↓ *Up or Down Month*   ⬛ *Cyclical Declines*   ⬤ *Recovery (to pre-decline level)*   ⬭ *Net New Advancement*

REWARD*

Total Return (1960-1997)	12.7%
Riskless Return (T-bills)	< 6.1%>
AVERAGE ANNUAL REWARD OF DOMESTIC 100% STOCKS PORTFOLIO	6.6%

*Annualized

RISK PROFILE

Mega Bear Market Decline	<46%>
Average Bear Market Decline	<22%>

CHART 10-7

Global Portfolios

Second Period of Study (1972-1997)

A second set of model portfolios will now be developed by adding international stocks and equity REITs to domestic stocks, U.S. Treasury bonds and T-bills. Although not possessing the very long-term, reliable data of the other asset classes, international stocks (U.S. dollars) and equity REITs were found in Chapter 8 to possess very good risk/reward characteristics.

The Global Model Portfolios ("global" here meaning a broader and more international scope) take further advantage of the lack of correlation between asset classes. Three balanced portfolios: Global Conservative, Global Moderate, Global Aggressive and a 100% Global Stocks Model Portfolio will be constructed. **The objective of each global model is to match the reward of its domestic model counterpart while further** *lessening its risk* **(exposure to bear market declines).**

Due to the constraints of the available data for equity REITs and international stocks (as discussed in Chapter 8), the period of analysis for Global Model Portfolios will be the 26-year period of 1972 through 1997.

Countless combinations of the seven participating asset classes were tested. Each combination was held constant by rebalancing at the end of each calendar year, selling some of that year's asset class winners and using the proceeds to buy more of that year's asset class losers to bring the portfolio back into alignment with its fixed asset allocation policy.

The Very Best Portfolio Designs

Based on the guidelines set forth (page 261), the following four Global Model Portfolios are the most favorable combination of all seven qualifying asset classes. These model portfolios have offered very high rewards for their respective levels of risk.

Conservative Balanced Portfolio (Global)

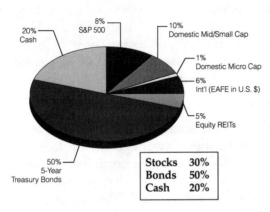

20% Cash

8% S&P 500

10% Domestic Mid/Small Cap

1% Domestic Micro Cap

6% Int'l (EAFE in U.S. $)

5% Equity REITs

50% 5-Year Treasury Bonds

Stocks	30%
Bonds	50%
Cash	20%

Primary Objective: The asset allocation which (approximately) matches the return of the Domestic Conservative Portfolio (for 1972-1997) with the *least* risk.

Performance Highlights: (1972-1997)

Rate of Return	10.3%
Riskless Rate (T-bills)	-6.9%
Reward	**3.4%**

Mega Bear Market Decline: 10%

Average Bear Market Decline: 6%

Moderate Balanced Portfolio (Global)

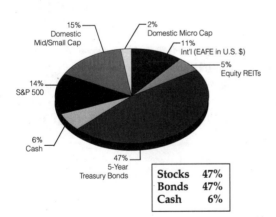

15% Domestic Mid/Small Cap

2% Domestic Micro Cap

11% Int'l (EAFE in U.S. $)

5% Equity REITs

14% S&P 500

6% Cash

47% 5-Year Treasury Bonds

Stocks	47%
Bonds	47%
Cash	6%

Primary Objective: The asset allocation which (approximately) matches the return of the Domestic Moderate Portfolio (for 1972-1997) with the *least* risk.

Performance Highlights: (1972-1997)

Rate of Return	11.5%
Riskless Rate (T-bills)	-6.9%
Reward	**4.6%**

Mega Bear Market Decline: 19%

Average Bear Market Decline: 9%

Aggressive Balanced Portfolio (Global)

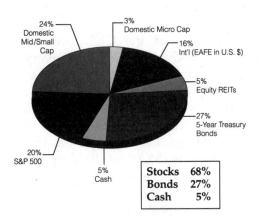

24% — Domestic Mid/Small Cap

3% — Domestic Micro Cap

16% — Int'l (EAFE in U.S. $)

5% — Equity REITs

27% — 5-Year Treasury Bonds

20% — S&P 500

5% — Cash

Stocks	68%
Bonds	27%
Cash	5%

Primary Objective: The asset allocation which (approximately) matches the return of the Domestic Aggressive Portfolio (for 1972-1997) with the *least* risk.

Performance Highlights: (1972-1997)

Rate of Return	12.6%
Riskless Rate (T-bills)	-6.9%
Reward	**5.7%**

Mega Bear Market Decline: 28%
Average Bear Market Decline: 12%

100% Stocks Portfolio (Global)

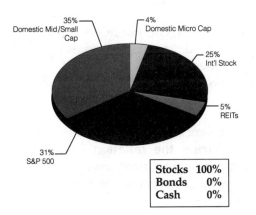

35% — Domestic Mid/Small Cap

4% — Domestic Micro Cap

25% — Int'l Stock

5% — REITs

31% — S&P 500

Stocks	100%
Bonds	0%
Cash	0%

Primary Objective: The asset allocation which (approximately) matches the return of the Domestic 100% Stocks Portfolio (for 1972-1997) with the *least* risk.

Performance Highlights: (1972-1997)

Rate of Return	14.1%
Riskless Rate (T-bills)	-6.9%
Reward	**7.2%**

Mega Bear Market Decline: 42%
Average Bear Market Decline: 17%

Excess Return from Rebalancing Uncorrelated Asset Classes

Balanced asset allocations generally provide higher long-term returns than the underlying asset classes. How's that possible... it sounds like 2 + 2 = 5?! It's made possible by rebalancing a portfolio of uncorrelated asset classes back to its fixed weightings on a periodic basis.

In calculating the historical performance of the Global Model Portfolios, each portfolio was rebalanced at the end of every calendar year to bring it back into alignment with its fixed asset allocation policy. For example, if at the end of one year, Mr. Smith's Global Conservative Balanced Portfolio values are 35% stocks, 47% bonds and 18% cash, he will shift his investments so that they once again reflect his chosen 30-50-20 weightings. He accomplishes this by selling a little of his stock mutual funds (5%) and dividing the proceeds between bond funds and money market accounts.

Rebalancing portfolios in this way produces an *additional* incremental rate of return. The *free* or enhanced returns for the balanced model portfolios from annual rebalancing in the Inflation Era were as follows:

Conservative Balanced	0.5% annually
Moderate Balanced	0.6% annually
Aggressive Balanced	0.6% annually

This is the difference between the actual compounded annual performance of these models (rebalanced annually) and simply adding up the individual compounded annual returns of the underlying asset classes (by their weighting within the model portfolio).

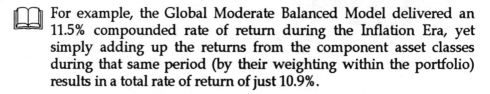 For example, the Global Moderate Balanced Model delivered an 11.5% compounded rate of return during the Inflation Era, yet simply adding up the returns from the component asset classes during that same period (by their weighting within the portfolio) results in a total rate of return of just 10.9%.

Charts 10-8 through 10-11 are Historical Risk/Reward charts for the four Global Model Portfolios covering the period 1972-1997.

Historical Risk/Reward Chart

Conservative Balanced (Global) Portfolio
30% Stocks* (21% U.S./6% Intl/5% REITs) – 50% Bonds (5-Yr Treasury) – 20% T-bills
Growth of $100,000
(12/31/71 – 12/31/97)

Year	Jan	Feb	Mar	Apr	May	Jun	Jul	Aug	Sep	Oct	Nov	Dec	Annual Returns
1972	$100,000	↑	↑	↑	↑	+10% 22 mo.		↑	↓	↑	↑	↑	8.9%
1973	↓	↓	↑	↓	↓	→	↓	↑	↑	$109,900			-2.4
1974					<10%> 11 mo.				$98,900	↑	↑	↑	-2.9
1975	↑	↑	↑	↑	↑	↑	↓	↓	↓	↑	↑	↑	18.3
1976	↑	↑	↑	↑	↓	↑	↑	↑	↑	↓	↑	↑	15.8
1977	↓	↑	↑	↑	↑	+80% 64 mo.		↑	→	↓	↑	↑	3.4
1978	↓	↑	↑	↑	↑	↑	↑	↑	↑	↓	↑	↑	8.1
1979	↑	↓	↑	↑	↑	↑	↑	↑	↑	↓	↑	↑	11.3
1980	$178,200	<6%> 2 mo.		↑	↑	↑	↑	↓	↑	↑	↑	↑	13.2
1981	↓	↓	↑	↓	↑	↓	↓	↓	↓	↑	↑	↓	7.8
1982	↓	↓	↓	↑	↑	↓	↑	↑	↑	↑	↑	↑	22.0
1983	↑	↑	↑	↑	↑	↑	↓	↑	↑	↓	↑	↑	13.4
1984	↑	↓	↑	↓	↓	+214% 89 mo.		↑	↑	↑	↑	↑	10.3
1985	↑	↓	↑	↑	↑	↑	↑	↑	↑	↑	↑	↑	22.9
1986	↑	↑	↑	↑	↓	↑	↓	↑	↓	↑	↑	↑	17.5
1987	↑	↑	↑	↓	→	↑	↑	$525,900	<8%> 3 mo.	$483,400		↑	4.6
1988	↑	↑	↑	↑	↓	↑	↓	↑	↑	↑	↓	↑	10.9
1989	↑	↓	↑	↑	↑	+33% 32 mo.		↓	↑	↑	↑	↑	14.7
1990	↓	→	↑	↓	↑	↑	$642,300	<5%> 2 mo.		↑	↑	↑	2.5
1991	↑	↑	↑	↑	↑	↓	↑	↑	↑	↑	↓	↑	18.4
1992	↓	↑	↓	↑	↑	+52% 40 mo.		↑	↑	↓	↑	↑	6.4
1993	↑	↑	↑	↑	↑	↑	↑	↑	↑	↑	↓	↑	11.9
1994	$928,800	<4%> 5 mo.			$887,100		↑	↑	↓	↑	↓	↑	-1.2
1995	↑	↑	↑	↑	↑	↑	↑	↑	↑	→	↑	↑	17.9
1996	↑	↓	→	↑	↑	+43% 42 mo.		↑	↑	↑	↑	↓	7.3
1997	↑	↑	↓	↑	↑	↑	↑	↓	↑	↓	↑	$1,268,000	11.6%

Total Return: Includes dividends, interest and capital gains reinvested   **Standard Deviation: 6.9**

U.S. Stocks=Domestic 100% Stocks Model; International Stocks=MSCI EAFE Index in U.S. $; REITs=NAREIT Equity REIT Index

↑ ↓ *Up or Down Month*　　⬛ *Cyclical Declines*　　⬭ *Recovery (to pre-decline level)*　　⬭ *Net New Advancement*

REWARD**

Total Return (1972-1997)	10.3%
Riskless Return (T-bills)	< 6.9%>
AVERAGE ANNUAL REWARD OF CONSERVATIVE BALANCED GLOBAL PORTFOLIO	3.4%

**Annualized*

RISK PROFILE

Mega Bear Market Decline	<10%>
Average Bear Market Decline	< 6%>

CHART 10-8

Historical Risk/Reward Chart

Moderate Balanced (Global) Portfolio (50-40-10)
47% Stocks* (31% U.S./11% Intl/5% REITs) – 47% Bonds (5-Yr Treasury) – 6% T-bills
Growth of $100,000
(12/31/71 – 12/31/97)

Year	Jan	Feb	Mar	Apr	May	Jun	Jul	Aug	Sep	Oct	Nov	Dec	Annual Returns
1972	$100,000	↑	↑	↑	↑	+11% 12 mo.		↑	↓	↑	↑	$111,400	11.4%
1973					<19%> 21 mo.								-6.9
1974									$90,600	↑	↑	↓	-8.3
1975	↑	↑	↑	↑	↑	↑	↓	↓	↓	↑	↑	↑	24.7
1976	↑	↑	↑	↑	↓	↑	↑	↑	↑	↓	↑	↑	19.5
1977	↓	→	↑	↑	→	+107% 64 mo.		↑	↓	↓	↑	↑	3.6
1978	↓	↑	↑	↑	↑	↑	↑	↑	↑	↓	↑	↑	9.8
1979	↑	↓	↑	↑	↑	↑	↑	↑	↑	↓	↑	↑	13.8
1980	$187,300	<8%> 2 mo.		↑	↑	+29% 15 mo.		↓	↑	↑	↑	↓	16.7
1981	↓	↓	↑	↓	↑	$221,300	<7%> 3 mo.	$206,000	↑	↑	↓		5.5
1982	↓	↓	↓	↑	↓	↓	↑	↑	↑	↑	↑	↑	22.6
1983	↑	↑	↑	↑	↑	↑	↓	↑	↑	↓	↑	↑	16.4
1984	↑	↓	↑	↓	↓	+208% 71 mo.		↑	↑	↑	↑	↑	9.2
1985	↑	↑	↑	↑	↑	↑	↑	↑	↓	↑	↑	↑	27.5
1986	↑	↑	↑	↑	↑	↑	↓	↑	↓	↑	↑	↓	21.1
1987	↑	↑	↑	↓	↑	↑	↑	$634,100	<13%> 3 mo.	$551,600	↑		4.9
1988	↑	↑	↑	↑	↓	↑	↓	↓	↑	↑	↓	↑	13.5
1989	↑	↓	↑	↑	↑	+38% 32 mo.		↓	↑	↓	↑	↑	16.8
1990	↓	↓	↓	↓	↑	↑	$761,300	<8%> 2 mo.		↑	↑	↑	-1.0
1991	↑	↑	↑	↑	↑	↓	↑	↑	↑	↑	↓	↑	22.5
1992	↓	↑	↓	↑	↑	↓	↑	↓	↑	↓	↑	↑	6.9
1993	↑	↑	↑	↑	↑	↑	↑	↑	↑	↑	↓	↑	14.4
1994	↑	↓	↓	↑	↑	+139% 87 mo.		↑	↓	↑	↓	↑	-1.3
1995	↑	↑	↑	↑	↑	↑	↑	↑	↑	↓	↑	↑	21.4
1996	↑	↑	↑	↑	↑	→	↓	↑	↑	↑	↑	↓	9.4
1997	↑	→	↓	↑	↑	↑	↑	↓	↑	↓	↑	$1,676,500	14.2%

Total Return: Includes dividends, interest and capital gains reinvested   **Standard Deviation: 9.3**

*U.S. Stocks=Domestic 100% Stocks Model; International Stocks=MSCI EAFE Index in U.S. $; REITs=NAREIT Equity REIT Index

↑ ↓ Up or Down Month ⬛ Cyclical Declines ⬤ Recovery (to pre-decline level) ⬭ Net New Advancement

REWARD**

Total Return (1972-1997)	11.5%
Riskless Return (T-bills)	< 6.9%>
AVERAGE ANNUAL REWARD OF MODERATE BALANCED GLOBAL PORTFOLIO	4.6%

**Annualized

RISK PROFILE

Mega Bear Market Decline   <19%>
Average Bear Market Decline < 9%>

CHART 10-9

Historical Risk/Reward Chart

Aggressive Balanced (Global) Portfolio (70-25-5)
68% Stocks* (47% U.S./16% Intl/5%REITs) – 27% Bonds (5-Yr Treasury) – 5% T-bills
Growth of $100,000
(12/31/71 – 12/31/97)

Year	Jan	Feb	Mar	Apr	May	Jun	Jul	Aug	Sep	Oct	Nov	Dec	Annual Returns
1972	$100,000	↑	↑	↑	↑	+14% 12 mo.		↑	↓	↑	↑	$114,200	14.2%
1973					<28%> 21 mo.								-12.1
1974									$81,700	↑	↓	↓	-14.6
1975	↑	↑	↑	↑	↑	↑	↓	↓	↓	↑	↑	↑	32.3
1976	↑	↑	↑	↓	↓	↑	↓	↑	↑	↓	↑	↑	22.7
1977	↓	↓	↑	↑	↓	+144% 64 mo.		↑	↓	↓	↑	↑	4.5
1978	↓	↑	↑	↑	↑	↑	↑	↑	↑	↓	→	↑	12.5
1979	↑	↓	↑	↑	↓	↑	↑	↑	↑	↓	↑	↑	17.8
1980	$199,700	<10%> 2 mo.		↑	↑	+37% 14 mo.		↑	↑	↑	↑	↓	22.1
1981	↓	↑	↑	↓	$245,300	<9%> 4 mo.			$223,200	↑	↑	↓	3.5
1982	↓	↓	↓	↑	↓	↓	↑	↑	↑	↑	↑	↑	20.4
1983	↑	↑	↑	↑	↑	↑	↓	↓	↑	↓	↑	↑	20.4
1984	↑	↓	↑	↓	↓	+243% 71 mo.		↑	↑	↑	↑	↑	7.2
1985	↑	↑	↑	↑	↑	↑	↑	↑	↓	↑	↑	↑	31.2
1986	↑	↑	↑	↑	↑	↑	↓	↑	↓	↑	↑	↓	24.2
1987	↑	↑	↑	↑	↑	↑	↑	$765,300	<18%> 3 mo.		$623,700	↑	5.7
1988	↑	↑	↑	↑	↓	↑	↓	↓	↑	↑	↓	↑	16.8
1989	↑	↓	↑	↑	↑	+44% 31 mo.		↑	↑	↓	↑	↑	18.5
1990	↓	↓	↓	↓	↑	$896,300	<12%> 3 mo. $792,100			↑	↑	↑	-5.8
1991	↑	↑	↑	↑	↑	↓	↑	↑	↑	↑	↓	↑	26.0
1992	↑	↑	↓	↑	↑	↓	↑	↑	↑	↓	↑	↑	6.8
1993	↑	↑	↑	↑	↑	↑	↑	↑	↑	↑	↓	↑	16.2
1994	↑	↓	↓	↑	↑	+174% 87 mo.		↑	↓	↑	↓	↑	0.1
1995	↑	↑	↑	↑	↑	↑	↑	↑	↑	↓	↑	↑	23.8
1996	↑	↑	↑	↑	↑	↓	↑	↑	↑	↑	↑	↓	12.6
1997	↑	↓	↓	↑	↑	↑	↑	↓	↑	↓	↑	$2,167,400	16.9%

Total Return: Includes dividends, interest and capital gains reinvested   **Standard Deviation: 11.9**

*U.S. Stocks=Domestic 100% Stocks Model; International Stocks=MSCI EAFE Index in U.S. $; REITs=NAREIT Equity REIT Index

↑ ↓ *Up or Down Month*   ⬛ *Cyclical Declines*   ⬤ *Recovery (to pre-decline level)*   ⬭ *Net New Advancement*

REWARD**

Total Return (1972-1997)	12.6%
Riskless Return (T-bills)	< 6.9%>
AVERAGE ANNUAL REWARD OF AGGRESSIVE BALANCED GLOBAL PORTFOLIO	5.7%

**Annualized

RISK PROFILE

Mega Bear Market Decline	<28%>
Average Bear Market Decline	<12%>

CHART 10-10

Historical Risk/Reward Chart

Global 100% Stocks Portfolio (100-0-0)
100% Stocks* (70% U.S./25% Intl/5% REITs) – 0% Bonds – 0% T-bills
Growth of $100,000
(12/31/71 – 12/31/97)

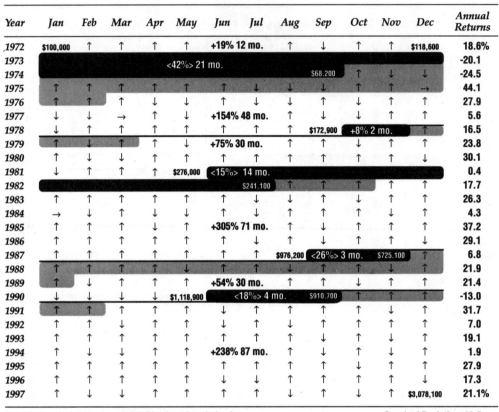

Year	Jan	Feb	Mar	Apr	May	Jun	Jul	Aug	Sep	Oct	Nov	Dec	Annual Returns
1972	$100,000	↑	↑	↑	↑	+19% 12 mo.		↑	↓	↑	↑	$118,600	18.6%
1973					<42%> 21 mo.								-20.1
1974									$68.200	↑	↓	↓	-24.5
1975	↑	↑	↑	↑	↑	↑	↓	↓	↓	↑	↑	→	44.1
1976	↑	↑	↑	↓	↓	↑	↓	↓	↑	↓	↑	↑	27.9
1977	↓	↓	→	↑	↓	+154% 48 mo.		↑	↓	↓	↑	↑	5.6
1978	↓	↑	↑	↑	↑	↑	↑	↑	$172,900	+8% 2 mo.		↑	16.5
1979	↑	↓	↑	↑	↓	+75% 30 mo.		↑	↑	↓	↑	↑	23.8
1980	↑	↓	↓	↑	↑	↑	↑	↑	↑	↑	↑	↓	30.1
1981	↓	↑	↑	↑	$276,000	<15%> 14 mo.							0.4
1982							$241.100	↑	↑	↑	↑	↑	17.7
1983	↑	↑	↑	↑	↑	↑	↓	↓	↑	↓	↑	↑	26.3
1984	→	↓	↑	↓	↓	↑	↓	↑	↑	↑	↓	↑	4.3
1985	↑	↑	↑	↓	↑	+305% 71 mo.		↓	↑	↑	↑	↑	37.2
1986	↑	↑	↑	↓	↑	↑	↓	↑	↓	↑	↑	↓	29.1
1987	↑	↑	↑	↑	↑	↑	↑	$976,200	<26%> 3 mo.		$725.100	↑	6.8
1988	↑	↑	↑	↑	↓	↑	↓	↓	↑	↑	↓	↑	21.9
1989	↑	↓	↑	↑	↑	+54% 30 mo.		↑	↑	↓	↑	↑	21.4
1990	↓	↓	↓	↓	$1,118,900	<18%> 4 mo.			$910.700	↑	↑	↑	-13.0
1991	↑	↑	↑	↑	↑	↓	↑	↑	↑	↑	↓	↑	31.7
1992	↑	↑	↓	↑	↑	↓	↑	↓	↑	↑	↑	↑	7.0
1993	↑	↑	↑	↑	↑	↑	↑	↑	↓	↑	↓	↑	19.1
1994	↑	↓	↓	↑	↑	+238% 87 mo.		↑	↓	↑	↓	↑	1.9
1995	↑	↑	↑	↑	↑	↑	↑	↑	↑	↓	↑	↑	27.9
1996	↑	↑	↑	↑	↑	↓	↓	↑	↑	↑	↑	↓	17.3
1997	↑	↓	↓	↑	↑	↑	↑	↓	↑	↓	↑	$3,078,100	21.1%

Total Return: Includes reinvested dividends and capital gains   **Standard Deviation: 16.5**

*U.S. Stocks=Domestic 100% Stocks Model; International Stocks=MSCI EAFE Index in U.S. $; REITs=NAREIT Equity REIT Index

↑ ↓ *Up or Down Month*   ⬛ *Cyclical Declines*   ⬮ *Recovery (to pre-decline level)*   ⬭ *Net New Advancement*

REWARD**   ### RISK PROFILE

Total Return (1972-1997)	14.1%	Mega Bear Market Decline	<42%>
Riskless Return (T-bills)	< 6.9%>	Average Bear Market Decline	<17%>
AVERAGE ANNUAL REWARD OF GLOBAL 100% STOCKS PORTFOLIO	7.2%		

**Annualized

CHART 10-11

Evaluating the Global Model Portfolios

In order to compare the Global Model Portfolios to the Domestic-Only Model Portfolios, the domestic models must first be recomputed for this new time period of analysis (1972-1997). As noted earlier, cross-comparisons among asset classes or portfolios are only accurate if comparing over the same time periods.

Global asset allocation policies have been able to match the long-term rewards of the Domestic-Only Model Portfolios with reduced risk. This is illustrated in Chart 10-12 by comparing the performances of the Global and Domestic Model Portfolios in the 1972-1997 period.

Comparing the Global and Domestic-Only Model Portfolios
Risks and Reward Highlights - 1972-1997

Model	Return	Mega Bear Market	Average Bear Market
Model Portfolios			
Domestic 100% Stocks	14.2%	<46%>	<20%>
Global 100% Stocks	14.1%	<42%>	<17%>
Domestic Aggressive Balanced	12.6%	<30%>	<14%>
Global Aggressive Balanced	12.6%	<28%>	<12%>
Domestic Moderate Balanced	11.5%	<20%>	<10%>
Global Moderate Balanced	11.5%	<19%>	<9%>
Domestic Conservative Balanced	10.3%	<10%>	<7%>
Global Conservative Balanced	10.3%	<10%>	<6%>

CHART 10-12

As stated earlier, assembling portfolios of reliable but uncorrelated asset classes improves the risk/reward relationship. This is a central feature of determining the best asset allocation policies.

Comparing the global models to each other brings the risk/reward relationship into clear view once again. An investor in a Global Conservative Balanced portfolio earned an annualized reward of 3.4% over U.S. Treasury bills for which the investor experienced a decline in his portfolio value of 6% (on average) approximately once every five years. An investor in a Global Moderate Balanced portfolio provided an annualized reward of 4.6% for which the investor had to endure a 9% decline in his portfolio value about twice per decade.

A Global Aggressive Balanced portfolio delivered a reward of 5.7% but suffered through cyclical bear markets averaging 12%. A Global 100% Stocks portfolio enjoyed a reward of 7.2%, while having to see 17% of his portfolio temporarily disappear (on average) about once every five years.

The Wind at Your Back

Selecting and adhering to one of the model portfolios puts the wind at your back as you sail through the years with your Wealth and Retirement Portfolio. You have channeled all of the best information from the history of investing right into the structure of your portfolio. **You are adopting the asset allocation policy that delivered the highest historical reward for your comfortable level of risk.** You also have a powerful ally in that you have a thorough insight into the major risks to which your own portfolio is exposed...*in advance.*

Just how good are the model portfolios? The S&P 500 is rightfully credited with outstanding performance, yet both the domestic aggressive and global aggressive portfolios with approximately 30% allocated to bonds provided similar returns to the S&P 500 over the past 38- and 26-year periods with significantly reduced risk. And the Global 100% Stocks Model provided a significantly higher rate of return than the S&P 500 with identical risk characteristics.

Merely indexing each component of these portfolios means you could outperform the S&P 500! (Both index mutual funds and managed mutual funds will be evaluated in Section IV.)

11

The Ultimate Test:
The Great Depression

How did the Domestic Model Portfolios introduced in Chapter 10 perform during the Great Depression? Say you invested at the top of the market in 1929. You were convinced of the logic of maintaining a disciplined strategy, so you stayed the course with your chosen portfolio throughout the Great Depression. What then?

Each Domestic Model Portfolio's performance is examined in both nominal and real U.S. dollars through the full market cycle from 1929 through 1937 with interesting and counter-intuitive results.

"In the main, therefore, slumps are experiences to be lived through... with as much equanimity and patience as possible."
— John Maynard Keynes (1938)

What is your greatest *fear* when it comes to your investments? For many investors, a possible replay of the Great Depression tops the list. Therefore, a careful study of how the Domestic Model Portfolios performed during that tragic period should be of great value.

Investing a Million Before the Crash

Assume you inherit $1,000,000 in August 1929. The feel-good era of the Roaring '20s is still going strong. The U.S. has blossomed in the post-War years, and there is a general sense of pride in American industry—its strength and potential. Stock market investors in the U.S. are euphoric after years of sensational returns. The stocks leading the market are not speculative, they are industry leaders: Radio Corp. (RCA), General Electric, American Telephone, General Motors and United States Steel. These companies seemed irrevocably poised to deliver on America's bright promise.

Without hesitation, you invest your new wealth following the criteria of one of the Domestic Model Portfolios presented in Chapter 10. Unknowingly, you have just invested 100% of your portfolio at the very top of a major bull market! Disaster strikes with the stock market crash of October 1929, followed by the worst bear market of this century. A horrifying and debilitating period of relentlessly declining stock prices unfolds (see Chart 11-1).

Fortunately, you have a comprehensive understanding of the risks and rewards of your model portfolio. You stay the course and *rebalance* your stock, bond and cash allocations at the end of each calendar year to bring them back into alignment with your portfolio's asset allocation weightings. It certainly isn't easy; the gloom and doomers are out in force (as usual), and the voice of calm reason is scoffed at and even ridiculed. Yet you stick to your guns....How bad is it? What happens to your $1,000,000? Did you blow your inheritance?

A Complete Market Cycle

 The proper way to measure your results is over a full market cycle. Far too many market evaluations are hopelessly biased by either their starting date or ending date or both. The history of the U.S.

stock market is one of sustained overall upward progress in market prices, which unfolds in periods of general advancement (bull markets), punctuated by sharp setbacks (bear markets).

The only fair evaluation of the stock market over spans of less than 15 to 20 years is to both begin and end at the exact same point in the market cycle—from one bull market peak to the next or one bear market trough to the following one.

As you entered the markets at the very peak in stock prices (September 1, 1929), the fair evaluation of your results would include the entire bear market (through June 1932) and the complete bull market that follows (through February 1937)—one full market cycle.

The Great Depression Market Cycle
(August 1929 through February 1937)
Annual Returns* from Stocks, Bonds, Cash and Inflation

Year	Inflation/ <Deflation>	U.S. Treasury Bills	U.S. 5-Year Treasury Bonds	Large Cap Stocks	Mid/ Small Cap Stocks	Micro Cap Stocks
1929**	-0.9%	1.6%	3.8%	-31.2%	-33.9%	-47.0%
1930	-6.0	2.4	6.7	-24.9	-35.2	-38.1
1931	-9.5	1.1	-2.3	-43.3	-46.5	-49.7
1932	-10.3	1.0	8.8	-8.2	-6.0	-5.4
1933	0.5	0.3	1.8	54.0	107.0	142.4
1934	2.0	0.2	9.0	-1.4	12.3	24.2
1935	3.0	0.2	7.0	47.7	43.8	40.2
1936	1.2	0.2	3.1	33.9	38.6	64.7
1937***	1.0	0.0	-0.2	5.9	8.2	20.1

Sources: © *Computed using data from* Stocks, Bonds, Bills & Inflation 1996 Yearbook™ *with data updated January 1997, Ibbotson Associates, Chicago; Center for Research in Security Prices (CRSP) University of Chicago*

*   Total returns include interest, dividends and capital gains or losses.
**   September through December
*** January through February

CHART 11-1

Historical Note:

The bull market of the 1920s peaked in August 1929. The worst bear market of this century began in earnest with the infamous crash of October that same year. It was not straight down as there were substantial rallies to the upside along the way. The market finally bottomed in the summer of 1932. From that very low point, the stock market turned around and began one of its most rewarding bull markets. This bull market experienced several steep setbacks on its way to a peak in February 1937.

In Chart 11-2 the progress of the four domestic model portfolios is followed on a year-by-year basis from the very top of the Roaring '20s bull market, through the devastation of the Great Depression's vicious bear market and on through the completion of the awesome bull market that peaked in February 1937. This is one complete market cycle. Each domestic model begins with $1,000,000 as of September 1, 1929. Returns are reflected on both a nominal basis (what shows up on your brokerage statement) and on a real return basis (the change in your wealth).

Domestic Model Portfolios in the Great Depression
(September 1929 through February 1937)
$1,000,000 Portfolio: Change in Value Over the Market Cycle**

End of Year	Value of Sept. '29 U.S. $*	CONSERVATIVE (30-50-20)		MODERATE (47-47-6)		AGGRESSIVE (67-28-5)		100% STOCKS (100-0-0)	
		Nominal U.S. $	Real* U.S. $	Nominal U.S. $	Real* U.S. $	Nominal U.S. $	Real* U.S. $	Nominal $	Real* U.S. $
1929[†]	1.01	922,000	931,000	863,000	872,000	778,000	786,000	668,000	675,000
1930	1.07	875,000	936,000	769,000	823,000	629,000	673,000	466,000	499,000
1931	1.19	748,000	890,000	598,000	712,000	426,000	507,000	256,000	305,000
1932	1.33	767,000	1,020,000	603,000	802,000	416,000	553,000	238,000	317,000
1933	1.32	963,000	1,271,000	842,000	1,111,000	658,000	868,000	434,000	573,000
1934	1.30	1,024,000	1,331,000	901,000	1,171,000	702,000	913,000	460,000	598,000
1935	1.26	1,200,000	1,512,000	1,124,000	1,416,000	940,000	1,184,000	669,000	843,000
1936	1.24	1,354,000	1,679,000	1,339,000	1,660,000	1,195,000	1,482,000	921,000	1,142,000
1937[††]	1.23	1,384,000	1,702,000	1,386,000	1,705,000	1,258,000	1,547,000	991,000	1,219,000
Avg. Annual Returns:		4.4%	7.3%	4.4%	7.4%	3.1%	6.0%	-0.1%	2.7%
For Comparison: Returns from 1960-1997		9.1%	4.4%	10.2%	5.5%	11.2%	6.5%	12.7%	8.0%

* *Reflects Deflation/Inflation of Period*

** *Rebalanced Annually Utilizing Data from Chart 11-1*

[†] *September through December*

[††] *January and February*

Source: © *Computed using data from* Stocks, Bonds, Bills & Inflation 1997 Yearbook™ *with data updated January 1998, Ibbotson Associates, Chicago; Center for Research in Security Prices (CRSP) University of Chicago*

CHART 11–2

Deflation's Effect

There is one other factor that has an unusual bearing on this particular market cycle. As was discussed in Chapter 4, the bear market of September 1929 through the end of 1932 is perhaps as noteworthy for its sustained **deflation** as for its falling stock prices.

Deflation is the opposite of inflation, i.e. the value or purchasing power of a dollar goes *up*, not down. Take a close look at Chart 11-1. The deflation from August 1929 to the end of 1932 added one-third to the purchasing power of every U.S. dollar. In isolation, this is a wonderful experience. Unfortunately, the accompanying economic conditions that bring about and sustain a period of deflation may not be pleasant at all. (Just look at Japan's experience with deflation in the 1990s to see that this is still true.)

As was also discussed in Chapter 4, *real* returns, those adjusted for a change in the value of the currency unit, are much more important than nominal returns as far as measuring increases or decreases in wealth. It is the purchasing power of your portfolio you wish to increase. The same principle applies during this unusual period of deflation. The real return (buying power) is still more important than the nominal return. However, for deflation, returns are adjusted upward to reflect the increased purchasing power of the U.S. dollar.

Moderate Balanced Portfolio: Step-By-Step

Assume your chosen portfolio was **47% domestic stocks** (21% large cap, 23% mid/small cap and 3% micro cap), **47% bonds** (5-year U.S. treasuries) and **6% cash** (30-day T-bills)—the Domestic Moderate Balanced portfolio. Let's see how you navigated the full Great Depression cycle that unfolded after you invested your $1,000,000. The bottom-line results are shown in Chart 11-2 along with those of the other asset allocations. [To see how these results were actually developed, Chart A11-1 on page 262 in the Appendix provides a detailed presentation of the year-by-year gains and losses of each asset class, as well as the year-end rebalancing to maintain the desired asset allocation.]

Starting with $1,000,000 at the beginning of September 1929, your portfolio falls to $863,000 in just four months (a loss of almost 14% during the crash). In 1930, your portfolio falls to $769,000—about 23% below where it was just 16 months before. The year 1931 is worse still; your rebalanced portfolio declines to $598,000 by year-end—down 40% from your original $1,000,000 in nominal terms. The vicious bear market reaches its low point at the end of May 1932. Your moderate portfolio is valued at $486,000, more than 51% below its beginning value.

 Good news! (And you need it.) The value of the U.S. dollar has experienced a substantial bull market. The number on your year-end 1932 brokerage statement—$603,000—will actually purchase in goods and services what $802,000 would have purchased in August 1929. Therefore, the real value of your portfolio has declined only a little over 19%.

The bull market for stocks, which began in the summer of 1932, now begins to significantly improve the numbers on your brokerage statement. By the end of 1933, your portfolio is up to $842,000, while your wealth (purchasing power) now exceeds that of your original inheritance.

The year 1934 sees further improvement, and 1935 is a truly banner year. Even your brokerage statement now shows your account to be above your initial investment. The year 1936 and the first two months of 1937 provide more big returns for your portfolio. By the end of February 1937, your brokerage statement reads $1,386,000…a 38% nominal gain from September 1929.

 Taking into consideration the deflation/inflation for the entire 7½-year cycle, your wealth in August 1929 dollars stands at $1,705,000—a 70% real gain—or 7.4% compounded annually! In an inflationary environment similar to the 1990s, it would take a 10.5% compounded annual return to produce this result. (This adds a 3.1% inflation rate to the 7.4% real return). This outcome is probably much better than most people would believe possible for the market cycle that included the worst stock market conditions of this century.

Observations and Lessons

Economic Tragedy

The Great Depression was the worst economic period of this century. The financial dislocations reached much further and deeper than the stock market alone. Joblessness reached 25 percent. The size of the American economy shrunk by *one-third*. Much of the confidence in the new American dream of perpetual prosperity was greatly eroded.

There is no one source to blame for a tragedy of such immense proportions. The relatively new Federal Reserve made serious mistakes, both in the boom period of the late 1920s and in the first few years of the Depression (shrinking the money supply by over 30%) and Congress thought it could dictate trade rules to the world (Smoot-Hawley Tariff).

The unsupervised stock market (the Securities and Exchange Commission and the National Association of Securities Dealers did not yet exist) encouraged highly speculative commodities-style stock trading. Stocks could be bought with as little as 10% of the purchase price paid in cash (margin) and 90% borrowed from the broker. Therefore, a minimal 10% decline in the value of a stock would force additional principal to be paid in (margin call) or the whole position would be lost. Thankfully, much has changed since that unfortunate period in U.S. history.[19]

Stock Market Lessons

For long-term investors (as opposed to speculators or traders), the stock market's ebb and flow in this period should provide important lessons and confirmations.

> **Bull markets**, no matter how apparently sound the underpinnings, no matter how good the economic conditions, are followed by bear markets.

> **Bear markets**, no matter how pernicious the economic conditions, no matter how deep the damage, are followed by bull markets.

There are no guarantees. Even a full market cycle does not guarantee that stocks will always be the best portfolio investment. It takes a period of 20 years for history to prove stocks are *always* the better investment over bonds and cash.

Do not buy stocks on margin. Buying stocks on margin leaves you vulnerable to complete loss during periods of major market declines. It robs you of your ability to stay the course with your plan.

Stocks were truly devastated by the bear market of 1929-1932. Even the following bull market (1932-1937) did not quite restore the full loss in nominal dollars. Fortunately, this was a one-of-a-kind event so far in this century.

Balanced Portfolio Lessons

The conventional wisdom is that the Great Depression virtually wiped out all investors and that there was no clear path to avoid the destruction in paper assets. This leaves many investors with a deep-seated, gripping fear of a repeat of 1929. The facts from the full period paint a somewhat different picture. The balanced portfolio designs performed remarkably well in the full market cycle.

In fact, the 4.4% average annual nominal returns from both the Conservative and Moderate Models were substantially better than the 0.9% average annual riskless return from T-bills and not too much below the 5.0% annual return from 5-year U.S. Treasury bonds. Even the Aggressive Portfolio's 3.1% average annual return was substantially better than that of cash. Balanced portfolios more than held their own—even in the market cycle containing the worst bear market of the modern financial era.

 This performance from balanced portfolio designs is one of the least known attributes of investment history. Balanced portfolios have wonderful risk-squelching characteristics that can serve the long-term investor.

12

The Right Portfolio
For You

The model portfolios introduced in Chapter 10 provide a wide cross-section of risks and rewards. One of those models is likely a sound choice to serve as the fundamental structure of your Wealth and Retirement Portfolio. You may already know which one is right for you. If you are uncertain as to a choice, there are three very important factors to consider: your personal financial situation, your likely reaction to market setbacks of varying intensity and the specific time horizon over which your investment portfolio will be held.

"Know thyself"
— Socrates

Before You Select a Model Portfolio

As stated in the introduction, this is not a book about financial planning, as important as that area is. Therefore, you need to undertake the following, either by yourself or with the help of a financial planning expert.

- **Analyze your financial situation.** Put your Wealth and Retirement Portfolio on paper (or on computer).

- **Determine your major financial objectives.** Partial or full retirement? Early or later retirement? The idea is to estimate how many years of growth and new investment you anticipate versus the number of years you will be taking an income from your Wealth and Retirement Portfolio.

- **Prepare a retirement budget.** A realistic projection of your expenses that provides for your basic needs and a separate calculation of the non-essentials that will make your retirement enjoyable.

Charts A1-1 through A1-6 in the Appendix (pages 252-257) will help you evaluate the other side of your ledger—the maximum sustainable income that your current portfolio and your current percentage of compensation set aside into 401(k)-type programs could provide you during retirement. These charts illustrate varying average annual returns on your investments. Determine the retirement income that is possible from a full range of long-term rates of return. (Chapter 13 will evaluate in detail the maximum sustainable retirement income from each of the domestic model portfolios.)

The critical decision as to which model portfolio may be most appropriate for your Wealth and Retirement Portfolio is also influenced by the following:

- **Diversification.** The model portfolios set forth in Chapter 10 assume broad diversification within each stock asset class. However, your particular portfolio may not make this possible. For example, you may have a substantial commitment to your company's stock. A single stock has an undiversifiable risk that results from factors unique to a particular company. You may want to reduce risks in the balance of your portfolio to offset any such unavoidable and unique risks.

- **Income.** Once your Wealth and Retirement Portfolio begins to distribute income for your retirement, a greater prudence may be necessary.

  As will be discussed thoroughly in Chapter 13, the percentage of income you can comfortably take from your retirement portfolio is subject to several assumptions including market conditions.

Simple "Formulas" That Don't Work

Regrettably, there is no black box you can plug some numbers into that will spit out the right portfolio for you. One-size-fits-all formulas should be ignored.

For instance, one such formula in the popular media is to establish a portfolio in which the percentage allocated to bonds is equal to your current age, with the balance to be put in stocks. This implies that it is appropriate for every 40-year-old to hold 40% in bonds. And, likewise, that every 60-year-old should allocate 60% to bonds.

Such a naïve formula would result in substantial and needless opportunity loss in wealth or retirement income for most of its followers.

For those 40-year-olds and even 60-year-olds who understand and accept market fluctuations, both emotionally and intellectually, the much higher long-term returns of Aggressive Balanced or 100% Stocks model portfolios may be more appropriate choices for many years to come in their lives.

After all, 40-year-olds should be building retirement portfolios planned to last for 50 years! This combines their remaining wealth building years (before retirement) and income distribution years (after retirement). And those who are 60 years of age should plan for a time horizon of 30 years for their retirement portfolios.

The Voice of Experience

And what about Phil Carret? This legendary investor turned age 100 in November 1996. He is truly the most experienced investment manager in America. He started the Pioneer Mutual Fund in 1928 and has managed client funds ever since—from the 1929 crash to the 1987 crash and every bull and bear market in between.

In his 55-year tenure as manager of the Pioneer Fund, a $10,000 investment in the fund would have grown to $28.3 million. By contrast, the same investment in the Dow Jones Industrial Average would have grown to only $3.8 million. (This record inspired market wizard Warren Buffett to praise Carret as having "the best long-term investment record of anyone in America.") Should Carret avoid stocks altogether because of his age? Let's hear what he had to say at age 98 on "Wall $treet Week With Louis Rukeyser," April 28, 1995.

> RUKEYSER: "What would be your (investment policy) advice to some kid of, say, 65?"
>
> CARRET: "Buy 30% bonds and 70% common stocks." (Basically, the Aggressive Model Portfolios—domestic and global.)
>
> RUKEYSER: "And that would be the same (advice for someone of age) 75 and 85?
>
> CARRET: "Same thing."

This has been a winning investment policy for Carret *because* of his personal comfort with its risks and rewards. Even at age 100, he is not tempted to change what works for him. This is the level of commitment to which every long-term investor should aspire.

Where is Your Threshold for Pain?

A basic premise of this book is that the more prepared you are for the inevitable setbacks that are cooked-in-the-mix of your asset allocation, the less likely you will be foiled by the great enemy of long-term investment success — fear.

> "Fear leads to panic, panic breeds the inability to distinguish between temporary declines and permanent losses. That, in turn, leads to the well-documented

propensity of investors to be massive sellers of good investments near market bottoms.

"Success is purely a function of two things: (1) recognition of the inevitability of major market declines; and (2) emotional/behavioral preparation to regard such declines as...non-events..."

—*Nick Murray, Investment Advisor magazine, April, 1996*

Not every investor has the same threshold for pain. To some investors, a 10% decline in their Wealth and Retirement Portfolio is extremely painful—prepared or not. Others, once prepared, can treat 30% declines as non-events.

Where do you fit? Numbers on a page have a way of appealing to your left brain, your intelligence. If they appeal to your emotions at all, it is usually to the other emotion that drives investment decisions — greed.

Right (Brain) Choice

Right now, you need to fully activate your right brain, your feelings. Call up any of your investment fears.

Select the model portfolio that you think most closely matches your financial facts and objectives or is simply your intuitive choice. Open this book to that portfolio's Historical Risk/Reward chart in Chapter 10. Look at the setbacks that this portfolio has incurred on its way to delivering its long-term return. Your Wealth and Retirement Portfolio will more than likely last that many years— and randomly incur setbacks of that same magnitude.

How will you feel when these losses unfold over periods of up to 22 months in your Wealth and Retirement Portfolio? Stomach-turning reactions are normal. As Richard Thaler, the economist at the University of Chicago, has pointed out, "Losing $100 hurts about twice as much as winning $100 gives you pleasure." Could this feeling induce fear or panic that will cause you to take actions that are inappropriate for your long-term success?

"Successful investment management depends to a large extent on the emotional stability of the individual, particularly during periods of strain and stress, and on his ability to overcome the severe psychological hurdles present during crucial periods." —*Ragnar D. Naess, Readings in Financial Analysis and Investment Management,* 1963

Many financial plans are foiled by poor emotional planning. Don't let your plan be overturned during the next stressful market period. At a minimum, decide on an investment policy for your Wealth and Retirement Portfolio. And if you are seeking to maximize the predictability of your long-term performance, go the next step with a fixed asset allocation. Any one of the model portfolios is an excellent choice depending on the rewards you want and the risks you are willing to live with through all its inherent ups and downs.

Time Horizon

It has been stressed that the principles of this book only apply to long-term portfolios, i.e. portfolios expected to see you throughout your retirement and perhaps to be left to your heirs. Not knowing how long your needs for retirement income will last, plan on your portfolio providing an inflation adjusted income well beyond the life expectancy of you and your spouse. Therefore, if you or your spouse are under 65 years of age, your Wealth and Retirement Portfolio is definitely long-term.

If you are older than 65 or are planning for a portfolio that will last less than 20 years, you should take into consideration the full *range* of possible returns from your selected asset allocation policy for the time period you have allocated.

 Each model portfolio's long-term reward (as shown in Chapter 10) is the historic average toward which it has gravitated over the very long run. However, the shorter the time period being evaluated, the higher the variance in average annual returns. Charts 12-1 through 12-4 illustrate the range of average annual returns from the domestic model portfolios for all 5-year, 10-year, 15-year and 20-year periods within the Inflation Era. Commentary and investment suggestions follow each chart. Pay close attention to the range of returns that each model portfolio has provided over your investment time horizon. Your planning should take all of the possible outcomes into consideration.

How Long is Your Investment Horizon?

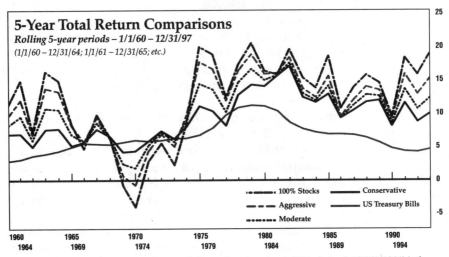

5-Year Total Return Comparisons
Rolling 5-year periods – 1/1/60 – 12/31/97
(1/1/60 – 12/31/64; 1/1/61 – 12/31/65; etc.)

● ─ ─ 100% Stocks   ─── Conservative
─ ─ ─ Aggressive   ─── US Treasury Bills
●●●●●● Moderate

| 1960 | 1965 | 1970 | 1975 | 1980 | 1985 | 1990 |
| 1964 | 1969 | 1974 | 1979 | 1984 | 1989 | 1994 |

Each point on this graph represents the start of a 5-year investment period. The first point (1960-1964) is the 5-year total return (annualized) for each portfolio beginning 1/1/60.

CHART 12-1

- **5-Year Investment Horizon.** Each domestic model portfolio has provided a wide range of 5-year returns. The Conservative Balanced portfolio has provided average annual returns from as low as 4% to as high as 16% for the 33 5-year periods beginning with 1960. The range of annualized returns for 5-year periods from the other domestic model portfolios are as follows: 2% to 17% for Moderate Balanced, -1% to 18% for Aggressive Balanced and -4% to 20% for 100% Stocks. As you can see, there is nothing predictable in such a short investment period.

  Another way of looking at a 5-year horizon may be summed up by the question, "How often and by how much did each domestic model portfolio underperform the riskless return of cash equivalents (30-day U.S. Treasury bills)?" (The return from Treasury bills is included on each of these four charts.) Whereas each model portfolio underperformed Treasury bills in either four or five of the 33 5-year periods shown, the degree of underperformance is quite different among the four models.

For *any* 5-year period in the Inflation Era, the maximum annualized percentage return *under* that of U.S. Treasury bills for the Conservative Balanced portfolio is only 1% annualized. By contrast, the Moderate Balanced portfolio has underperformed U.S. Treasury bills by as much as 4% per year in a 5-year period, while the Aggressive Balanced portfolio has underperformed cash by as much as 6% per year and the 100% Stocks portfolio by a whopping 10% per year.

With a 5-year time horizon, the Conservative Balanced portfolio is the best choice. It provides both a low *risk* of underperforming cash (four periods out of 33) and a low *degree* of underperformance during such periods. Yet, on average, the Conservative Balanced model has outperformed Treasury bills by an average of 3%, annualized over all 5-year periods.

Each of the other model portfolios should be approached much more cautiously for such a short investment horizon as five years. Although the risk of underperformance may be low, the degree of underperformance is substantial and may jeopardize the achievement of the goal for which the money is invested.

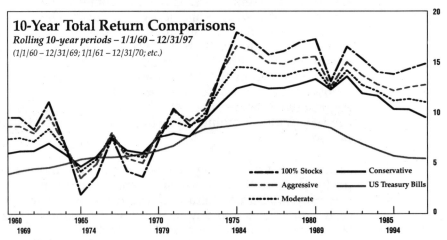

Each point on this graph represents the start of a 10-year investment period. The first point (1960-1969) is the 10-year total return (annualized) for each portfolio beginning 1/1/60.

CHART 12-2

10-Year Investment Horizon. Each domestic model portfolio continues to deliver a large range of returns in the 29 10-year periods reflected in Chart 12-2. The Conservative Balanced portfolio ranges from a low 10-year return of 4% to a high of 14%, not that much different from its range of 5-year returns. The Moderate Balanced portfolio's 10-year average annual returns range from a low of 4% to a high of 16%. The Aggressive Balanced portfolio ranges from 3% to 17%, and 100% Stocks has a range of 2% to 18%. The most noticeable improvement at a 10-year time horizon over that of a 5-year horizon is the progressively better low-end of the range of returns as one moves from Conservative Balanced to 100% Stocks.

As for the degree of underperforming cash, the Conservative Balanced portfolio just barely underperforms Treasury bills in two of the 29 10-year periods. The Moderate Balanced portfolio underperforms Treasury bills by as much as 1% per year in only one 10-year period. Even the Aggressive Balanced portfolio underperforms Treasury bills by more than 1% per year in only one 10-year period. By contrast, the 100% Stocks model portfolio substantially underperforms cash in four 10-year periods, the worst being a full 3% average annual underperformance. (Stocks have *not* always been the best investment in a given 10-year period.)

 Therefore, with a 10-year time horizon, it appears that either the Conservative Balanced or Moderate Balanced portfolios are quite acceptable and the additional risk of an Aggressive Balanced portfolio would not likely discourage investors who would normally choose this model based on all the other factors in their decision. On the other hand, the 100% Stocks portfolio in a 10-year time horizon carries substantial risk of underperforming Treasury bills and by a margin great enough to jeopardize the goals set for the portfolio based on a minimum return of at least that provided by cash equivalents.

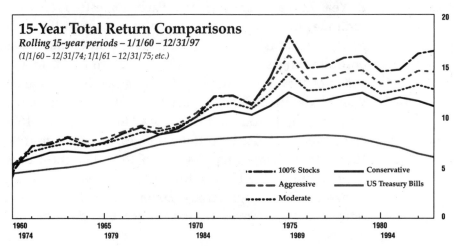

Each point on this graph represents the start of a 15-year investment period. The first point (1960-1974) is the
15-year total return (annualized) for each portfolio beginning 1/1/60.

CHART 12-3

- **15-Year Time Horizon.** The graph of 15-year returns (Chart 12-3) begins to smooth out considerably compared to the five-year and 10-year charts. Yet there is still a considerable range of returns. The Conservative Balanced portfolio produces average annual returns of between 5.5% at the low end and 11.5% at the high end. The range for the Moderate Balanced portfolio is between 5.5% and 14.0%. For the Aggressive Balanced portfolio it is between 5.5% and 16.0%, and for 100% Stocks the range is from 5.0% to 18.0%.

Fifteen years turns out to be a significant time horizon in two respects. All four domestic models outperform U.S. Treasury bills in each of the 24 15-year periods shown. In addition, at 15 years, the Aggressive Balanced portfolio always outperformed the Moderate Balanced portfolio, which in turn always outperformed the Conservative Balanced portfolio. However, the same cannot be said of the 100% Stocks portfolio whose 15-year rate of return dipped below that of the Aggressive Balanced—and even the Moderate Balanced portfolio—for extended periods.

Whereas any of the four domestic models are acceptable with a 15-year investment horizon, the Aggressive Balanced portfolio appears to be a better choice than 100% Stocks.

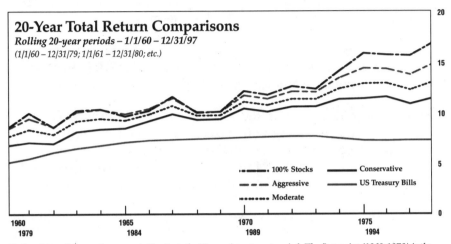

20-Year Total Return Comparisons
Rolling 20-year periods – 1/1/60 – 12/31/97
(1/1/60 – 12/31/79; 1/1/61 – 12/31/80; etc.)

Legend:
- ▪—▪ 100% Stocks
- — — Aggressive
- ▪▪▪▪▪ Moderate
- —— Conservative
- —— US Treasury Bills

Each point on this graph represents the start of a 20-year investment period. The first point (1960-1979) is the 20-year total return (annualized) for each portfolio beginning 1/1/60.

CHART 12-4

- **20-Year Time Horizon.** Contrasting Chart 12-4 with the other three charts demonstrates why this book has chosen a 20-year time horizon or greater as the appropriate time horizon for long-term portfolios. By 20 years, the returns from the various model portfolios have flattened out considerably.

 When planning for time periods of 20 years or less, perhaps a variation in an old saying is appropriate, "Plan for the worst, expect the average." In other words, you may want to prepare two estimated return calculations, one utilizing the long-term average annual rate of return from Chapter 10 and one utilizing the worst-case scenario as indicated by the bottom portion of the range depicted on these charts. If your time horizon is longer than 20 years, then the *average* annual return shown for each model portfolio in Chapter 10 is most likely your best planning choice.

Real Returns

Charts 12-1 through 12-4 reflect "nominal returns," those not adjusted for inflation/deflation. Even though this is the way we usually think about rates of return, it is not always the best way — particularly when planning long-term.

The discussion in Chapter 4 points out the overriding importance of "real returns" (those adjusted for inflation/deflation) in providing for a reliable standard of living during a long retirement.

 Chart 12-5 reflects the annualized *real* returns over 20-year time periods beginning with 1926-1945 and ending with 1978-1997. This chart covers both the Inflation Era and the prior Deflation Era. The returns reflected in this chart are those above or below the actual inflation/deflation of that particular 20-year period.

For example, the average annual real returns for the 20-year period 1934 through 1953 are circled on the chart. An investment in the Conservative Balanced portfolio at the beginning of 1934 experienced a real return of 1.5% over the next 20 years. For a Moderate Balanced portfolio, the real return was 3.4%, for Aggressive Balanced it was 5.4% and for 100% Stocks it was 7.5%.

Notice that the average annual real return from 30-day U.S. Treasury bills was a negative -3.3% per year for 20 years! This chart demonstrates clearly that cash equivalents alone are a poor choice for financing a retirement income need or creating wealth.

A big part of the price tag for higher returns has been increased *volatility*. As this study demonstrates, volatility is not the same as being *at risk* of not achieving your retirement goals. Over the past seven decades, a more aggressive asset allocation nearly always outperformed a more conservative one when viewed from time periods of 20 years or longer.

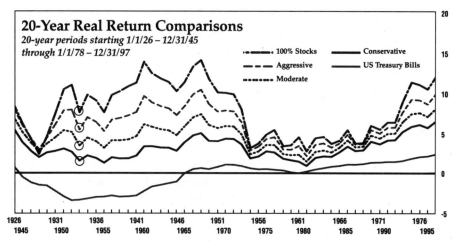

Each point on this graph represents the average annualized real return for a particular 20-year period. Real returns measure wealth accumulation by removing the inflation component from nominal rates of return.

Viewed from the perspective of 20-year real returns, the Conservative Balanced and Moderate Balanced asset allocation policies have been relatively stable, whereas Aggressive Balanced and particularly 100% Stocks have provided a wide variation in real returns.

CHART 12-5

13

Maximizing Your Retirement Income

How much income can your portfolio reasonably provide throughout your retirement? This is a critically important question to answer *before* you begin taking out income. Certain choices will have a dramatic affect on the answer. Do you wish to leave a legacy to your heirs? Do you want to fully or partially increase your income to reflect changes in the cost of living?

You should also take into consideration factors over which you have no control but still may significantly influence the amount that your portfolio can distribute during your full retirement. One such factor is the unfolding of worst-case market conditions early in your retirement. This chapter will explore the impact of each of these choices and factors on the four Domestic Model Portfolios.

"Nine-tenths of wisdom is being wise in time."
— Theodore Roosevelt

No Room for Error

Many retirees face the financial side of their retirement with an understandable touch of fear. Before retiring, employment income paid the bills. Investments were for the future, and there was time to make up for any mistakes. Suddenly, it's very different.

One of the biggest challenges for those contemplating retirement is to determine how much income they can comfortably take out of their portfolio. While there is no precise answer, a realistic approximation is far better than no estimate at all.

Four Considerations in Calculating Retirement Income

There are four major considerations in determining the maximum amount of income your retirement portfolio can provide.

- Your portfolio's expected long-term rate of return;

- The appropriate adjustment to your retirement income for inflation;

- Your intention with regard to maintaining or depleting the principal of your retirement portfolio; and

- Your life expectancy (or how long your portfolio will provide an income).

Notice that your expenses or spending level are not considered here. Although your retirement spending level is a critical, separate variable, it really does not influence what a portfolio *can* pay out over its full term.

Assumptions for Each Model Portfolio

In order to calculate the maximum percentage of income that each domestic model portfolio (introduced in Chapter 10) could pay out annually during retirement, the following assumptions are made.

Historical Performance in the Inflation Era. The actual performance of the model portfolios and the Consumer Price Index (CPI) in the Inflation Era (1960-1997) is the best platform for this study. (The rationale for this assumption is laid out in Chapter 4.)

Life Expectancy. Each model portfolio is assumed to provide income for 30 years. (This is well beyond the average number of years a retiree takes income out of his/her portfolio.)

Principal: Maintain or Deplete. Each model portfolio is looked at both ways. A *Legacy Portfolio* in which principal is more or less maintained intact (adjusted for inflation) is presented, as well as a *Spendthrift Portfolio* (Spending My Children's Inheritance) in which principal is used to enhance income over 30 years before being depleted.

Income. The maximum income for the *first* year of retirement is shown as a percentage of the Wealth and Retirement Portfolio just prior to retirement. The purchasing power of this income is held constant throughout retirement by adjusting the original income level by the full measure of inflation.

Chart 13-1 below shows the maximum percentage that each model portfolio could pay out as retirement income and still satisfy all of the assumptions above. (Charts A13-1 through A13-8 in the Appendix illustrate the year-by-year calculations and results for the Domestic Moderate Model Portfolio that are summarized within this chapter.) Real returns for any long period of time are likely to approximate those of the Inflation Era, therefore these percentages of distributable income are appropriate for your own future planning.

Maximum Retirement Income – Full CPI Adjustment

Retirement income, once set by this percentage, adjusts annually by the full change in CPI.

Domestic Model Portfolios	Spendthrift Portfolio (30 Years' Income)	Legacy Portfolio (Perpetual Income)
Conservative Balanced (30-50-20)	4.9%	3.2%
Moderate Balanced (47-47-6)	5.4%	3.9%
Aggressive Balanced (67-28-5)	6.0%	4.6%
100% Stocks (100-0-0)	6.5%	5.3%

CHART 13-1

Example: A new retiree that has selected a Moderate Balanced (domestic) allocation for her Wealth and Retirement Portfolio of $500,000 could take up to $27,000 of income in her first year of retirement (500,000 x 5.4%) and adjust this income upward by the full change in the CPI index for 30 years before her principal is depleted. Or, she could take an income of $19,500 in her first year of retirement ($500,000 x 3.9%) and adjust this income upward by the full change in the CPI index in perpetuity. Under this last scenario, the full inflation-adjusted value of the $500,000 portfolio would be more or less maintained indefinitely.

Your Inflation Rate

Suppose you want a higher level of income from your portfolio than that shown by the model closest to your own portfolio design in Chart 13-1. One obvious choice would be to adopt a more aggressive returning model for your retirement portfolio.

Another change of assumptions that may be appropriate is in the inflation adjustment. It is quite possible that the pay-out from your Wealth and Retirement Portfolio will not require an automatic raise by the full percentage increase in the CPI each year. Some of your expenses may be fixed, some may be stable, some may decline as your retirement unfolds. Obviously, you will gauge your actual expenses and raise your income accordingly. Perhaps your own personal inflation rate may only be two-thirds of the general rate *as registered by the CPI statistic.*

In addition, the CPI itself has come under criticism by noted economists; and even Alan Greenspan, the Chairman of the Federal Reserve, stated in testimony to congress in August 1996, "The (CPI) statistic is but an imprecise statistical proxy for inflation." He is also on record as stating that the reported CPI may overstate inflation by a full percentage point—about one-third of the projected 3.1% inflation rate. Therefore, estimating your personal inflation rate at two-thirds of the CPI rate may better recognize the U.S. economy's true rate of inflation and particularly your own.

Therefore, for each of the stated objectives above, a second set of maximum initial retirement incomes have been calculated assuming your retirement income need only increase at 67% of reported CPI. These numbers are reflected in Chart 13-2.

Maximum Retirement Income – Two-Thirds CPI Adjustment

Retirement income, once set by this percentage, adjusts annually by two-thirds of the change in CPI.

Domestic Model Portfolios	Spendthrift Portfolio (30 Years' Income)	Legacy Portfolio (Perpetual Income)
Conservative Balanced (30-50-20)	5.8%	4.6%
Moderate Balanced (47-47-6)	6.4%	5.3%
Aggressive Balanced (67-28-5)	7.0%	6.0%
100% Stocks (100-0-0)	7.5%	6.7%

CHART 13-2

For any Spendthrift Model Portfolio, this particular change in your long-term planning allows for a one percentage increase in the initial pay-out from your portfolio at retirement. In our prior example, the new retiree with a portfolio of $500,000 can add $5,000 to her beginning income at retirement (from $27,000 to $32,000) if she adjusts this higher initial income by only two-thirds of the CPI index over time. However, she will want to carefully monitor her actual increase in expense level and determine if it is indeed only two-thirds of reported CPI over a reasonable period.

Worst-Case Market Conditions

One other consideration needs to be addressed. As pointed out, the calculations in this chapter follow the thesis presented in Chapter 4 that the year 1960 is perhaps the best representative year for beginning a long-term market analysis, i.e. normal market conditions relative to the 1990s. But what if it isn't?

A search of the data reveals that 1968 was the worst year to begin retirement in the Inflation Era. Not only was the stock market beginning one of its worst six-year periods ever, but inflation was just starting a long, dramatic rise. The impact of retiring at just the wrong time is calculated for each model portfolio in Chart 13-3. Like Chart 13-2, this chart assumes retirement income is adjusted by two-thirds of the annual change in CPI.

Maximum Retirement Income – Worst-Case Initial Market Conditions

Retirement income, beginning in the worst conditions of the Inflation Era, adjusts annually by two-thirds of the change in CPI.

Domestic Model Portfolios	Spendthrift Portfolio (30 Years' Income)	Legacy Portfolio (Perpetual Income)
Conservative Balanced (30-50-20)	5.5%	4.5%
Moderate Balanced (47-47-6)	5.7%	4.9%
Aggressive Balanced (67-28-5)	5.7%	5.0%
100% Stocks (100-0-0)	5.5%	5.0%

CHART 13-3

Comparing Chart 13-3 with Chart 13-2 vividly demonstrates the impact of *initial* market conditions on the amount of income a portfolio can afford to pay-out. Keep in mind that both sets of portfolios in these two charts experienced the poor market conditions of 1968-1974. The difference is that those portfolios in Chart 13-3 *began* with them.

Also notice the unevenness of the effect on the four model portfolios. As with Chapter 11's discussion of portfolios in the Great Depression, the less growth-oriented the model portfolio (percentage of stocks), the less damage inflicted by worst-case market conditions—inflationary or deflationary. For example, the Conservative model's maximum pay-out was only reduced by three-tenths of one percent (5.8%→5.5%), while the 100% Stocks model suffered a full two percent reduction (7.5%→5.5%).

Considering the Choices

There is a good deal of information within this chapter that can help anyone in formulating their plans for retirement.

Model Portfolio Choice. These charts provide valuable additional input in choosing a model portfolio to emulate during retirement. Under normal market conditions, looking from one model portfolio to the next (as measured by a higher percentage dedicated to stocks) adds between 10% to 20% to your sustainable retirement income.

Inflation Adjustment. Planning for a retirement income that fully adjusts for annual changes in CPI has a big price tag. It may be worth it, but perhaps it isn't. In the 1960-1997 period and likely in any future period, adjusting your retirement income by 67% of the annual change in CPI (instead of 100%) allows for between 15% and 30% higher initial retirement income.

Legacy or Spendthrift. This decision has a substantial effect on your retirement income. For those who wish to leave an estate behind approximately equal to the real value of their portfolio at retirement, the reduction in the maximum retirement income that could be paid out in the 1960-1997 period was between 35% (from 4.9% to 3.2% in a Conservative Model Portfolio) and 18% (from 6.5% to 5.3% in a 100% Stocks portfolio). This is also a likely consequence going forward.

Market Conditions. Market conditions are a more troubling topic. Certainly those who retired in 1968 did not know at the time that they were looking down a double-barreled shotgun of much higher inflation and extremely poor market performance for the next six years (as a whole). Those 1968 retirees, who were anticipating a continuance of market conditions similar to 1960, would face some unhappy choices if they paid out the maximum retirement income allowed by more normal market conditions. They would run out of retirement income well short of the 30 years anticipated.

The impact of poor market conditions diminishes the further in the future they unfold. The retirees of 1960 also experienced the 1968-1974 bear market and accelerating inflation of that period, yet were much less affected.

The best advice is **be prepared.** Know your worst-case scenario and be prepared to live within it. If extremely poor market conditions do unfold early in your retirement, you will be glad you were ready.

Section IV

Three Portfolio Strategies:
Executing Your Asset Allocation

Overview
of Section IV

Whereas your asset allocation policy provides the structure for your portfolio, you still need to choose a comprehensive strategy to implement it. The three primary strategies discussed in this Section are:

- *Passive Strategy* - employing index mutual funds (the most certain strategy of precisely fulfilling your asset allocation policy)

- *Active Strategy* - employing various *styles* of actively managed mutual funds (the most challenging yet potentially rewarding strategy) and

- *Managed Account Strategy* - employing your own money manager (the most disciplined strategy, removing emotionally motivated decisions).

Index funds need to be fully understood as to the exact asset class or combination of asset classes they are attempting to capture. Actively managed mutual funds require special attention as to their ability to add value to the asset class(es) in which they invest. Money managers should be evaluated on a host of important criteria to make sure they are both professionally competent and *right for you*.

14

The Certainty of Index Funds

Index funds are designed to track an entire asset class by buying and holding a very large cross-section of all of the securities within it. They are a low-cost alternative for those individuals with limited time for, or interest in, investing. They are also appropriate for those who want the most certain strategy for meeting the results anticipated by their asset allocation.

For all other investors, the appropriate combination of index funds provides an excellent "benchmark" to measure the performance of their own Wealth and Retirement Portfolios.

"Simplicity or singleness of approach is a greatly underestimated factor of market success."
— Garfield Drew, <u>New Methods of Profit in the Stock Market</u> (1941)

Simple and Certain Strategy

The simplest and most certain way to put your asset allocation policy in action is with **index mutual funds**. Indexing, or *passive* management, virtually guarantees that you will achieve results that closely parallel those of your asset allocation.

It's that simple! Whether your retirement portfolio is $10,000 or $10,000,000, you can put it all into index mutual funds allocated according to your chosen asset allocation and be done with it (except for annual rebalancing). You have achieved broad diversification within each of your chosen asset classes.

Is an index fund strategy right for you? Your orientation toward investing is the main determinant. A general profile of a good candidate for an index fund strategy is shown below:

Issues to Consider	*Candidate for Index Fund Strategy*
Time for Investments	"I want to spend as little time on my investments as possible."
Interest Level in Investing	"Investments are boring."
Stress Level	"Uncertainties of investing are stressful."
Goals for Investment Performance	"Capturing market returns with normal ups and downs is okay with me."
Attitude Toward Fees	"I don't like paying any more in fees than I absolutely have to."

CHART 14-1

If you choose this elegantly simple strategy of capturing average returns and average setbacks, you will never suffer below average performance! You will have completely harnessed the full long-term predictability of your asset allocation policy.

Benchmark Portfolio

 This leads into one of the most important observations of this book. Any other strategy you employ should add value to the performance of a pure index approach, otherwise, *What's the Point?!*

Therefore, if you do *not* choose to use an index fund strategy, assemble it on paper anyway. This will be your own benchmark to gauge the performance of your actual Wealth and Retirement Portfolio. Appropriate benchmark portfolios for the asset allocation policies (model portfolios) developed in Chapter 10 are shown in Chart 14-2 utilizing Vanguard Index Funds.

Your Benchmark Portfolio is now the track that your portfolio is following and attempting to improve upon. **It is the only valid yardstick by which to measure your Wealth and Retirement Portfolio's performance.** Every time you compute the total return of your portfolio, also compute the return over the same period for your benchmark portfolio. Compare the two. How are you doing? Now you know for sure. No wishful thinking. No inappropriate yardsticks.

Right and Wrong Yardsticks

Applying the wrong yardstick to portfolio performance is very common among individual investors and professionals alike.

By far the most common mis-measuring tool is the Dow Jones Industrial Average ("Dow"). When virtually anyone asks, "How did the market do today?" the appropriate response is the gain or loss in the Dow that day. In other words, the performance of the Giant Cap component (just 30 very large cap stocks) of the total domestic stock market is the expected answer.

This may seem innocent enough because everyone knows what is meant. Perhaps it would be safe if this were the end of it. Unfortunately, this is just the beginning, for the very next question is, "How are you doing vs. 'the market'?" This pits your portfolio's performance against that of the Dow.

Benchmark Portfolios - Using Vanguard Index Funds

Domestic Conservative (30-50-20)

13%	S&P 500 Trust
17%	Extended Market
50%	Intermediate-Term Treasury Bond
20%	Money Market
100%	Total Portfolio

Domestic Aggressive (67-28-5)

30%	S&P 500 Trust
37%	Extended Market
28%	Intermediate-Term Treasury Bond
5%	Money Market
100%	Total Portfolio

Domestic Moderate (47-47-6)

21%	S&P 500 Trust
26%	Extended Market
47%	Intermediate-Term Treasury Bond
6%	Money Market
100%	Total Portfolio

Domestic 100% Stocks (100-0-0)

44%	S&P 500 Trust
56%	Extended Market
100%	Total Portfolio

Global Conservative (30-50-20)

8%	S&P 500 Trust
11%	Extended Market
6%	Total International
5%	REIT
50%	Intermediate-Term Treasury Bond
20%	Money Market
100%	Total Portfolio

Global Aggressive (68-27-5)

20%	S&P 500 Trust
27%	Extended Market
16%	Total International
5%	REIT
27%	Intermediate-Term Treasury Bond
5%	Money Market
100%	Total Portfolio

Global Moderate (47-47-6)

14%	S&P 500 Trust
17%	Extended Market
11%	Total International
5%	REIT
47%	Intermediate-Term Treasury Bond
6%	Money Market
100%	Total Portfolio

Global 100% Stocks (100-0-0)

31%	S&P 500 Trust
39%	Extended Market
25%	Total International
5%	REIT
100%	Total Portfolio

CHART 14-2

Definitions – Chart 14-2

Vanguard 500 Index. This fund seeks investment results that correspond with the price and yield performance of the S&P 500 index, the most commonly used proxy for domestic large cap stocks. Similar S&P 500 index funds are widely available from mutual fund providers such as **Charles Schwab & Company, Inc., Fidelity, Dreyfus, Stagecoach** and many others.

Vanguard Extended Market Index. This fund seeks to replicate the performance of the Wilshire 4500 Index. Basically, this fund captures the performance of the entire mid/small cap and micro cap asset classes. (If overweighting the micro cap asset class is desired, Dimensional Fund Advisors' 9-10 Fund is the best representative index fund.)

Vanguard Total International Index. This fund seeks a broad balance of international equities designed to track the performance of the Morgan Stanley EAFE Index, including approximately 15% in Emerging Markets.

Note: For investors desiring a more conservative index to international equity markets, the **Schwab International Index** is a good alternative. In lieu of country weightings, the Schwab International Index fund primarily invests in the 350 largest companies outside of the U.S.

Vanguard Intermediate-Term U.S. Treasury. This managed fund invests exclusively in U.S. government securities and ordinarily maintains a weighted maturity of between five and ten years. An alternative fund that comes even closer to the 5-Year U.S. Treasury bond index used in this book is the **Dreyfus 100% U.S. Treasury Intermediate Term** fund.

Vanguard REIT Index. This index fund seeks to replicate the performance of the Morgan Stanley Equity REIT index (excluding healthcare properties). This index has closely paralleled the NAREIT equity index over its short existence.

This is appropriate only if your portfolio (or the stocks portion thereof) is made up of but one asset class—the giant Dow stocks. With any other asset allocation policy, such a comparison is apples to oranges. Using the wrong yardstick leads to the wrong conclusions about your portfolio's performance and soon may lead you to make changes within your portfolio that are completely uncalled for.

S&P 500 Index Vs. General Equity Funds

An index—or index fund—is nothing more, nothing less than an average for the asset class being indexed. Can average be *better* than average? This question may sound nonsensical; yet, the S&P 500 Index is frequently touted (since the mid-1990s) as superior to 70-80% of all actively managed general equity mutual funds.

One obvious problem with such a comparison is that most mutual fund portfolio managers do not invest exclusively in domestic large cap stocks and many do not use the S&P 500 as their fund's benchmark (target asset class).

Many general equity mutual funds today exclusively or predominantly invest in mid cap, small cap or micro cap stocks. Many of these funds invest in the full range of stock asset classes. Therefore, if the S&P 500 is outperforming more than 50% of managed domestic stock portfolios, it is likely that the domestic large cap asset class is simply the best performing asset class for the period used for comparison.

And this was the case through the mid-to-late 1990s. As pointed out in Chapter 4, the bull markets in the period 1982-1997+ have been led by domestic large cap stocks—those that dominate the S&P 500. This asset class outperformed the other three domestic asset classes and international stocks (disregarding currency effects) and REITs. **The average of the best performing asset class (whichever one it is for the time period being measured) will *always* outperform most money managers or mutual funds.**

A comparison of the S&P 500 Index with the average performance of all general equity funds for the full Inflation Era (1960-1997+) paints a truer picture. During that time period, there were periods when each one did far better than the other. However, in the end, each one's outperformance periods were canceled out by its underperformance periods. And, as might have been expected, the S&P 500 *average* just about equaled the equity fund *average* (Chart 14-3). There is no implicit guarantee that either is a better long-term choice based on performance alone.

Gus Sauter, principal at the Vanguard Group and manager of all the company's index funds had this to say in the February 18, 1997, issue of Financial World magazine, "Markets are a zero sum game. All investors are the market and by definition half will outperform and half will underperform — before fees. Once fees are added to the equation, the marginal outperformers will fall below average."

Note: These performance figures for general equity funds do not account for "survivorship bias." This means that the results from discontinued funds are not included in the equity fund average. Some studies indicate that when all funds are included that were available to investors, the long-term average may be reduced by as much as 0.5% per year.

Your Domestic Stocks Can Beat the S&P 500 Index

Do you want 95% probability that the domestic stocks portion of your Wealth and Retirement Portfolio will beat the S&P 500 over a 20-year period? Easy. Utilize only micro cap stocks in your asset allocation. Micro cap stocks have outperformed large cap stocks (S&P 500) in 49 out of a possible 52 20-year time periods since 1926 and hold a 2.0% annualized advantage for the whole time period (1926-1997).

Average performance for the micro cap asset class is easily attainable for many investors. DFA's Small 9-10 Fund is the micro cap asset class (since 1981) as used by Ibbotson Associates in their SBBI Yearbook. Before you opt for this solution, however, be sure to study the fluctuation pattern of micro caps in their Historical Risk/Reward [Chart 5-6 on page 70] and pay particular attention to their degree of temporary losses during setbacks. Micro cap stocks have been very volatile, which would make a portfolio comprised of only these very small company stocks difficult to live with over time. (See pages 32-38 for more information on micro cap stocks.)

Mutual Fund Managers Versus S&P 500

Calendar Year	General Equity Funds (%)	S&P 500 Reinvested (%)
1997	24.2	33.3
1996	19.5	23.1
1995	31.3	37.5
1994	-1.4	1.3
1993	13.0	10.1
1992	9.1	7.6
1991	35.9	30.4
1990	-6.0	-3.1
1989	24.9	31.6
1988	15.4	16.6
1987	0.9	5.2
1986	14.4	18.7
1985	28.1	31.7
1984	-1.2	6.3
1983	21.6	22.6
1982	26.0	21.6
1981	-0.6	-4.9
1980	34.8	32.5
1979	29.5	18.6
1978	11.9	6.6
1977	2.5	-7.1
1976	26.7	23.9
1975	35.0	37.2
1974	-24.2	-26.5
1973	-22.3	-14.7
1972	13.2	19.0
1971	21.3	14.3
1970	-7.2	3.9
1969	-13.0	-8.4
1968	18.1	11.0
1967	37.2	23.9
1966	-4.9	-10.0
1965	23.3	12.5
1964	14.3	16.5
1963	19.2	22.8
1962	-13.6	-8.7
1961	25.9	26.9
1960	3.6	0.5

AVERAGE ANNUAL RETURN PERFORMANCE (%)
1960-97   11.3%   11.6%

Source: Lipper Analytical Services, Inc.

CHART 14-3

As a more desirable alternative, either the Domestic 100% Stocks Model Portfolio or the Global 100% Stocks Model Portfolio has been a far less-risky choice for outperforming the mighty S&P 500 (Charts 10-7 and 10-11).

Indexes Are No Panaceas

An index fund strategy is perfect for the investor who is interested in a simple, yet certain, method of capturing the average returns—and accepting the average setbacks—of his/her asset allocation policy. An added plus is the minimum amount of time required to maintain an index portfolio. Just don't be deceived into believing that an index strategy is better than average.

 In fact, when viewed from the perspective of indexes other than the S&P 500 Index, the more appropriate question may be, "Can average be *worse* than average?" While mutual funds that specialize in domestic large cap stocks have in fact had difficulty in outperforming the S&P 500 (recently), there has been no such difficulty in virtually any other equity asset class.

Studies conducted by Morningstar Mutual Funds have found that actively managed mutual funds that target the other domestic equity asset classes or the broad based EAFE international stock index have enjoyed better average performance than the indexes or comparable index funds. Figures from Lipper Analytical back this up: 74 percent of actively managed small-company funds beat their benchmark—the Russell 2000 Index—for the 10 years ended December 1996. In the international arena, 70 percent of actively managed funds beat the EAFE international index over the past five years.[20]

The capitalization weighted Vanguard Extended Market Index Fund, which invests in all U.S. companies except the S&P 500, is an ideal index of domestic mid/small and micro cap asset classes combined. Yet, this index fund has never (in the 10 years of its existence through 1997) scored in the top 25% of Morningstar's

Small Company Universe, and only three times has it been in the top half.

These time periods of comparison are too short to be conclusive. Until proved otherwise, it is best to assume that a stock index or equity index fund provides no more, no less than the average returns with the average setbacks of the underlying assets in that class and that close to half of all actively managed funds will improve on this average and the others will underperform over long time periods.

Bond Indexing

Index mutual funds are also available to match various bond indexes prepared by Lehman Brothers, Merrill Lynch, Salomon Brothers and other Wall Street firms. Included in the diverse group of bond index funds are specific offerings that target a "constant maturity" U.S. Treasury bond.

Bond index funds are perhaps even more appropriate than equity index funds for the predictable portfolios developed with this book. Bonds offer fewer options to fund managers for "adding value" than do stocks, particularly in U.S. Treasury bonds of intermediate maturity. Therefore, the low level of fees within bond index funds (about one-fourth of broad-based bond funds) are more likely to impact final performance.

The early results of these relatively new investment vehicles appear to verify this observation. "Mutual funds linked to bond indexes have outperformed at least two-thirds of comparable non-indexed funds in seven of the last eight years."[21]

Other Attributes of Index Funds

Index funds are passively managed and, therefore, do not need the breadth and depth of personnel that actively managed funds require to be competitive. This shows up in much lower fund management fees. Trading securities is held to a minimum so brokerage costs are also held down. The total cost differential between an index fund and an actively managed fund can easily run between 0.5% and 1.0% per year. This is a head start with which index funds begin each year.

The lower fee structure of index funds provides a definite advantage to their long-term return. Offsetting this return advantage is the somewhat higher risk that index funds sport relative to the average managed fund. This is primarily due to the fully invested nature of index funds through all market declines.

Some comparisons also attribute tax savings to index funds in taxable accounts. This is due to their low turnover of securities creating little in the way of capital gains. However, recent studies, including one conducted by the No-Load Fund Analyst in 1995 and updated again in 1997, have raised clouds over this issue. Many actively managed funds that produced superior returns to index funds have actually distributed less in taxable gains and dividends.

Tactical Asset Allocation

The index fund strategy is an ideal extension of the fixed asset allocation policy developed in Chapters 9 and 10. They offer market certainty, low costs and fees and the possibility of an average or lower tax bite.

These attributes of an index strategy disappear if you attempt to achieve short-term advantages by rotating among the asset classes. This adds an element of market timing.

This is not just a subtle change or enhancement; it is an entirely different strategy. The enforced discipline of rebalancing is rendered moot. As Gus Sauter was quoted as saying, "(Asset class) rotating is like betting, pure and simple. It's silly to choose a strategy that guarantees market returns and then use it in a way that risks (opportunity) loss."

Conclusion

Implementing your investment strategy with index mutual funds is the most reliable way to achieve your asset allocation's performance. From a long-term perspective, this is your most predictable portfolio.

15

Managed Funds: Adding Value to Your Asset Allocation

Like many investors, you may be invigorated by the challenge of outperforming the index averages. Assembling a portfolio of mutual funds with superior managers at the helm offers the potential of higher returns and/or lower risk than that of your benchmark (index) portfolio. This chapter lays out a unique approach to evaluating fund managers so as to identify those few who have demonstrated success at consistently outperforming their targeted asset class.

"It is impossible to produce superior performance unless you do something different from the majority."
— Sir John Templeton

Actively Managed Mutual Funds

The prior chapter examined a portfolio strategy built around the advantages and long-term predictability of index mutual funds. As pointed out, if index funds are not employed directly, every investor and investment professional should strongly consider establishing and monitoring a benchmark portfolio of index funds that best fits his/her asset allocation policy. Your benchmark portfolio will be the guiding light—the appropriate yardstick—for your personal Wealth and Retirement Portfolio.

This chapter will focus on adding value to your benchmark portfolio with actively managed mutual funds. These mutual funds rely on the judgment of their portfolio manager to attempt to *improve on the performance of the asset class* or asset classes they are targeting. As with the index fund strategy, it is your orientation toward investing that should help guide your decision. Before taking on the challenge of active management, consider the following:

Issues to Consider	*Candidate for Active Management Strategy*
Time for Investments	"My schedule affords ample time for researching, evaluating and selecting investments."
Interest Level in Investing	"Investing is fun, interesting, challenging."
Stress Level	"Being totally at the mercy of the market (in index funds) is stressful."
Goals for Investment Performance	"I want to try to beat my benchmark"; AND/OR "I want benchmark returns with less fluctuation in values."
Attitude Toward Fees	"Risk and returns are far more important than fees."

CHART 15-1

Of course, there is nothing wrong with building a portfolio of mutual funds that includes both index funds and actively managed funds. Many investors and professionals alike choose to index their large cap stock position with an S&P 500 Index Fund, but choose to actively manage their allocations to all other equity asset classes, reasoning that there is more opportunity in mid/small, micro cap or international funds for individual judgment on stock selection to pay off.

Random Walk

In the previous chapter, it was pointed out that domestic large cap stocks have been the best performing asset class since the early 1980s. Because of this, the primary index of large cap stocks—the S&P 500 Index—has outperformed the majority of general equity mutual funds, as would be expected.

Unfortunately, many industry observers have confused the performance of the large cap *asset class* with the performance of *passive* or *index investing*. Thus, passive management has been given undeserved credit for being able to outperform the average actively managed general U.S. stock fund. As was shown in Chapter 14, this is based on the false premise that all general equity funds target the S&P 500.

Yet, the success of the S&P 500 Index for so many years has given renewed credence to the original theory that led to the development of index funds—the "efficient market theory" popularized by Burton Malkiel in his now famous A Random Walk Down Wall Street in 1973.

This theory suggests that neither a person nor a system of stock selection can consistently beat random selection of stocks over time. The foundation for this theory is that all public knowledge is instantaneously known by market participants and immediately reflected in equity prices, i.e. no one can know more than the all-knowing market. To its logical conclusion, random walk means that *every* fully invested portfolio of large cap stocks, for example, would eventually gravitate to the large cap market average, less fees and costs.

Common Sense Prevails

Until very recently, random walk was becoming entrenched as accepted wisdom, yet it defies common sense. It's as if Warren Buffett, Michael Price, Ben Graham, Ralph Wanger, Shelby Davis, Peter Lynch and all the other long-term "winners" never lived! Individual investment managers have indeed outperformed their target markets over very long time periods!

Recent exhaustive research has also proved that superior *methods* of stock selection have consistently outperformed their target asset class over time.

A landmark study conducted by professors Eugene Fama and Kenneth French of the University of Chicago scrutinized the performance of 2,000 stocks from 1941 to 1990. Whereas efficient market theory suggests that no criterion of stock selection (other than market capitalization and volatility) would accurately predict *future* performance, the Fama/French study published in the Journal of Finance (June 1992) found that selection criteria such as the current market price of a stock as a multiple of its book value did in fact predict *future* performance.

Even more impressive is James O'Shaughnessy's study of every stock in Standard & Poor's (S&P) database from 1954 through 1994 as published in What Works on Wall Street (McGraw Hill, 1996). In his study, O'Shaughnessy pitted 40 combinations of selection criteria, i.e. *methods* of stock selection, against the S&P 500 Index and against a universe of all stocks for that 40-year period.

What Works on Wall Street, as its preface notes, "is the first all-inclusive, definitive guide to the long-term efficacy of Wall Street's favorite strategies." Using vast computer power and a method devoid of outside influences, O'Shaughnessy tested these 40 well-known strategies for returns, risk (standard deviations and Sharpe ratios) and consistency of performance. The result: "Forty years of data prove that the market follows a purposeful stride, not a random walk. The stock market consistently rewards some strategies and consistently punishes others."

Active management employing disciplined strategies can add value to the relevant combination of indexes and, as importantly, can do so with *less risk* than that of a comparable index. Better still, certain methods of adding value to index performance are predictable!

Superior Mutual Fund Managers

Now that the air has been let out of the efficient market theory, it should be pointed out that there is some validity to the theory with regard to actively managed mutual funds. Among all mutual funds, there is an observable gravitation toward the mean (average) over time. Perhaps the theory could be restated as follows:

> Most mutual funds and other managed portfolios will trend toward the average performance of the asset classes they are employing. Winners in one period may lose in the next—or just win with less margin over average. From the other side, losers in one time period may win in the next— or just lose with less margin. Over many time periods, perhaps 80% of mutual funds will cluster around the average; *less than* 10% will be persistent winners and *more than* 10% will be consistent losers.

This really should come as no great surprise. Money management is as fiercely competitive as professional sports. There are few— very few—who possess the remarkable talent, the work ethic and discipline to stand out like Michael Jordan, Martina Navratilova, Carl Lewis or Jack Nicklaus have in their respective professions over long careers.

Managing a Portfolio of Mutual Funds

 The conclusion of these studies and of those cited in Chapter 14 is that a small proportion of actively managed mutual funds will consistently add value to the index returns of the asset class within which they invest. The key word is *consistently*. Anyone can look at one-year, three-year and five-year performance charts and point out those mutual funds that beat their relevant index. But without consistency it has questionable meaning with regard to predicting *future* superior performance.

As a long-term investor in actively managed mutual funds, you want a selection criteria that identifies one or two mutual fund managers that are more likely than not to outperform the asset class they are filling within your Wealth and Retirement Portfolio...over the long haul.

Put simply, can *you* identify such consistent, long-term, superior mutual fund managers? And, once identified, can you stay with them? The second question will be dealt with in Chapters 16 and 17. The first question is the subject of the balance of this chapter. Before addressing the question directly, there is one other characteristic of equity mutual funds with which you need to be aware.

Your Stock Fund Has Style

Benjamin Graham is known today as the father of value investing. This is a *style* of investing characterized by the goal of buying out-of-favor individual stocks for less than a third-party buyer would pay for the whole company or for less than the cash-out value of the company if it were liquidated.

Graham's credentials are impeccable. He wrote the bible of investment evaluation technique for professionals in 1934, Security Analysis. He also wrote what is still among the best investment books for individuals, The Intelligent Investor (1973). His personal and professional investment track record is among the very best of this century and perhaps the best of the Deflation Era.

T. Rowe Price is thought by many students of 20th century investing to be the father of growth investing. This is the *style* of investing noted by its attachment to the stocks of companies well-positioned for long-term growth of revenues and earnings.

Price wrote some of the most insightful pieces ever written on investing and broad economic trends, including a series of articles written for Barron's in 1939 entitled "Picking Growth Stocks." More than anyone else, he influenced investors to look beyond the balance sheet and toward the future and the positioning of each company for sustainable growth. His personal investment record and that of the mutual funds he founded are a testament to his successful methods.

Growth Vs. Value

The two schools of investing have spawned the so-called growth-versus-value debate. There are many dimensions to this debate that have ramifications for your mutual fund evaluation, selection and performance measurement.

 As this book takes a long-term focus, it should be stated quite clearly that this debate has no winner...or loser. When applied consistently, investing techniques based on both philosophies have produced superior results. In other words, superior mutual fund managers have emerged from both the growth and value camps.

A study in the September 26, 1997, Morningstar Mutual Funds came to the same conclusion. "....we found that broad trends in investment style didn't play much of a role in long-term returns. Over a three- or a five-year period, style can have a huge impact on returns. Over the 10-year period covered in the study, however, there were several countervailing trends, causing many of the style effects to cancel each other out."

Also, superior fund managers may have elements of both investment philosophies within their stock selection criteria. Warren Buffett confessed that he was caught up in the growth vs. value debate early in his career, but after a point, learned that "they are joined at the hip." Few superior value managers totally ignore the earnings prospects of a company and few superior growth managers will pay any price for perceived future growth. Mutual fund managers who acknowledge that their investment philosophy incorporates elements of both camps are referred to as "growth-at-a-price" managers, and Morningstar categorizes them under the style box heading "blend."

So why pay any attention to this particular debate? Because one style or the other—or even a subset style—may be dominating short-term performance statistics. Therefore, diversifying your equity mutual funds among the distinctive style categories serves to smooth out short-term portfolio performance without sacrificing long-term returns.

How do you know what style a particular domestic stock fund falls into? Each individual mutual fund's prospectus and marketing materials, as well as analytical industry observers like Morningstar and Value Line, available at many public libraries, will prove helpful in determining a fund's style. Possibly the best source of style comparisons by asset class is the No-Load Fund Analyst (Orinda, California). This firm pioneered much of the research in this area of mutual fund analysis. As their name suggests, however, they analyze selected no-load mutual funds only.

Identifying Consistently Superior Mutual Fund Managers

Focus on the Manager

This book focuses on evaluating mutual fund *managers*—not mutual funds themselves. In most cases, the performance that a mutual fund delivers (above or below its target asset class) is a direct result of the judgment of the fund manager. The mutual fund organization may provide terrific technical support, insightful research and talented analysts, yet in the end, it is up to the portfolio manager to make the decisions that are the primary determinant of the fund's results during his or her tenure. This has two notable ramifications:

- Mutual fund performance records are valid only back to the inception of the current (lead) portfolio manager and

- A manager's track record may be pieced together from prior mutual fund or private money management experience if the manager was the primary manager with the same investment mandate as held currently.

As a consequence, a mutual fund with a great long-term track record but with a new, unproven portfolio manager is of no interest, while a brand new mutual fund with a proven superior manager may be quite appealing.

Historical Risk/Reward

Historical Risk/Reward charts are especially designed for long-term analysis and therefore are of great value in evaluating the risks and rewards of asset classes and asset allocation policies. Unfortunately, few mutual fund managers have been at the helm for the requisite 20-year period or longer. Of those that do qualify, there are some outstanding performers.

Chart 15-2 is a Historical Risk/Reward chart of a superior large cap growth-at-a-price fund, Davis New York Venture, continuously managed since 1969 by Shelby Davis. (Davis has also managed no-load Selected American Shares since 1993. In 1997, he turned over the role of lead portfolio manager to his son, Chris, with whom he had worked closely for several years. Now, Shelby calls himself the "coach," and Chris the "quarterback" as Shelby focuses on the big picture and Chris performs day-to-day management.) Shelby's official title is Chief Investment Officer.

Chart 15-3 compares the performance of Shelby Davis's New York Venture Fund against that of the S&P 500, his targeted asset class, for the 1972-1997 period of study.

Chart 15-4 is a Historical Risk/Reward chart of a superior mid/small cap growth fund, Acorn, continuously managed since 1970 by Ralph Wanger.

Chart 15-5 compares the performance of Ralph Wanger's Acorn Fund against that of mid/small caps, his targeted asset class, for the 1972-1997 period of study.

Historical Risk/Reward Chart

Davis NY Venture A: Shelby Davis
Growth of $100,000
(12/31/71 – 12/31/97)

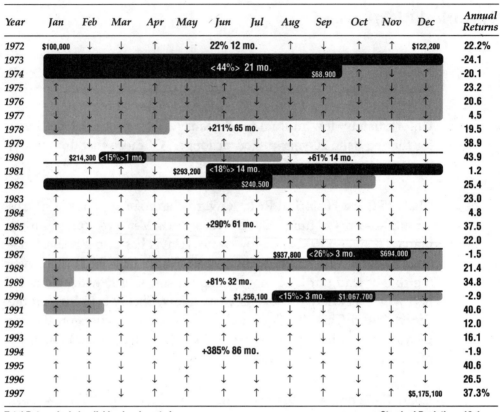

Year	Jan	Feb	Mar	Apr	May	Jun	Jul	Aug	Sep	Oct	Nov	Dec	Annual Returns
1972	$100,000	↓	↓	↑	↓	22% 12 mo.		↑	↓	↑	↑	$122,200	22.2%
1973													-24.1
1974					<44%> 21 mo.				$68.900	↑	↓	↑	-20.1
1975	↑	↓	↓	↑	↓	↑	↓	↓	↑	↑	↓	↓	23.2
1976	↑	↓	↓	↓	↓	↑	↓	↓	↑	↑	↑	↑	20.6
1977	↓	↓	↑	↑	↓	↑	↓	↓	↓	↑	↑	↓	4.5
1978	↓	↑	↑	↑	↓	+211% 65 mo.		↑	↓	↓	↑	↓	19.5
1979	↑	↓	↑	↓	↓	↑	↓	↑	↓	↑	↓		38.9
1980	↑	$214,300	<15%>1 mo.	↑	↑	↑	↑	↓	+61% 14 mo.		↑	↓	43.9
1981	↓	↑	↑	↓	$293,200	<18%> 14 mo.							1.2
1982						$240,500		↑	↓	↑	↓	↓	25.4
1983	↑	↓	↑	↑	↓	↑	↓	↑	↑	↓	↑	↓	23.0
1984	↑	↓	↑	↓	↓	↑	↓	↑	↑	↓	↓	↑	4.8
1985	↑	↓	↓	↑	↓	+290% 61 mo.		↑	↓	↑	↑	↓	37.5
1986	↑	↑	↓	↓	↑	↓	↓	↑	↓	↑	↓		22.0
1987	↑	↓	↓	↓	↑	↑	↓	$937,800	<26%> 3 mo.	$694.000	↑		-1.5
1988	↓	↑	↑	↑	↑	↑	↑	↑	↓	↓	↑		21.4
1989	↑	↓	↑	↑	↑	↓	+81% 32 mo.	↓	↑	↓	↑	↑	34.8
1990	↓	↑	↓	↓	↑	↓	$1,256,100	<15%> 3 mo.	$1,067.700	↑	↓		-2.9
1991	↑	↑	↓	↑	↑	↓	↑	↓	↓	↓	↓	↑	40.6
1992	↓	↑	↑	↓	↑	↑	↓	↑	↑	↓	↑	↑	12.0
1993	↑	↑	↑	↓	↑	↑	↓	↑	↓	↓	↓	↑	16.1
1994	↑	↓	↓	↑	↑	+385% 86 mo.		↑	↓	↑	↓	↑	-1.9
1995	↑	↑	↓	↑	↓	↓	↓	↑	↓	↑	↓		40.6
1996	↑	↓	↓	↓	↑	↓	↓	↑	↑	↓	↑	↓	26.5
1997	↑	↑	↓	↑	↑	↑	↑	↓	↑	↓	↑	$5,175,100	37.3%

Total Return: Includes dividends reinvested   **Standard Deviation: 18.1**

Source: Davis Selected Advisors

↑ ↓ *Up or Down Month* ⬛ *Cyclical Declines* ⬤ *Recovery (to pre-decline level)* ⬭ *Net New Advancement*

REWARD*	**RISK PROFILE**
Total Return (1972-1997) 16.4%	Mega Bear Market Decline <44%>
Riskless Return (T-bills) < 6.9%>	Average Bear Market Decline <19%>
AVERAGE ANNUAL REWARD OF	
DAVIS NY VENTURE A: 9.5%	
SHELBY DAVIS	

*Annualized

CHART 15-2

For information on larger or updated versions of these charts, call 800-772-0072.

Face Off: Shelby Davis vs. S&P 500 (1972-1997)

		S&P 500	Shelby Davis Davis NY Venture Fund
Advances & Declines			
Jan 1972→Dec 1972	End of Advance	19%	22%
Jan 1973→Sep 1974	(Worst-Case Decline)	-43%	-44%
Oct 1974→Feb 1980	Advance	132%	211%
Mar 1980	(Cyclical Decline)	-10%	-15%
Apr 1980→Nov 1980	Advance	43%	61%
Dec 1980→Jul 1982	(Cyclical Decline)	-17%	-18%
Aug 1982→Aug 1987	Advance	282%	290%
Sep 1987→Nov 1987	(Cyclical Decline)	-30%	-26%
Dec 1987→May 1990	Advance	71%	81%
Jun 1990→Oct 1990	(Cyclical Decline)	-15%	-15%
Nov 1990→Dec 1997	Advance	286%	385%
Jan 1972→Dec 1997:	**Total Gain**	**2460%**	**5075%**
	Annualized Gain	**13.3%**	**16.4%**
Full Market Cycles			
Jan 1973→Feb 1980	High to High	30%	74%
Oct 1974→Mar 1980	Low to Low	109%	164%
Mar 1980→Nov 1980	High to High	29%	37%
Apr 1980→Jul 1982	Low to Low	19%	32%
Dec 1980→Aug 1987	High to High	217%	220%
Aug 1982→Nov 1987	Low to Low	167%	189%
Sep 1987→May 1990	High to High	20%	34%
Dec 1987→Oct 1990	Low to Low	45%	54%
Jun 1990→Dec 1997	High to High Point	243%	327%
Reward (annualized return above T-bills)		**6.4%**	**9.5%**

CHART 15-3

Historical Risk/Reward Chart

Acorn: Ralph Wanger
Growth of $100,000
(12/31/71 – 12/31/97)

Year	Jan	Feb	Mar	Apr	May	Jun	Jul	Aug	Sep	Oct	Nov	Dec	Annual Returns
1972	$100,000	↑	↓	↑	↓	+11% 11 mo.		↑	↑	↑	$110,850		8.9%
1973					<45%> 22 mo.								-24.0
1974									$61,000	↑	↓	↓	-27.7
1975	↑	↓	↓	↑	↑	↑	↓	↓	↑	↓	↓	↓	30.2
1976	↑	↓	↓	↓	↑	↑	↓	↑	↑	↓	↑	↑	66.0
1977	↓	↓	↑	↓	+265% 47 mo.		↓	↓	↑	↓	↑	↓	18.1
1978	↓	↑	↑	↑	↓	↓	↑	$222,500	<20%> 2 mo.	↑	↑	↓	16.9
1979	↑	↓	↑	↓	↑	↑	↓	↑	↑	↓	↑	↑	50.2
1980	↑	↓	↓	↑ +134% 31 mo. ↓		↑	↓	↑	↓	↑	↑	↓	30.9
1981	↓	↑	↑	↓	$416,600	<21%> 14 mo.							-7.3
1982							$329,100	↑	↓	↑	↓	↓	17.6
1983	↑	↓	↓	↑	↑	↓	↓	↑	↑	↓	↑	↓	25.2
1984	↓	↓	↑	↓	↓	↑	↓	↑	↓	→	↓	↑	4.4
1985	↑	↓	↓	↑	↑	+242% 62 mo.	↓	↓	↑	↑	↑	↓	31.4
1986	↑	↑	↓	↓	↑	↓	↓	↑	↓	↑	↓	↓	17.0
1987	↑	↑	↓	↓	↑	↑	↓	↑ $1,125,600	<26%> 2 mo.		↑		4.5
1988	↑	↑	↓	↑	↓	↑	↓	↓	↑	↓	↓	↑	24.8
1989	↑	↓	↓	↑	↓	+70% 31 mo.	↓	↓	↑	↓	↑	↑	24.9
1990	↓	↑	↑	↓	↑ $1,415,000	<26%> 4 mo.			$1,047,800	↑	↓	↓	-17.6
1991	↑	↑	↓	↓	↑	↓	↑	↓	↓	↓	↓	↑	47.4
1992	↑	↑	↓	↓	↑	↓	↑	↓	↑	↑	↑	↑	24.2
1993	↑	↓	↑	↓	↑	+346% 86 mo.	↑	↓	↑	↓	↑		32.4
1994	↓	↓	↓	↑	↓	↓	↑	↑	↓	↑	↓	↑	-7.5
1995	↓	↑	↓	↓	↑	↑	↑	↓	↑	↓	↑	↓	20.8
1996	↓	↑	↓	↑	↓	↓	↓	↑	↓	↓	↑	↑	22.6
1997	↑	↓	↓	↑	↑	↑	↑	↑	↑	↓	→	$4,669,300	25.0%

Total Return: Includes dividends reinvested   **Standard Deviation: 21.5**

Source: Morningstar Principa ™ Plus for Mutual Funds

↑ ↓ *Up or Down Month* ■ *Cyclical Declines* ◼ *Recovery (to pre-decline level)* ◻ *Net New Advancement*

REWARD*		RISK PROFILE	
Total Return (1972-1997)	15.9%	Mega Bear Market Decline	<45%>
Riskless Return (T-bills)	< 6.9%>	Average Bear Market Decline	<23%>
AVERAGE ANNUAL REWARD OF ACORN: RALPH WANGER	9.0%		

*Annualized

CHART 15-4

For information on larger or updated versions of these charts, call 800-772-0072.

Face Off: Ralph Wanger vs. Mid/Small Cap Stocks (1972-1997)

		Domestic Mid/ Small Cap Stocks (Asset Class)	Ralph Wanger Acorn Fund
Advances & Declines			
Jan 1972→Nov 1972	(End of Advance)	9%	11%
Dec 1972→Sep 1974	(Worst-Case Decline)	-50%	-45%
Oct 1974→Aug 1978	Advance	225%	265%
Sep 1978→Oct 1978	(Cyclical Decline)	-17%	-20%
Nov 1978→May 1981	Advance	115%	134%
Jun 1981→Jul 1982	(Cyclical Decline)	-19%	-21%
Aug 1982→Aug 1987	Advance	256%	242%
Sep 1987→Nov 1987	(Cyclical Decline)	-31%	-26%
Dec 1987→May 1990	Advance	65%	70%
Jun 1990→Oct 1990	(Cyclical Decline)	-24%	-24%
Nov 1990→Dec 1997	Advance	325%	346%
Jan 1972→Dec 1997:	**Total Gain**	**3266%**	**4569%**
	Annualized Gain	**14.5%**	**15.9%**
Full Market Cycles			
Jan 1972→Aug 1978	High to High	63%	101%
Oct 1974→Oct 1978	Low to Low	170%	192%
Sep 1978→May 1981	High to High	78%	87%
Nov 1978→Jul 1982	Low to Low	74%	85%
Jun 1981→Aug 1987	High to High	188%	170%
Aug 1982→Nov 1987	Low to Low	146%	153%
Sep 1987→May 1990	High to High	14%	26%
Dec 1987→Oct 1990	Low to Low	25%	29%
Jun 1990→Dec 1997	High to High Point	247%	256%
Reward (annualized return above T-bills)		**7.6%**	**9.0%**

CHART 15-5

Winning the War

Neither Shelby Davis nor Ralph Wanger won every skirmish, but they did win most battles and in the end they won the war. Each manager trailed his target asset class occasionally during a particular advance or decline, but Davis *never* trailed during a full market cycle and Wanger fell short only once. This is the picture of consistency.

Chart 15-6 summarizes their risks and rewards along with those of their target asset classes over the entire 26-year period. It demonstrates clearly that superior risk-adjusted performance is not only possible but also sustainable.

Two Superior Mutual Fund Managers vs. Their Target Asset Class (1972-1997)

	Shelby Davis	vs.	S&P 500	Ralph Wanger	vs.	Mid/Small Cap
Return (Annualized)	16.4%		13.3%	15.9%		14.5%
Riskless Return (T-bills)	-6.9%		-6.9%	-6.9%		-6.9%
Reward	9.5%		6.4%	9.0%		7.6%
Mega Bear Market Decline	<44%>		<43%>	<45%>		<50%>
Average Bear Market Decline	<18%>		<18%>	<23%>		<23%>

CHART 15-6

Target Asset Class

Some proponents of asset allocation will not invest in Ralph Wanger's Acorn Fund because in recent years he has invested between 15% and 20% of the fund's assets internationally. These asset allocation purists want to strip away from their fund managers the right to exercise investment judgment outside of the confines of their primary asset class, i.e. to only invest within one asset class.

This book takes a different view. For such purists, the index fund strategy outlined in Chapter 14 should be ideal. With index funds, they can control the asset class representations within their portfolio precisely. With index funds, companies are routinely bought and sold as they enter and leave the applicable universe of the specific asset class.

What separates actively managed funds from index funds is the exercise of *judgment*. Of course, much of this judgment is aimed at discerning which securities within a target asset class best fit a manager's own specifications of exceptional stocks. However, there are good reasons to allow a fund manager to exercise judgment in a wider field of vision.

For example, suppose a mid/small cap domestic stock manager has owned a specific company for some time, understands its growth prospects, knows its management well and is very satisfied with the current value of its stock and the prospects for a higher price. If this company's market cap grows to large cap status, should she automatically sell the stock like an index fund would (and pay a large capital gains tax), or should she continue to own this stock for as long as she continues to judge the stock as a particularly good stock for her portfolio?

Another example. Many exceptional managers like Ralph Wanger and Michael Price of the Mutual Series Funds do buy international stocks for their primarily U.S. stock funds. As Price puts it, "If I can buy a company in Europe for a 40-50% discount over the price I would pay for a similar stock of a U.S. company, it makes sense for me to buy it."

 Superior managers like Wanger, Price and Davis know their target asset classes very well. If their judgment leads them to a purchase outside of that asset class, you can be sure that they believe it will add value to their portfolio. Therefore, **a fund manager's performance may be judged against that of his or her target asset class even if some percentage of the fund's portfolio falls into other asset classes.**

The earlier cited study by Morningstar Mutual Funds supports this conclusion "....the factors most directly controlled by the fund manager—a fund's aggressiveness, shorter-term shifts in style and stock selection—appear to make a significant difference in returns. ....At the very least, it's clear that the benefits of maintaining an asset-allocation policy to the last decimal point may not be as great as those offered by finding fund managers....who consistently add value...."

Full Market Cycle

As was stated earlier, very few mutual fund managers offer a 20+-year track record to evaluate as do Shelby Davis and Ralph Wanger. Therefore, a method for identifying the truly superior mutual fund managers over a somewhat shorter time period is needed.

Recall the discussion of asset classes and model portfolios during the Great Depression (Chapter 11). It was stated then that the only fair evaluation of a shorter time period than 20 years would be that of a full market cycle, i.e. one full bull market and one complete bear market. The same logic applies to the evaluation of mutual fund managers. Obviously, the more market cycles over which a fund manager can be evaluated relative to his or her target asset class the better.

One particularly relevant argument for evaluating a fund manager's performance over a market cycle is that various styles of fund management tend to earn their rewards at different times. Therefore, beginning mid-cycle will unfairly penalize managers employing one style while benefiting managers with different styles. Another reason to look at full cycles is that some managers do their best during the advancing half of the cycle and others are at their best during the declining part of the cycle.

 The bottom line is simply this: fund managers cannot be considered "superior" until they have *proved* their ability to outperform their target asset class over at least one full market cycle. The more full cycles of continuous outperformance by a manager, the more confidence you can develop in their ability to keep delivering superior long-term performance.

The Cream of the Crop

Charts 15-7 through 15-11 compare the full market cycle performance of proven superior mutual fund managers with that of their target asset class. The comparisons begin with the earliest bull market peak or bear market trough for which performance information on the manager is available.

Face Off: Michael Price vs. Mid/Small Cap Stocks   *VALUE STYLE*
(June 1981 - December 1997)

		Domestic Mid/ Small Cap Stocks (Asset Class)	Michael Price Mutual Qualified Fund
Advances & Declines			
Jun 1981→Jul 1982	(Cyclical Decline)	-19%	15%
Aug 1982→Aug 1987	Advance	256%	242%
Sep 1987→Nov 1987	(Cyclical Decline)	-31%	-20%
Dec 1987→May 1990	Advance	65%	55%
Jun 1990→Oct 1990	(Cyclical Decline)	-24%	-14%
Nov 1990→Dec 1997	Advance	325%	292%
Jun 1981→Dec 1997:	**Total Gain**	960%	1544%
	Annualized Gain	15.4%	18.5%
Full Market Cycles			
Jun 1981→Aug 1987	High to High	188%	293%
Aug 1982→Nov 1987	Low to Low	146%	174%
Sep 1987→May 1990	High to High	14%	24%
Dec 1987→Oct 1990	Low to Low	25%	33%
Jun 1990→Dec 1997	High to High Point	223%	237%

Sources: Morningstar, Inc., Advanced Analytics for Principia™ and Center for Research in Security Prices (CRSP)

CHART 15-7

Mutual Qualified is a value-style mutual fund that has been continuously managed by Michael Price since inception. The performance of the fund is compared here to the fund's target asset class, mid/small cap stocks, beginning with the first market peak after the fund's inception. As you can see, Michael Price has greatly outdistanced the total return of his target asset class while *underperforming* every single major advance. Price's superiority clearly is a function of significant outperformance during cyclical declines. This downside focus did not keep Price from winning all five full market cycles. This is an example of how to evaluate the performance histories that are presented herein.

The next four superior mutual fund manager candidates are compared to their target asset class over the last three full market cycles. Mason Hawkins (value) and Ron Baron (growth) represent mid/small cap stocks while Bill Nasgovitz (value) and Larry

Auriana (growth) represent micro caps. Two very successful aggressive growth managers, Gary Pilgrim and Foster Friess, are also shown.

Face Off: Mason. Hawkins vs. Mid/Small Cap Stocks   *VALUE STYLE*
(September 1987 - December 1997)

		Domestic Mid/ Small Cap Stocks (Asset Class)	Mason Hawkins Longleaf Partners Fund
Advances & Declines			
Sep 1987→Nov 1987	(Cyclical Decline)	-31%	-25%
Dec 1987→May 1990	Advance	65%	69%
Jun 1990→Oct 1990	(Cyclical Decline)	-24%	-23%
Nov 1990→Dec 1997	Advance	325%	399%
Sep 1987→Dec 1997:	**Total Gain**	268%	387%
	Annualized Gain	13.5%	16.7%
Full Market Cycles			
Sep 1987→May 1990	High to High	14%	27%
Dec 1987→Oct 1990	Low to Low	25%	30%
Jun 1990→Dec 1997	High to High Point	247%	300%

Face Off: Ron Baron vs. Mid/Small Cap Stocks   *GROWTH STYLE*
(September 1987 - December 1997)

		Domestic Mid/ Small Cap Stocks (Asset Class)	Ron Baron Baron Asset Fund
Advances & Declines			
Sep 1987→Nov 1987	(Cyclical Decline)	-31%	-20%
Dec 1987→May 1990	Advance	65%	76%
Jun 1990→Oct 1990	(Cyclical Decline)	-24%	-28%
Nov 1990→Dec 1997	Advance	325%	438%
Sep 1987→Dec 1997:	**Total Gain**	268%	491%
	Annualized Gain	13.5%	18.9%
Full Market Cycles			
Sep 1987→May 1990	High to High	14%	41%
Dec 1987→Oct 1990	Low to Low	25%	27%
Jun 1990→Dec 1997	High to High Point	247%	320%

Sources: Morningstar, Inc., Advanced Analytics for Principia™ and Center for Research in Security Prices (CRSP)

CHART 15–8

Face Off: Bill Nasgovitz vs. Micro Cap Stocks   *VALUE STYLE*
(September 1987 - December 1997)

		Domestic Micro Cap Stocks (Asset Class)	Bill Nasgovitz Heartland Value Fund
Advances & Declines			
Sep 1987→Nov 1987	(Cyclical Decline)	-33%	-32%
Dec 1987→Sep 1989	Advance	54%	58%
Oct 1989→Oct 1990	(Cyclical Decline)	-32%	-28%
Nov 1990→Dec 1997	Advance	360%	421%
Sep 1987→Dec 1997:	**Total Gain**	**223%**	**303%**
	Annualized Gain	**12.1%**	**14.5%**
Full Market Cycles			
Sep 1987→Sep 1989	High to High	3%	9%
Dec 1987→Oct 1990	Low to Low	5%	14%
Oct 1989→Dec 1997	High to High Point	213%	275%

Face Off: L. Auriana & H. Utsch vs. Micro Cap Stocks   *GROWTH STYLE*
(September 1987 - December 1997)

		Domestic Micro Cap Stocks (Asset Class)	Auriana and Utsch Kaufmann Fund
Advances & Declines			
Sep 1987→Nov 1987	(Cyclical Decline)	-33%	-39%
Dec 1987→Sep 1989	Advance	54%	174%
Oct 1989→Oct 1990	(Cyclical Decline)	-32%	-30%
Nov 1990→Dec 1997	Advance	360%	464%
Sep 1987→Dec 1997:	**Total Gain**	**223%**	**560%**
	Annualized Gain	**12.1%**	**20.2%**
Full Market Cycles			
Sep 1987→Sep 1989	High to High	3%	67%
Dec 1987→Oct 1990	Low to Low	5%	92%
Oct 1989→Dec 1997	High to High Point	213%	295%

Sources: Morningstar, Inc., Advanced Analytics for Principia™ and © computed using data from Stocks, Bonds, Bills & Inflation 1997 Yearbook™ with data updated January 1998, Ibbotson Associates, Chicago

CHART 15-9

Face Off: G. Pilgrim vs. Mid/Small Cap Stocks *AGGRESSIVE GROWTH*
(September 1987 - December 1997)

		Domestic Mid/ Small Cap Stocks (Asset Class)	Gary Pilgrim PBHG Growth
Advances & Declines			
Sep 1987→Nov 1987	(Cyclical Decline)	-31%	-33%
Dec 1987→May 1990	Advance	65%	86%
Jun 1990→Oct 1990	(Cyclical Decline)	-24%	-32%
Nov 1990→Dec 1997	Advance	325%	458%
Sep 1987→Dec 1997:	**Total Gain**	**268%**	**373%**
	Annualized Gain	**13.5%**	**16.3%**
Full Market Cycles			
Sep 1987→May 1990	High to High	14%	25%
Dec 1987→Oct 1990	Low to Low	25%	26%
Jun 1990→Dec 1997	High to High Point	247%	279%

Face Off: F. Friess vs. Mid/Small Cap Stocks *AGGRESSIVE GROWTH*
(September 1987 - December 1997)

		Domestic Mid/ Small Cap Stocks (Asset Class)	Foster Friess Brandywine Fund
Advances & Declines			
Sep 1987→Nov 1987	(Cyclical Decline)	-31%	-41%
Dec 1987→May 1990	Advance	65%	114%
Jun 1990→Oct 1990	(Cyclical Decline)	-24%	-18%
Nov 1990→Dec 1997	Advance	325%	323%
Sep 1987→Dec 1997:	**Total Gain**	**268%**	**338%**
	Annualized Gain	**13.5%**	**15.5%**
Full Market Cycles			
Sep 1987→May 1990	High to High	14%	26%
Dec 1987→Oct 1990	Low to Low	25%	75%
Jun 1990→Dec 1997	High to High Point	247%	247%

Sources: Morningstar, Inc., Advanced Analytics for Principia™ and Center for Research in Security Prices (CRSP)

CHART 15-10

Note: Aggressive Growth is a subset of the Growth style employing a combination of earnings and price momentum strategies. Brandywine may now be categorized as large cap, yet its track record was built primarily with mid/small cap stocks.

Face Off: H. Castegren vs. Int'l Stocks (EAFE)
(September 1987 - December 1997)

		International Stocks (EAFE) (Asset Class)	Hakan Castegren Ivy International A
Advances & Declines			
Sep 1987→Oct 1987	(Cyclical Decline)	-15%	-25%
Nov 1987→Dec 1989	Advance	48%	73%
Jan 1990→Sep 1990	(Cyclical Decline)	-31%	-14%
Oct 1990→Dec 1997	Advance	90%	170%
Sep 1987→Dec 1997:	**Total Gain**	65%	201%
	Annualized Gain	5.0%	11.4%
Full Market Cycles			
Sep 1987→Dec 1989	High to High	26%	30%
Nov 1987→Sep 1990	Low to Low	2%	49%
Jan 1990→Dec 1997	High to High Point	31%	132%

Sources: Morningstar, Inc., Advanced Analytics for Principia™ and Morgan Stanley Capital International

CHART 15-11

International stock funds present a quandry. Few, if any, managers that were active during the 1980s outperformed the EAFE international stock index in U.S. dollars. On the other hand, the vast majority of active international fund managers have outperformed this index in the 1990s. The primary reason for both the 1980s underperformance and the 1990s outperformance lies with the dominance of one country in the index—Japan—and the tendency of international fund managers to underweight Japanese stocks in their portfolios.

During the 1980s when the Japanese market was flying high, the underweighting of Japan could not be made up from the performance of stocks in lesser performing markets. During the 1990s, the exact opposite has occurred. The Japanese market has been a woeful underperformer, and therefore, the underweighting of this market has boosted fund performance relative to the EAFE index. Castegren is one of the few to outperform the index in the late 1980s.

Note: The general market advance that began in November of
        1990 for most domestic stock asset classes is still in progress
        as this book is completed in January 1998. At over seven
        years in duration, this particular advance qualifies as a
        complete advance for the purposes herein, as virtually
        every style of management has come into and out of vogue
        at least once during this long advance.

Managed Mutual Fund Portfolios - Pairing

Earlier in this chapter, it was pointed out that superior fund
managers have emerged from both the *growth* and *value* camps.
This is now clearly evident from the performance of the managers
illustrated herein. It was also noted that the reason for recognizing
the different styles was that each tended to outperform at different
times.

The performance histories of these funds show that growth
managers tend to outperform during the advancing portion of the
market cycle, while value managers typically outperform during
major market declines. Therefore, pairing two superior managers in
each equity asset class, one with a growth style and the other from
the value camp, should smooth your overall performance and offer
the opportunity of outperforming the results from the asset class in
both the advancing and declining portions of the target asset class's
market cycle.

The following charts, 15-12, 15-13 and 15-14, pair a growth
manager and a value manager and illustrate their combined results
against that of their target asset class. One pairing is represented for
each of the three domestic asset classes: large cap (S&P 500),
mid/small cap and micro cap. Each pairing demonstrates that
outstanding results relative to those of the asset class are possible
and with a smoother overall delivery than that provided by the
index of the asset class. This is truly the best of all worlds.

Mutual Fund Pairing: Large Cap Stocks (S&P 500)

		S&P 500	Paired Performance	GROWTH: Spiros Segalas	VALUE: Shelby Davis
Advances & Declines					
Sep 1987→Nov 1987	(Cyclical Decline)	-30%	-28%	-30%	-26%
Dec 1987→May 1990	Advance	71%	77%	73%	81%
Jun 1990→Oct 1990	(Cyclical Decline)	-15%	-18%	-21%	-15%
Nov 1990→Dec 1997	Advance	286%	385%	386%	385%
Sep 1987→Dec 1997:	**Total Gain**	**293%**	**409%**	**365%**	**452%**
	Annualized Gain	**14.3%**	**17.2%**	**16.2%**	**18.1%**
Full Market Cycles					
Sep 1987→May 1990	High to High	20%	27%		
Dec 1987→Oct 1990	Low to Low	45%	45%		
Jun 1990→Dec 1997	High to High Point	243%	298%		

Sources: *Morningstar, Inc., Advanced Analytics for Principia™; Standard & Poor's; Davis Selected Advisors*

CHART 15-12

Selecting a superior value manager and a superior growth manager for each equity asset class comes closest to delivering on the goal of achieving both a reduced risk and a higher reward than that of the relevant asset class.

Mutual Fund Pairing: Mid/Small Cap Stocks

		Domestic Mid/Small Cap Stocks (Asset Class)	Paired Performance	VALUE: Mason Hawkins	GROWTH: Ron Baron
Advances & Declines					
Sep 1987→Nov 1987	(Cyclical Decline)	-31%	-22%	-25%	-20%
Dec 1987→May 1990	Advance	65%	72%	69%	76%
Jun 1990→Oct 1990	(Cyclical Decline)	-24%	-26%	-23%	-28%
Nov 1990→Dec 1997	Advance	325%	419%	399%	438%
Sep 1987→Dec 1997:	**Total Gain**	268%	439%	387%	491%
	Annualized Gain	13.5%	17.8%	16.7%	18.9%
Full Market Cycles					
Sep 1987→May 1990	High to High	14%	33%		
Dec 1987→Oct 1990	Low to Low	25%	27%		
Jun 1990→Dec 1997	High to High Point	247%	284%		

Sources: Morningstar, Inc., Advanced Analytics for Principia™ and Center for Research in Security Prices (CRSP)

CHART 15-13

Mutual Fund Pairing: Micro Cap Stocks

		Domestic Micro Cap Stocks* (Asset Class)	Paired Performance	VALUE: Bill Nasgovitz	GROWTH: L. Auriana H. Utsch
Advances & Declines					
Sep 1987→Nov 1987	(Cyclical Decline)	-33%	-36%	-32%	-39%
Dec 1987→Sept 1989	Advance	54%	116%	58%	174%
Oct 1989→Oct 1990	(Cyclical Decline)	-32%	-29%	-28%	-30%
Nov 1990→Dec 1997	Advance	360%	443%	421%	464%
Sep 1987→Dec 1997:	**Total Gain**	223%	432%	303%	560%
	Annualized Gain	12.1%	17.7%	14.5%	20.2%
Full Market Cycles					
Sep 1987→Sep 1989	High to High	3%	38%		
Dec 1987→Oct 1990	Low to Low	5%	53%		
Oct 1989→Dec 1997	High to High Point	213%	286%		

Sources: Morningstar, Inc., Advanced Analytics for Principia™ and © computed using data from Stocks, Bonds, Bills & Inflation 1997 Yearbook™ with data updated January 1998, Ibbotson Associates, Chicago

* DFA 9-10 Fund

CHART 15-14

Other Candidates

The following mutual fund managers also qualify as superior under the method outlined herein. Each has proved his ability to outperform his or her target asset class over at least two full market cycles, while bettering the performance of the target asset class over his or her entire management tenure. (Be aware that many of the best known, best performing fund managers over one-, three- and five-year periods *fail* this test and that many other *potentially* superior mutual fund managers have not proved themselves over this long of a time period.)

Asset Class	Manager	Style	Mutual Fund(s) Available Through:
Domestic Large Cap	Spiros Segalas[1]	Aggressive Growth	Harbor Capital Appreciation
	James Margard[1]	Growth-at-a-Price	Rainier Core Equity
	William Ruane/ Richard Cunniff	Value	Sequoia[2]
Domestic Mid/ Small Cap	Wilmot Kidd	Growth-at-a-Price	Central Securities (closed-end)
	James Margard[1]	Growth-at-a-Price	Rainier Small/Mid Cap Equity
	William Dutton	Growth at-a-Price	Skyline Special Equities[2]
	Kenneth Heebner	Aggressive Growth	CGM Capital Development
	Robert Rodriquez	Growth-at-a-Price	FPA Capital[2]
	Stephen Johnes	Growth	Merrill Lynch Growth B
Domestic Micro Cap	Mason Hawkins[1]	Value	Longleaf Small Cap[2]
	Jeanne Sinquefield[3]	N/A	DFA 9-10 Small Co.
International Stock	Jean-Marie Eveillard[1]	Value	SoGen Overseas
	Mark Holowesko	Value	Templeton Foreign
	Richard Foulkes	Growth	Vanguard International Growth

[1] *Track record partially developed outside of this mutual fund.*

[2] *Closed to new investors as of January 1998.*

[3] *Although used as the index for small companies in SBBI, this fund has substantially outperformed the complete micro cap asset class since its inception (see pages 34-38).*

Note: Our apologies to any mutual fund manager who qualified but did not come to our attention.

What Works on Wall Street – The "Dogs"

A new and different approach to actively managed mutual funds has recently become available. Instead of relying on the judgment and discipline of a human manager, these funds mechanically buy and sell stocks that fall within the guidelines of a proven long-term strategy.

In a sense, these new mutual funds are a variation of index funds. Instead of matching an entire asset class, they match a select group of stocks within an asset class that best meet the criteria of the strategy. Stocks are held only so long as they meet that criteria. The academic justification for such strategies began with the Fama/French study referred to on page 198.

The most well known strategy of this type is referred to as the "Dogs of the Dow" (Dogs). It was popularized by Michael O'Higgins in his 1992 book Beating the Dow. The essence of this strategy is to buy the 10 highest yielding stocks in the Dow Jones Industrial Average (Dow) and hold them exactly one year. At the end of the year, you merely repeat the process. O'Higgins demonstrated that this strategy, and several variations, have all outperformed the Dow since 1972—and with less risk.

Initially, this strategy was better suited to unit trusts than to mutual funds. A unit trust is not perpetual. The sponsor raises all of the money before employing the strategy, then closes the trust, executes the strategy and liquidates when the strategy is fulfilled (one year later in this case).

The results of the Dogs strategy were verified back to 1954 in James O'Shaughnessy's What Works on Wall Street. As discussed earlier (see page 198), his book illustrated the superior results of several "look ahead" strategies including this one. Each of O'Shaughnessy's strategies calls for the purchase of the 50 stocks within the domestic stock market (except Micro Caps) that best fit the criteria of that specific strategy. These stocks are held one full year, then sold and replaced by the 50 stocks that then best meet the strategy's criteria. There is no magic to the starting date for a strategy as long as the stocks are held only one full year.

In December 1996 O'Shaughnessy introduced four mutual funds, each based on one of the top-performing strategies illustrated in his book, including one variation of the Dogs strategy. What separates these funds from actively managed funds is the strict adherence to a defined long-term strategy without human judgment. The long-term element is fundamental. As O'Shaughnessy has stated, even the most superior of strategies can underperform for a period of years. Dedication to stay with any such strategy for a period of more than 10 years—the longer the better—has been necessary to ensure the superior results eventually were achieved.

Funds or unit trusts based on proven long-term strategies may one day become as popular as indexing. However, it should be apparent that such strategies are tax *insensitive* and belong in the tax-deferred or tax-sheltered slices of your Wealth and Retirement Portfolio.

Asset Class Integrity Funds

There is a new category of mutual funds that could be called "asset class integrity funds." (The author introduced this term at the Charles Schwab Advisors Conference in November, 1997.) These are mutual funds that aim at achieving both asset class purity *and* superior performance from active management.

Perhaps the two most prominent providers of these funds are the Frank Russell Company and SEI. In lieu of just indexing each asset class, these providers seek out the best money manager(s) they can uncover to select the securities for the fund—but the fund managers must stay within the defined parameters of the asset class. No straying to other asset classes! This is a new concept that bears watching for those who believe in both asset class purity and active management.

Bond Funds

5-Year U.S. Treasury Bond Asset Class

Intermediate-term government bond funds come closest to capturing the risks and rewards of the 5-year U.S. Treasury bond asset class used throughout this book. Individual funds within this group may vary their criteria to differentiate their fund from the others within the group. Typical of such distinguishing characteristics are:

- Lengthening or shortening the average maturity of the bonds within the fund

- Including government agency securities or mortgage notes issued or guaranteed by quasi-government agencies such as FNMA or GNMA (mortgage backed securities)

- Allowing illiquid securities and/or options, futures or warrants to be purchased and

- Adopting exotic or leveraged strategies in the hope of boosting yields and returns.

This book takes the view that it is preferable with this asset class to focus on reliability. Plain vanilla intermediate government bond funds with a very low fee structure, such as the index funds discussed in Chapter 14, are preferable to higher risk and uncertain strategies for most investors. Reaching for perhaps a one-quarter to one-half percent total return advantage over the index (if you were to be <u>very</u> successful over time) may not be worth the risk or time involved.

In fact, if your portfolio is large enough to allow it, purchases of U.S. Treasury bonds either directly or through a broker may be more desirable than a mutual fund for this asset class.

 However, for those investors who have the time and interest to evaluate bond funds that lie outside of the intermediate-term Treasury bond asset class, there may be opportunities to add value. Three bond fund managers that should be on the short-list of such research are Dan Fuss (Loomis Sayles Bond), Ernest Monrad (Northeast Investors) and Bill Gross (PIMCO bond funds). These three managers have provided consistently superior results relative to their target bond asset classes over several bond market cycles.

Mutual Funds' Rapid Growth

It is no secret that the mutual fund industry is enjoying a period of rapid growth. While good for the mutual fund sponsoring companies, it is not necessarily good news to fund shareholders.

Top-performing mutual fund managers are inundated with huge inflows of new money to manage. In just the first few months of 1996, many funds *doubled* in size or more. One fund manager started 1996 with no money under management yet had over $1 billion to manage before mid-year.

This can be harmful to fund shareholders. The new dollars must be put to work regardless of market conditions or available stock opportunities. If not, the dollars will pile up in the fund. Huge slugs of cash can dilute performance.

Mutual funds specializing in micro caps or the smaller stocks within the mid/small cap universe will find it particularly hard to put the new money to work in their favorite stocks without pressuring prices upward (getting less long-term value). Therefore, many successful managers in a smaller market cap universe are forced into bigger and bigger market cap stocks where they may not be able to get the same results.

A mutual fund organization has its internal business side, too. Operations, computer capability, shareholder services, custody and administration can easily consume more and more of the manager's time in a fast-growing fund. This obviously takes away from his ability to perform for the fund. And this does not even take into consideration the need to find, interview and hire good analysts to support the expanding needs for research.

This is not a new phenomenon. It is just in a very intense phase in the 1990s. One caveat to reviewing the historical performance of any mutual fund manager you are considering is simply, "How much of her exceptional performance was delivered when her fund was in its first year or managing substantially fewer dollars than now?" Many a fund is quick out of the gate only to deliver very average performance afterward. Yet, their 3-year, 5-year and "since inception" returns look good for years *after the great performance is over*!

One solution is to close the fund. This is the route taken by some of the fund managers most concerned about their existing shareholders. While often beneficial for these shareholders, it closes some very good opportunities to you in your evaluation of superior managers.

Ever so often, a great manager, whose primary fund is closed, does open a new, different fund that is still well within his/her expertise and experience. These occasions provide some exceptional opportunities to those looking to fill out their Wealth and Retirement Portfolios.

Tax Strategies

All That Matters

Sir John Templeton, the founder of the highly regarded Templeton Group of funds, was fond of saying throughout his career that "the only return that counts is the after-tax, after-inflation return on your investments." There is more than an element of truth in his insight. Whatever you pay Uncle Sam from your investments will not add to your wealth nor will it supplement your retirement income.

Therefore, it makes good sense to be aware of tax mistakes to avoid as well as smart moves to take advantage of in your Wealth and Retirement Portfolio.

Year-End Distributions

In order to eliminate double taxation, each mutual fund must distribute the net capital gains it has realized throughout the year, either by the end of December or at the end of October. The date chosen is at the option of each fund.

If you purchase a mutual fund in a taxable account just prior to its making a large taxable distribution, you may wish you had waited to purchase it...or had purchased this mutual fund in a tax deferred account (IRA, IRA rollover, 401(k), etc.). This is an area where you must be proactive. Mutual funds will rarely alert you as to either the exact date or the amount of such distributions.

Tax Efficiency

If some or all of your Wealth and Retirement Portfolio is in a taxable account, pay attention to a fund's tax efficiency. The pinnacle of tax efficiency would be having your after-tax returns equal your pre-tax returns. No taxes due. A mutual fund that delivered such a stellar result would be 100% tax efficient.

Many mutual funds—including some of the higher performing ones—have 85%+ tax efficient ratings. As a comparison, at the end of 1997 Morningstar reports that the Vanguard 500 Index Trust had a tax efficiency of 90% versus a below 80% rating for the average general equity mutual fund.

Two of the superior fund managers highlighted on the past few pages of this chapter have demonstrated exemplary after-tax returns. These two fund managers, their flagship fund and 10-year tax efficiency ratings are: Ron Baron's Baron Asset (95%) and Mason Hawkin's Longleaf Partners (87%). A discussion with either of these fund managers makes it clear that tax efficiency is not accidental; it is a primary focus of their individual mission statements.

Of course, a poor performing mutual fund would not jump into consideration just because it is highly tax efficient. (A "zero" total return with no tax due is 100% tax efficient!) In the same vein, a great fund should not be totally discounted just because it is somewhat below average in this area. (Hopefully, you could place such a fund in a tax-deferred *slice* within your portfolio.)

Tax efficiency ratings are included in Morningstar's individual mutual fund evaluations. Many periodicals pick up these ratings and include them in their own mutual fund rankings.

Another variation of this theme is the introduction of tax managed index funds. Vanguard Funds, Charles Schwab and others have introduced index mutual funds specifically designed to be highly tax efficient. The underlying strategy of these funds is to not sell any security unless forced to do so. If a sale is necessary, first sell the higher cost shares and, when possible, sell losing security positions to offset the gains. This relatively new wrinkle in the mutual fund world may prove to be a winner for those not averse to index funds for their taxable accounts.

Taxable Yields

If you have an IRA, 401(k) or other such tax-deferred account within your Wealth and Retirement Portfolio, attempt to place as many of your higher yielding mutual funds into this account. Bond funds and equity mutual funds of the value style, i.e. those that produce high levels of dividend and interest income, would typically be higher yielding than other types of funds.

The reason for this focus on yields is two-fold. First, the total tax bite on interest and dividend income typically exceeds that of long-term capital gains. Second, mutual fund managers cannot reduce the tax bill on interest and dividend income through strategies such as realizing offsetting capital losses discussed above.

Selling Funds

When you have a need to sell some portion of any one of several mutual funds within your taxable portfolio, check the tax basis of each mutual fund relative to its current market value. In other words, what percentage of the sales price will be taxable to you? All else being equal, sell the fund with the lowest tax hit (highest tax basis).

Once you build up significant tax-deferred gains within a particular mutual fund, think twice before selling it. This is particularly true if you are merely switching to a different but similar fund within your taxable portfolio. You will have a lot fewer dollars—after taxes—to invest in the new fund.

Getting Started

One final hurdle remains if you will be acting as your own investment manager. This is the question of how to commit new dollars to equity mutual funds. The stock market often seems high or vulnerable to a correction—or worse. The reality, of course, is that no one knows how high is too high or, for that matter, if a new low is low enough.

If this is a concern, there are two viable strategies:

- Begin with a defensive strategy, i.e. choose only actively managed funds from the value investing style. Even within these styles, some superior managers have proved more defensive than others, so do your homework.

- The other strategy is to phase in your new dollar commitment over a period of time (perhaps 6-18 months). This virtually guarantees you will not invest the bulk of the new investment dollars at a major top in the market cycle.

Dollar Cost Averaging

A commonly recommended stock market strategy is referred to as dollar cost averaging. This strategy can be boiled down to simply this: buy shares in stock mutual funds at regular intervals with a set dollar amount.

It is a very good strategy for those who are adding to their Wealth and Retirement Portfolio from wages—either through company-sponsored 401(k) plans or through direct purchases.

One of the advantages attributed to a dollar-cost-average program is that you buy more shares when the market is down and fewer when the market is up with your fixed commitment of dollars, thereby producing a lower average cost than the market average over time.

 Although this is true, the real strength of this strategy is the force of its discipline. Once set up, it takes on a life of its own. You will find it very hard to talk yourself out of continuing the program. This is the hallmark of a truly great strategy.

Maintain Controls

It was noted in Chapter 1 that most investors do not know how their portfolio is performing. Many investors know they don't know, many others think they know but really don't.

The only way you can control your portfolio properly and know if you are on track toward your objectives is to nail down the performance of your portfolio—and your benchmark portfolio's performance—at least once a year.

The easiest and perhaps best way to do this is to join the computer age in this area of your life if you haven't already done so. This is one of those areas where software is delivering on its promise of quality, flexibility, low cost and ease of use. Software such as Intuit's "Quicken" or Meca Software's "Managing Your Money" can track all of your investments quickly and easily. "Wealthbuilder" by Reality Technologies is also good. With these programs you can subscribe to on-line services which will provide automatic pricing and performance updates for your mutual funds. You can easily set up two portfolios and update them both when checking on your portfolio (actual and benchmark).

These software packages will not only do the math for you, they will properly differentiate between new contributions or withdrawals and those items that contribute to your total return (interest, dividends, capital gains, unrealized appreciation, etc.). They may also help you with tax planning and tax preparation.

Making it easy to see your investments *as a portfolio* and to track overall performance is much more than half the battle. You can't properly plan, you can't adjust, if you don't know the performance and status of your investments.

Conclusion

Superior mutual fund managers are available to your Wealth and Retirement Portfolio. These managers have proved themselves where it counts — over several full market cycles. Choosing superior fund managers to fill out your asset allocation policy offers the highest probability of providing long-term performance which outdistances that of your benchmark (index) portfolio.

There are many other benefits possible with an active management strategy. Among them are the personal enjoyment of active involvement in your financial future, the satisfaction of success and the ability to personalize the risks and rewards of your Wealth and Retirement Portfolio. But if you lack the time, interest or discipline, read on.

16

A "One Decision" Strategy that Works

Employing an investment advisor may be the best way for many investors to implement the ideas outlined in this book. A thorough evaluation of the professional's skills and services are critical to a successful long-term relationship. Other important factors include the advisor's compensation, the quality of his client communications (including performance reviews) and the rapport you establish with the advisor and his staff. A professional manager can assure the discipline, expertise and time required to execute your plan.

"The emergence of this new profession of disinterested investment [advisors], who have no allegiance or alliances and whose only job is to judge a security on its merits, is one of the most constructive and healthy developments of the last half century."
— Bernard Baruch (1957)

Do you know someone who has gone to a health spa?

People who just can't seem to eat right or exercise with consistency in their normal life seem to fall right in step with the spa's healthy lifestyle.

Why do these programs work? They succeed because it takes only one decision—the decision to do it. Once you have made that decision, paid the price, arranged the ticket, you don't have to make any more decisions. No temptations. No hesitations. You avoid the noise of the 1,000 and more distractions and excuses that come your way in your everyday "normal" life.

You surrender both your normal self and normal surroundings to be totally enmeshed in a culture that is completely supportive of your higher goal. Everything is lined up for success—the facility (all good stuff, no bad stuff), the staff (positive, goal-oriented, professionally competent) and your fellow campers ("we're all in this together") make it almost impossible to fail.

Best of all, you do it gladly. You know it works, it's what you want and this is the way to make sure it gets done, even if it costs more than doing it on your own.

One Decision

In the same sense, choosing a money manager can be your one decision that makes everything in this book work for you. The management firm can be your Health Spa of Finance. The professional money manager provides knowledge, confidence and experience in the development and execution of your personal financial game plan, as well as the ongoing management of your investments. No more hesitations to plan your financial future or temptations to tamper with a well-thought-out investment policy. The end result—peace of mind.

Candidates for a Money Manager

In Chapters 14 and 15 we looked at the types of investors who would be good candidates for investing with index funds and those that would be a better fit with actively managed mutual funds. The differences revolved around their attitude and expectations from investing. Let's look at who might be a good candidate for hiring a personal money manager.

Issue	Candidate for Money Manager
Time	"I wish to spend as little time on my investments as possible." (same as Index Investor)
Interest Level	"Investments are boring" or "too difficult to judge." (same as Index Investor)
Stress	"Being totally at the mercy of the market is stressful." (same as Active Fund Investor)
Market Returns	"I want to try to beat my benchmark." OR "I want benchmark returns but with less risk." (same as Active Fund Investor)
Fees	"Returns and fluctuations are far more important than fees." (same as Active Fund Investor)
Guidance	"I want personal consulting and guidance to make sure my objectives, asset allocation policy and related financial issues are on track." (unique to money manager)
Service	"I would like a complete package of account services that include consolidated performance reports, accounting, tax preparation, rebalancing and special services such as income distributions and tracking." (unique to money managers)
Discipline	"I'm not sure that I will have the discipline on my own to stay with my asset allocation policy or my mutual fund strategy during substantial changes in market conditions." (unique to money managers)

CHART 16-1

If you decide to hire an investment professional to manage some or all of your Wealth and Retirement Portfolio, understand that, at a minimum, you are still responsible for evaluating and selecting the appropriate investment policy that is right for you. The manager then selects the mutual funds (or individual securities) that best executes your plan.

Your investment manager should help you assemble your financial information to determine where you stand currently. He should also help clarify your future needs and objectives. And most importantly, your investment advisor should reinforce and personalize the market education you have received from this book; particularly in reaching the all important asset allocation decision.

 However, in the end, the investment policy that is the most appropriate trade-off between long-term returns and degree of market setbacks is *your* call. There is no escaping from the fact that this is your money, that the long-term returns will greatly affect your retirement or wealth and that only you know what degree of temporary loss (it will seem like a permanent loss when it occurs) you can tolerate without emotional trauma.

Once the asset allocation policy is in place, *you* can relax and turn over the reins to your investment manager. You don't have to watch the market on a day-to-day basis, and you are relieved of the stress and strain of having to make your own investment selections and placing your own transactions. You can focus on your own activities—even travel with confidence—because the management firm is there overseeing your plan on a daily basis.

Selecting a Professional Investment Manager

For those who hire a personal money manager, the most important determinant of long-term investment success will be in choosing the right manager to begin with. Start with the basics, screen out any candidates who are not:

- **Professional.** Is this money manager a full-time professional with an established counseling practice? There is no reason for your account to be a guinea pig or after-thought. A true professional should be registered with the Securities and Exchange Commission (SEC) by filing a form "ADV." Ask for a copy, review it thoroughly. It will detail all the nuts and bolts of the advisor's practice as well as his principal investment philosophy and experience.

- **Performance.** A good money manager is a craftsman, building a performance record that has unique risk and reward characteristics. Take a long, hard look at this track record for accounts with similar objectives to your own. How has the firm performed relative to its benchmark? This is the true test of the manager's investment skills.

- **Fee-Only.** Does the advisor charge an annual fee for managing your account or does he receive per-transaction commissions? The advisor's method(s) of compensation should be clearly set forth in the firm's ADV filing (see above). Fee-only managers are professionals whose interest is identical to your own—to maximize the value of your account relative to your risk parameters.

  There's no pressure to buy or sell investments and no conflict of interest in making investment recommendations. As transaction costs are a detriment to account growth, the money manager's interest will be to keep transaction costs to a minimum.

  Note: The fee-only rule need only apply to compensation related to investment selection and supervision. Other services that financial planners provide such as estate planning may be reasonably compensated in other ways.

- **Fee Conscious.** There is a trade-off to hiring your own money manager. The typical fee charged by a money manager is approximately one percent of the money under his direct management per year. Some investment advisors will charge as little as one-half of one percent per year and others as much as two percent per year or more. Buyer beware...cost and quality do not necessarily go hand in hand.

Initial Appointment

For those who pass this first screening and whose philosophies ring appropriate chords with you, speak directly with the prospective advisor either in person or by phone. The purpose of this investigatory meeting should include:

- **Quarterback.** Will this money manager help you evaluate your entire Wealth and Retirement Portfolio—including the parts not to be directly managed—in order to help formulate and adhere to the overall plan?

- **Asset Allocation.** Will the advisor help you establish your asset allocation? Will the advisor agree to stay within its boundaries? (Maintaining your portfolio's structure is fundamental to achieving the expected long-term returns with the anticipated degree of periodic setbacks in market values.) Will the advisor provide a suitable benchmark for performance comparisons?

- **Enjoyable Relationship.** This should be entered into as a long-term relationship. Make sure it feels right from the beginning. Is there a spirit of trust, cooperation and mutual respect?

If the results of this initial discussion are satisfactory for you, then ask the advisor for at least two referrals of long-term clients of the firm that share similar characteristics and objectives to your own. Call them. Ask them to speak candidly of their relationship with the advisor. Ask them to address the advisor's strengths and weaknesses. This may provide good insights and help you decide on—or prepare for—a second meeting.

Counseling and Communication

In our health spa analogy at the beginning of this chapter, it was pointed out that one of the reasons it works is the completely supportive atmosphere, including staff and fellow campers. Good money management firms will put a lot of effort into providing you with high-quality support for your Wealth and Retirement Portfolio objectives.

This is one area where there are significant differences between money management firms.

Your management firm should prepare simple, consolidated reports. These will illustrate your asset allocation, your individual securities and mutual fund holdings, your current-period performance and your historical performance. Your fee will be clearly shown and netted against your gross return to reflect your bottom-line return. Your net returns are then compared to those of your benchmark (see Chapter 14). This provides you with a measuring tool for both returns and setbacks.

This is important. Whether by phone or in person, conversations with your advisor should include complete discussions of just how your account is doing relative to its objectives. With appropriate benchmarks, you are not guessing, you are not at the mercy of your manager's presentation...*you know*!

Professional money managers prepare detailed quarterly reports to keep you informed of their current market insights and the reasoning behind any changes that have either just occurred or are anticipated within your portfolio. The quality of these reports varies widely.

Some money managers add interim client reports and special individual correspondence to highlight specific activity within the firm or within your individual portfolio.

Some professionals organize quarterly or annual meetings in which all clients are invited to participate. This is a great way to hear your money manager's broader views as well as interact with other clients of the firm and hear their questions and comments. This can be very positive reinforcement. (For those who cannot attend, a cassette tape may be offered.)

It is very important that you take advantage of all the counseling and communication that your money manager offers. It is both informing and supportive.

Making Life Easier - Other Services

A high-quality money management firm will provide other services that may not add to the long-term rate of return of your retirement portfolio but will surely add to your overall satisfaction by taking over all the minutiae and aggravations of servicing a portfolio.

Tax Reporting and Accounting. Your money manager should make life much easier at tax time. Many professionals provide full and complete accounting for your account(s).

Tax reports will be prepared that reconcile exactly with your 1099s. Preliminary reports can easily be put together in the fall of the year to help with any year-end planning you may wish to do.

Accounting reports can be prepared that comply with almost any needs either you or your accountant require. An underrated part of the money manager's all-around service is troubleshooting when problems occur—and they will occur.

Retirement Income and Other Payouts. Your money management firm will oversee the payment (from the Custodian) of your monthly retirement income—by check or wire. In addition, any non-recurring needs for money from your Wealth and Retirement Portfolio (new roof, new car, etc.) are easily handled with a phone call. All such transactions are a part of your permanent accounting record and show up on your statements in easy-to-read form.

Rebalancing. The financial markets are not symmetrical (correlated). Your Wealth and Retirement Portfolio needs periodic rebalancing to make sure it does in fact continue to meet your asset allocation. This is obviously a continuous and dynamic part of your manager's service.

Conclusion

A qualified money manager is an excellent strategy for those who want a third-party to enforce the discipline of their investment policy. Given the myriad temptations to alter a well-thought-out, long-term asset allocation *at just the wrong time,* using a professional's services may be a better choice than either utilizing index funds or developing your own portfolio of managed funds. In addition, your investment advisor can customize your strategy to focus on increasing the returns and/or decreasing the risks within your portfolio.

17

The Not-So-Secret Key Ingredient

Many investors are disappointed by the returns they make from their investments. The culprit is often either market timing or performance chasing (dumping a fund or stock that is currently out of favor in order to buy a hot one). The solution is to select an investment strategy you can rely upon and then stay the course. This is the most important ingredient in attaining investment success and the one in least supply.

"Our stay-put behavior reflects our view that the stock market serves as a relocation center at which money is moved from the active to the patient."
— Warren Buffett

Have you ever sat on a river bank, one with a fast-moving current and scattered rapids? Perhaps you threw pieces of bark or branches into the water. If your "ship" made it to the main current—off it went—caught in the major force of the river. It bobbed and weaved wildly, but its course was undeniable. You had no doubt where it was heading.

If your ship did not make the main current, it may have been caught in swirling eddies, or in dead-end side streams or even in the calm water near the edge. Not being part of the major force of the river, your ship might end up anywhere, while the major rush of the river passed it by.

We want our *investment* ships in the main current. The ride may be spirited, but we know where we're going, and we know we'll get there.

Prediction Deficit

An asset allocation policy is arguably the most predictable approach to long-term investing. In Chapter 10, a set of model portfolios employing fixed asset allocation policies were introduced that spanned the range from low risk with low rewards to high risk with high rewards.

Therein lies a fundamental truth about intelligent asset allocation using reliable asset classes. Higher long-term returns go hand-in-hand with larger declines during bear markets. Yet, it *seems* sensible to go for the high returns of an aggressive portfolio allocation during bull markets and to retreat to a more conservative allocation during bear markets. If only one could divine the major movements of the markets.

Financial publications and various market gurus oblige this desire by offering market forecasts that appear logical and well founded based upon analysis of economic and market data. The problem is consistency. **No publication or market analyst has ever consistently forecast the direction of the economy or the market!**

Examples could not only fill a book, they could fill a reference library! However, two examples from otherwise highly reliable sources should make the point.

One of the most respected leaders of the mutual fund industry, John Bogle, Chairman of Vanguard Mutual Funds, had this to say on the Dow Jones Industrial Average (October 15, 1996). "I think it is at least possible that we will be sitting here around 6000 for some years. The market fundamentals just aren't very good."[22] Less than 10 months later, the Dow was above 8300—almost 40% higher!

Another example comes from the 1998 Forecast issue of Money magazine, the most widely circulated magazine on investments. "...We've warned readers for the past three years that stocks could decline 15% to 20% before bouncing back again. So far, the market has defied those predictions. In last year's Forecast issue, we were correct that long-term interest rates would fall. But we were far off the mark predicting that economic growth would drop to 2% in 1997; instead the economy figures to expand at 3.7%. And rather than returning the feeble 7% we expected, top quality stocks gained around 24% in 1997."

One-time gurus such as Joe Granville, Elaine Garzarelli and Marty Zweig had their 15 minutes of fame with uncanny market calls only to fall to earth on subsequent lousy ones. Their forecasts were based on their "proprietary" market indicators and technical analysis.

However, even Ned Davis, one of the better known market timers, is "candid about the limitations of technical analysis. He once gave a seminar in which he used a series of indicators to argue that the Dow Jones Industrial Average would rise by 1000 points over the next 12 months. After a short break, he returned to the podium and used another set of indicators to argue that the Dow would shed 1000 points in the coming 12 months. 'The point being,' says Davis, 'that at any time there are enough indicators to make a credible case in either direction.' "[23]

Market forecasting comes in many different venues, but the long-term results are always the same. Whether based on technical indicators, fundamental values, market sentiment (moods), cycles or even jumping from one strategy to another...they just rob you of your valuables: *time* and *compounding*.

Peter Lynch put it in different terms: "Far more money has been lost by investors in preparing for corrections, or anticipating corrections, than has been lost in the corrections themselves."

Performance Chasing

Chasing hot stocks or mutual funds is the bane of other investors. In fact, based upon the average holding period for all mutual funds being only 21 months, it appears most investors might follow this strategy to one extent or another. Morningstar has conducted several studies in recent years to determine the net effect on investors' portfolios from all this chasing and switching. The results from each study have been the same—*lower* returns.

In a report titled "The Plight of the Fickle Investor" (December, 1997), Morningstar stated, "We found that investors across all fund types—both stocks and bonds—have paid a price for being fickle. …Swapping in and out of funds wouldn't be so bad if we were actually good at it. But…we're not. Instead of buying low and selling high, we do the opposite. So rather than checking fund prices first thing each morning, let's show some restraint, develop an investment plan, and stick to it. As Warren Buffett said, "Inactivity strikes us as intelligent behavior." If it works for him…"

 Research continually shows that, among individuals and professionals alike, those with a consistent approach win, and those who keep changing strategies lose.

Twist on Load Vs. No-Load Mutual Funds

For mutual fund investors, another interesting proof of maintaining a strict discipline comes from combining the results of two different studies on mutual funds and their investors.[24]

The first study was conducted by finance professor Mark Carhart of the University of Southern California. He constructed a comprehensive mutual fund database that included virtually every diversified equity mutual fund that has existed since 1962—

including those that no longer exist (to eliminate survivorship bias). See page 189.

The study concluded that the average no-load mutual fund outperformed the average load mutual fund by 0.6% per year. And that does not take into consideration the commissions load fund investors must pay. All other fund expenses were included so that the net results would be comparing apples to apples.

The second study was conducted by Dalbar Financial Services, a Boston-based consulting firm. Dalbar studied the actual returns of *investors*, as opposed to the returns of the funds themselves (much like the Morningstar study previously cited). Dalbar found that the average load fund investor (before loads) made 1.2% per year more than the average no-load fund investor!

How can this be? Don't the two studies indicate opposite results? No. The average load fund investor earned more than the average no-load fund investor simply because he/she stayed put longer…even though the load funds themselves did not perform as well. (It appears that investors are less likely to sell a fund for which they have incurred a sales charge.) **The real lesson is that discipline is far more important than any other aspect of your investment strategy.**

Experience Builds Patience

Investing is not easy, and the most difficult part of all is in mastering our own emotions. Let's listen in again on another part of Louis Rukeyser's insightful interview on April 28, 1995, with Phil Carret, the voice of 77 years of investment management experience.

RUKEYSER: "What is the most important thing that you have learned about investing over the past three-quarters of a century?"

CARRET: "Patience."

RUKEYSER: "What do you think of this stock market today?"

CARRET: "I think it is dangerous at current levels. There's a lot of froth on the bloom. I think we're in for maybe something like 1987 when the market went down 500 points in one day…But in the long run…the market will recover, and people who buy the right stocks and sit on them are going to do very well."

RUKEYSER: "What do you do, given your experience, when you think there may be too much froth, when you think there may be a major correction, even a crash? Do you sell all your stocks?"

CARRET: *"No, I really don't do anything."*

Don't Just Sit There — Do Nothing!

It appears that the great philosopher Blaise Pascal could have been discussing investment philosophy in 1670 when he said, "I have discovered that all human evil comes from this, man's being unable to sit still in a room."[25]

Your asset allocation policy will control your risks—let it! Any market timing or performance chasing you attempt to enhance returns and/or reduce setbacks has a very high probability of doing exactly the opposite—lower your long-term returns and increase the risk that you will fall well short of your retirement income objective.

 Your asset allocation policy is much more powerful and predictable than any ad hoc system of investing! Let it work for you.

> *"We have striven throughout to guard the student against over emphasis upon the superficial and the temporary...this over emphasis is at once the delusion and the nemesis of the world of finance."*
> — Benjamin Graham and David Dodd,
> Security Analysis, 1934

Action Summary

Here is a simple summary of the important points in this book. Understanding and acting upon them will help assure your investment success.

Motivate yourself to invest better. Understand that the rate of return you achieve on your investments may be the single most important determinant of the retirement income available to you.

Organize your retirement portfolio—all of it—on one page. Begin thinking of it as an entity in itself, not a collection of separate investments. Purchase financial software that makes this much easier.

Educate yourself as to the long-term returns that asset classes and combinations of asset classes are likely to provide. Also, appreciate the interim fluctuations in market values that are a part of each class. Be armed and prepared *not to act*!

Select an asset allocation that is appropriate for your Wealth and Retirement Portfolio—the right combination of long-term return and fluctuation in market values that is satisfying and livable for you.

Choose your strategy for investing within the asset allocation you select. Index funds? Actively managed funds? Your own personal money manager? One of these is the best choice for you. Size yourself up based on your attitude and expectations from investing.

Research and uncover those few superior mutual fund managers experienced in the styles appropriate to your objective (actively managed fund strategy)—OR—select a professional money manager to do this for you.

Stay put with your asset allocation and investment strategy. To get the benefits of a well-thought-out investing program, you still need the patience and discipline to stay the course—either on your own or with help from an advisor.

Rebalance your asset allocation annually.

Build Wealth and. . . .Have a Great Retirement!

Appendix

Note: Charts in the Appendix are the letter A (for Appendix) followed by the chapter number in which the chart is introduced or to which it is referred. A hyphen follows these two digits which is followed by the individual chart number.

How Much Retirement Income Will Your Current Tax-Sheltered Account Provide?

(Inflation-Adjusted, Retirement Income as a Percentage of Your Current Tax-Sheltered Retirement Account)

Years to Retirement	Annual Rates of Return							
	5%	6%	7%	8%	9%	10%	11%	12%
0	4.3%	4.9%	5.5%	6.2%	7.0%	7.8%	8.6%	9.4%
10	5.2%	6.6%	8.1%	10.1%	12.4%	14.9%	18.0%	21.8%
15	5.7%	7.6%	9.8%	12.8%	16.4%	20.7%	26.2%	33.1%
20	6.3%	8.7%	11.9%	16.2%	21.8%	28.8%	38.0%	50.4%
25	6.9%	10.1%	14.4%	20.6%	28.9%	40.0%	55.3%	76.6%
30	7.6%	11.7%	17.4%	26.1%	38.4%	55.6%	80.4%	116.4%
35	8.4%	13.5%	21.1%	33.1%	50.9%	77.2%	116.8%	176.9%
40	9.2%	15.5%	25.5%	41.9%	67.6%	107.2%	169.8%	269.0%

CHART A1-1

Note: In order to estimate future income from a portfolio, it is necessary to make certain assumptions:
- Inflation is assumed to be 3.0% per year (both before and after retirement).
- Retirement income will be adjusted annually by the increase in inflation.
- Retirement income will be paid out for 30 years before the investment principal is depleted.

Example: Assume you currently have $300,000 in a tax-deferred account, such as a Rollover IRA, 401(k), profit sharing plan or deferred annuity. Further assume you are 15 years away from beginning to take retirement distributions from this account (shaded on chart). Based on the assumptions noted, your maximum level of retirement income will be determined by the rate of return from your investments both before and after retirement. Assume your investment return averages 7% per year (shaded on chart). At this rate of return, your maximum retirement income will be $29,400 ($300,000 x 9.8%) per year *in today's dollars* for 30 years. A year-by-year illustration of this example is shown on Chart A1-2.

This chart is designed to illustrate the impact on your retirement income of merely changing the rate of return on your current investment portfolio. Changing your rate of return has a dramatic impact on your available retirement income. In the example above, a 5% annual rate of return reduces retirement income to only $17,100 per year in current dollars, whereas increasing the rate of return to 9% results in an annual retirement income of $49,200 per year in present value dollars.

Tax Sheltered Net Worth

Lump Sum:	$300,000
Years to Retirement:	15
Inflation Rate:	3%
Pre-Retirement Total Return:	7%
Post-Retirement Total Return	7%

Years Before and After Retirement	Accumulated Wealth	Retirement Income	
1	$321,000	N/A	
2	343,470	N/A	
3	367,513	N/A	
4	393,239	N/A	
5	420,766	N/A	
6	450,219	N/A	
7	481,734	N/A	
8	515,456	N/A	
9	551,538	N/A	
10	590,145	N/A	
11	631,456	N/A	*$46,027 equates to $29,400 in present dollars at 3% inflation. Each annual retirement income distribution increases by 3%; however, the buying power of each year's income remains $29,400 in present dollars.*
12	675,657	N/A	
13	722,954	N/A	
14	773,560	N/A	
15	$827,709	$46,027	
1	838,241	47,408	
2	848,089	48,830	
3	857,160	50,295	
4	865,358	51,804	
5	872,575	53,358	
6	878,697	54,958	
7	883,598	56,607	
8	887,145	58,305	
9	889,190	60,055	
10	889,577	61,856	
11	888,136	63,712	
12	884,682	65,623	
13	879,018	67,592	
14	870,929	69,620	
15	860,186	71,708	
16	846,540	73,860	
17	829,722	76,075	
18	809,445	78,358	***30 Years of Retirement Distributions***
19	785,398	80,708	
20	757,246	83,130	
21	724,630	85,623	
22	687,162	88,192	
23	644,425	90,838	
24	595,972	93,563	
25	541,320	96,370	
26	479,951	99,261	
27	411,309	102,239	
28	334,794	105,306	
29	249,765	108,465	
30	155,529	111,719	

	$ 51,345	*Final Distribution - Principal Depleted*

CHART A1-2

10% SALARY DEFERRAL

What Percentage of Your "Final Salary" Will Your 401(k) Replace?

(Your Retirement Income as a Percentage of Your Final Compensation)

Years to Retirement	Annual Rates of Return							
	5%	6%	7%	8%	9%	10%	11%	12%
10	4.9%	5.9%	7.0%	8.4%	9.9%	11.6%	13.5%	15.6%
15	7.5%	9.3%	11.4%	13.9%	16.9%	20.2%	24.3%	29.0%
20	9.8%	12.3%	15.4%	19.2%	23.9%	29.3%	36.0%	44.0%
25	13.3%	17.3%	22.4%	28.8%	37.0%	47.2%	60.3%	76.5%
30	16.2%	21.7%	28.9%	38.4%	50.9%	67.8%	88.6%	116.5%
35	19.5%	26.8%	36.8%	50.4%	69.1%	94.0%	128.8%	175.7%
40	22.7%	32.1%	45.4%	64.1%	90.9%	129.7%	184.4%	261.3%

CHART A1-3

Assumptions:
- Annual rate of return is for both "years to retirement" *and* 30 years after retirement.
- Annual Inflation: 3.0% (both before and after retirement)
- Annual Salary Increases: 1.0% (over inflation)

Example: You anticipate you will retire in 20 years (shaded on chart). You and your employer together will set aside 10% of your growing annual salary each year. (Your salary is assumed to grow 1.0% per year above inflation.) If your investments average a 9% rate of return (shaded on chart) both before and after retirement, your investments from the 20 years of salary deferral will replace 23.9% (shaded on chart) of your *final* salary. Your retirement income will fully adjust for changes in the Consumer Price Index (CPI), that is the income paid out to you during your retirement will rise each year by the inflation rate. The income will last 30 years at which time all of the investment principal would be consumed. (See opposite page for a full illustration of this example.)

This chart is designed to illustrate the impact on your retirement income of merely changing the rate of return on your 401(k) investments.

Retirement Income as a % of Final Compensation

Compensation:	$25,000	Inflation Wage Adjustment:	3%
Contribution Level:	10%	Portfolio Rate of Return (Pre-Retirement):	9%
Merit Wage Adjustment:	1%	Portfolio Rate of Return (Post-Retirement):	9%

Years Before and After Retirement	Compensation	Plan Contribution	Plan Accumulation/ Retirement Fund	Retirement Income	
1	$26,000	$2,600	$ 2,834	0	
2	27,040	2,704	6,036	0	
3	28,122	2,812	9,645	0	
4	29,246	2,925	13,701	0	
5	30,416	3,042	18,249	0	
6	31,633	3,163	23,340	0	
7	32,898	3,290	29,026	0	
8	34,214	3,421	35,368	0	
9	35,583	3,558	42,430	0	
10	37,006	3,701	50,282	0	
11	38,486	3,849	59,002	0	
12	40,026	4,003	68,675	0	
13	41,627	4,163	79,393	0	
14	43,292	4,329	91,258	0	
15	45,024	4,502	104,378	0	
16	46,825	4,682	118,876	0	Each annual
17	48,698	4,870	134,883	0	retirement income
18	48,698	4,870	134,883	0	distribution increases
19	50,645	5,065	152,543	0	by 3%; however, the
20	$52,671	$5,267	$172,013	$12,081	buying power of each
1			175,050	12,444	year's income
2			177,988	12,817	remains at 23.9% of
3			180,805	13,202	final compensation.
4		Increasing/(Decreasing)	183,480	13,598	
5		Value of	185,987	14,006	
6		Retirement Fund	188,300	14,426	
7			190,389	14,859	
8			192,219	15,304	
9			193,756	15,764	
10			194,957	16,236	
11			195,780	16,724	
12			196,175	17,225	
13			196,089	17,742	
14			195,462	18,274	
15			194,231	18,822	
16			192,325	19,387	
17			189,666	19,969	30 Years of
18			186,168	20,568	Retirement
19			181,738	21,185	Distributions
20			176,274	21,820	
21			169,664	22,475	
22			161,784	23,149	
23			152,501	23,844	
24			141,667	24,559	
25			129,122	25,296	
26			114,688	26,055	
27			98,173	26,836	
28			79,368	27,641	
29			58,040	28,471	
30			33,939	29,325	

$ 6,789 Final Distribution - Principal Depleted

CHART A1-4

How Much Retirement Income Will Your Current After-Tax Account Provide?

(Inflation-Adjusted, Retirement Income as a Percentage of Your Current After-Tax Retirement Account)

Years to Retirement	Annual Rates of Return							
	5%	6%	7%	8%	9%	10%	11%	12%
0	3.5%	3.8%	4.2%	4.6%	5.1%	5.5%	6.1%	6.6%
10	3.6%	4.3%	5.1%	6.0%	7.0%	8.1%	9.5%	11.0%
15	3.7%	4.6%	5.6%	6.8%	8.2%	9.8%	11.9%	14.2%
20	3.8%	4.8%	6.1%	7.7%	9.6%	11.9%	14.8%	18.3%
25	3.9%	5.1%	6.7%	8.7%	11.2%	14.4%	18.5%	23.6%
30	4.0%	5.4%	7.4%	9.9%	13.1%	17.4%	23.2%	30.5%
35	4.1%	5.7%	8.1%	11.2%	15.4%	21.1%	29.0%	39.4%
40	4.2%	6.1%	8.8%	12.6%	18.0%	25.5%	36.2%	50.9%

CHART A1-5

Note: In order to estimate future income from a portfolio, it is necessary to make certain assumptions:
- Inflation is assumed to be 3.0% per year (both before and after retirement).
- Retirement income will be adjusted annually by the increase in inflation.
- Retirement income will be paid out for 30 years before the investment principal is depleted.

Example: You assume you will retire in 25 years (shaded on chart). You currently have a Wealth and Retirement Portfolio of $300,000. If your portfolio averages a 10% rate of return (shaded on chart) both before and after retirement, your after-tax retirement income (distributions from your portfolio) will have the same purchasing power as 14.4% (shaded on chart) of today's $300,000 throughout your retirement (30 years). In other words, your retirement income from your current nest egg is the equivalent of $43,200 per year (14.4% x $300,000) in today's dollars after taxes. (See opposite page for a full illustration of this example.)

This chart is designed to illustrate the impact on your retirement income of merely changing the rate of return on your current investment portfolio.

Non-Tax Sheltered Net Worth

Lump Sum:	$300,000
Years to Retirement:	25
Inflation Rate:	3%
Tax Rate:	30%
% Taxable (Accumulation):	100%
Pre- and Post-Retirement Total Return:	10%
Pre- and Post-Retirement After-Tax Return:	7%

Years Before and After Retirement	Accumulated Wealth	Retirement Income	
1	$ 321,000	N/A	
2	343,470	N/A	
3	367,513	N/A	
4	393,239	N/A	
5	420,766	N/A	
6	450,219	N/A	
7	481,734	N/A	
8	515,456	N/A	
9	551,538	N/A	
10	590,145	N/A	
11	631,456	N/A	
12	675,657	N/A	
13	722,954	N/A	
14	773,560	N/A	
15	827,709	N/A	
16	885,649	N/A	
17	947,645	N/A	
18	1,013,980	N/A	
19	1,084,958	N/A	*$90,542 equates to*
20	1,160,905	N/A	*$43,200 in present*
21	1,242,169	N/A	*dollars. Each annual*
22	1,329,121	N/A	*retirement income*
23	1,422,159	N/A	*distribution increases*
24	1,521,710	N/A	*by 3%; however, the*
25	$1,628,230	$ 90,542	*buying power of each*
1	1,648,948	93,258	*year's income remains*
2	1,668,318	96,056	*$43,200 in present*
3	1,686,163	98,937	*dollars.*
4	1,702,289	101,906	
5	1,716,487	104,963	
6	1,728,529	108,112	
7	1,738,171	111,355	
8	1,745,148	114,696	
9	1,749,172	118,136	
10	1,749,933	121,681	
11	1,747,098	125,331	
12	1,740,304	129,091	
13	1,729,161	132,964	
14	1,713,250	136,953	*30 Years of*
15	1,692,116	141,061	*Retirement*
16	1,665,272	145,293	*Distributions*
17	1,632,189	149,652	
18	1,592,301	154,141	
19	1,544,996	158,766	
20	1,489,618	163,528	
21	1,425,456	168,434	
22	1,351,751	173,487	
23	1,267,682	178,692	
24	1,172,367	184,053	
25	1,064,858	189,574	
26	944,137	195,262	
27	809,107	201,119	
28	658,591	207,153	
29	491,325	213,368	
30	305,949	219,769	
	$ 101,004	*Final Distribution - Principal Depleted*	

CHART A1-6

Measures of Risk

Risk Profile is an investor's tool, not an academic measurement, for portraying the long-term risks of an asset class or portfolio. It takes into consideration the two primary characteristics of risk as *felt* by long-term investors: the worst-case decline in market value (mega bear market) and the normal cyclical decline in market value (average bear market).

The number of major declines to be evaluated is determined by dividing by 5 the total number of years being studied. (Fractions of one-half or over add one additional decline to the study.) For example, in the 1960-1997 period of study (38 years), the eight most severe declines in market value are included (38 ÷ 5 = 7-3/5 — rounded up to 8).

The rationale for dividing by five is simply that the total U.S. stock market has incurred one major decline *on average* about every five years. These declines do not operate on a predictable cycle, and therefore some five-year periods have no major declines and some five-year periods have more than one major decline. See the Historical Risk/Reward Chart 5-3 to visually see this illustrated for the S&P 500.

Declines, recoveries and advances are measured from calendar month-ends to subsequent calendar month-ends. (This lines up with the timing of brokerage and custodial valuations, i.e. month-end statements.) The end of a decline is established when a recovery restores the entire market value temporarily lost in the decline. All calculations are made on a total return basis without consideration of taxes or costs.

The most significant decline in the period of study is dubbed the mega bear market decline. On Chart 5-3, the worst decline for the S&P 500 in the 1960-1997 period is the decline that began in January 1973 and ended 21 months later in September 1974. The S&P 500 fell a full 43% during the 21-month duration of this decline. In the bottom right-hand corner of Chart 5-3, the mega bear market decline shows as "43%."

All the remaining major declines (the next seven most severe declines in this period of study) are averaged together to determine the average cyclical decline to which an investor was exposed. On Chart 5-3, the average cyclical decline (without including the worst-case decline already illustrated) of the S&P 500 in the 1960-1997 period was 19%.

Standard deviation is a common measure of the volatility of annual returns. The standard deviation is defined as $\sigma = \{[(r_1 - r_A)^2 + (r_2 - r_A)^2 + \ldots (r_n - r_A)^2]/n\}^{1/2}$, where $r_1, r_2 \ldots r_n$ are the individual yearly returns and r_A is the average, or *mean* of the yearly returns (σ^2 is called the *variance*): if yearly returns follow a normal distribution, popularly known as the *bell-shaped curve*, then about two thirds of the time the asset will have a return equal to the mean plus or minus one standard deviation. That is, the return on the asset will be within one standard deviation of its average, or mean, about two thirds of the time. About 95 percent of the time, the return on the asset will be within two standard deviations of its mean.

Example of Standard Deviation "Predictions"

Suppose that the average of all the annual returns from an investment over a 20-year period of study is 10%[*]. Further assume that this investment produced a standard deviation of 18.5% for this 20-year period. The standard deviation for this investment predicts the following:

- **13** of the 20 annual returns likely fell within the range of **-8.5% to 28.5%**, the average annual return of 10% plus or minus one standard deviation

  (10% ± 18.5%)

- **19** of the 20 annual returns likely fell within the range of **-27% to 47%**, the average annual return of 10% plus or minus two standard deviations

  [10% ± (2 times 18.5%)]

---

[*] This is not the compounded average annual return from this investment, it is simply the arithmetic *mean* of all 20 of its annual returns.

- **1** annual return may be lower than **-27.0% or higher than 47.0%**

Standard deviation has one distinctive advantage—its precision. Academics and market commentators like the fact that any historical set of returns can produce this precise, annual measurement of volatility to match up with an investment's annual return.

Standard Deviation's Limitations

From an investor's viewpoint, standard deviation does have several insurmountable shortcomings as the measure of an asset class's risk, i.e. the intensity of its market declines.

- **Omission of Worst Case.** In the eyes of many investors, the most significant risk of an investment is defined by, "What's the worst that can happen?" A major handicap of standard deviation is that it leaves out the worst case. Over the long term, the standard deviation calculation will not predict or illustrate the very worst "bear market" decline that the investor will likely face.

Annual Risks vs. Total Risk. Standard deviation measures volatility in calendar year units. This has the effect of hiding or downplaying the real risks incurred. For example, in calculating the standard deviation for the S&P 500 index, a *positive* annual return is entered for 1987—the year of the crash! Is this an accurate portrayal of the risk that unfolded to investors in that year? Standard deviation also fails to prepare investors for the cumulative effect of back-to-back declines like 1973-1974.

Historical Risk/Reward charts are a better yardstick for illustrating the risk faced by a long-term investor within an asset class. On display are all the major market declines from beginning to end, regardless of calendar year starts and stops, as this is wh   the investor feels as his monthly brokerage statements arrive.

Model Portfolio Guidelines

Certain guidelines were adopted in order to prevent any model from being too lopsided toward any one particular asset class. These guidelines are:

- No asset class can represent more than 50% of a model portfolio (to ensure appropriate diversification).

- Every qualifying asset class must be represented in each model (except in the 100% Stocks Model Portfolio).

- No domestic stock asset class can represent more than twice its historically normal weighting in the U.S. stock market.

- International stocks may not exceed 50% of the stock portion of any model portfolio (approximately their total proportion of world markets).

- REITs may not exceed 5% of any model portfolio (approximately four times their total proportion of the domestic stock market).

Virtually every combination of domestic stock asset classes, 5-year Treasury bonds and 30-day T-bills that met the guidelines above was tested. The returns assumed a reinvestment of all dividends, interest and capital gains. The goal was to find the most favorable combination of the five asset classes that satisfied the objectives set out for each model portfolio.

If more than one asset allocation met the rate-of-return objective and produced an identical level of risk, the portfolio with the most even distribution of asset classes was selected as the domestic model.

All of the results of this study may be duplicated using the databases identified in Chart 8-1.

Domestic Model Portfolio: Moderate
(September 1929 through February 1937)
Illustrates annual gains/declines by asset class and annual rebalancing back to 47% Stocks, 47% Bonds, 6% Cash.

Year			47% Stocks	47% Bonds	6% Cash	Nominal Value of Total Portfolio	Value of U.S. $ Relative to 9/1/29	Real Value of Total Portfolio
1929	1-Sep		470,000	470,000	60,000	1,000,000	$1.00	$1,000,000
	Gain/<Loss>		<156,000>	18,000	1,000	<137,000>		
	31-Dec		314,000	488,000	61,000	863,000	$1.01	$ 872,000
1930	1-Jan	(Rebalanced)	405,000	405,000	52,000	863,000		
	Gain/<Loss>		<122,000>	28,000	1,000	< 94,000>		
	31-Dec		283,000	433,000	53,000	769,000	$1.07	$ 823,000
1931	1-Jan	(Rebalanced)	361,000	361,000	46,000	769,000		
	Gain/<Loss>		<163,000>	< 8,000>	1,000	<171,000>		
	31-Dec		198,000	353,000	47,000	598,000	$1.19	$ 712,000
1932	1-Jan	(Rebalanced)	281,000	281,000	36,000	598,000		
	Gain/<Loss>		< 20,000>	25,000	0	5,000		
	31-Dec		261,000	306,000	36,000	603,000	$1.33	$ 802,000
1933	1-Jan	(Rebalanced)	284,000	284,000	36,000	603,000		
	Gain/<Loss>		233,000	5,000	0	239,000		
	31-Dec		517,000	289,000	36,000	842,000	$1.32	$1,111,000
1934	1-Jan	(Rebalanced)	396,000	396,000	51,000	842,000		
	Gain/<Loss>		24,000	35,000	0	59,000		
	31-Dec		420,000	431,000	51,000	901,000	$1.30	$1,171,000
1935	1-Jan	(Rebalanced)	424,000	424,000	54,000	901,000		
	Gain/<Loss>		192,000	29,000	0	223,000		
	31-Dec		616,000	453,000	54,000	1,124,000	$1.26	$1,416,000
1936	1-Jan	(Rebalanced)	528,000	528,000	67,000	1,124,000		
	Gain/<Loss>		199,000	17,000	1,000	215,000		
	31-Dec		727,000	545,000	68,000	1,339,000	$1.24	$1,660,000
1937	1-Jan	(Rebalanced)	629,000	629,000	80,000	1,339,000		
	Gain/<Loss>		48,000	< 1,000>	0	47,000		
	28-Feb		677,000	628,000	80,000	1,386,000	$1.23	$1,705,000

Average Annual Return Over 90 Months: 4.4% (nominal)   **7.4%** (real)

CHART A11-1

Moderate Domestic Model
Maximum Perpetual "Real" Retirement Income
Full Adjustment for Inflation (CPI*) Increases

Initial Portfolio: $500,000   Initial Income: $19,500 (3.90% of Original Portfolio)

	The Numbers You See				The Numbers You Feel	
Year	The Portfolio Grows in Nominal $ Even After Paying Out Retiree Distributions	Retiree's Annual Distributions– Increasing Annually with the Full Change in Inflation	CPI: Annual Inflation Rate %	CPI: Cumulative Inflation %	This Portfolio Remains Fairly Stable in Real $ (Adjusted for Inflation)	Retiree's Annual Distributions in Real $ (Adjusted for Inflation)
1960	$ 509,967	$ 19,500	1.5%	1.5%	$ 502,431	$19,500
1961	562,999	19,637	0.7	2.2	550,823	19,500
1962	529,041	19,872	1.2	3.4	511,462	19,500
1963	563,889	20,190	1.6	5.1	536,567	19,500
1964	601,711	20,432	1.2	6.4	565,767	19,500
1965	644,378	20,821	1.9	8.4	594,588	19,500
1966	614,140	21,528	3.4	12.1	548,053	19,500
1967	703,480	22,174	3.0	15.4	609,494	19,500
1968	759,042	23,217	4.7	20.8	628,111	19,500
1969	687,265	24,633	6.1	28.2	536,019	19,500
1970	715,145	25,988	5.5	35.3	528,686	19,500
1971	777,341	26,871	3.4	39.9	555,769	19,500
1972	818,411	27,785	3.4	44.6	565,892	19,500
1973	725,864	30,230	8.8	57.3	461,305	19,500
1974	627,390	33,918	12.2	76.5	355,368	19,500
1975	755,586	36,292	7.0	88.9	399,982	19,500
1976	885,433	38,034	4.8	98.0	447,251	19,500
1977	857,795	40,620	6.8	111.4	405,703	19,500
1978	871,899	44,276	9.0	130.5	378,324	19,500
1979	959,098	50,165	13.3	161.1	367,308	19,500
1980	1,073,495	56,385	12.4	193.5	365,764	19,500
1981	1,068,402	61,404	8.9	219.6	334,278	19,500
1982	1,276,941	63,799	3.9	232.1	384,529	19,500
1983	1,418,857	66,223	3.8	244.7	411,623	19,500
1984	1,467,122	68,872	4.0	258.5	409,255	19,500
1985	1,760,697	71,489	3.8	272.1	473,167	19,500
1986	1,948,821	72,275	1.1	276.2	518,025	19,500
1987	1,920,013	75,455	4.4	292.8	488,858	19,500
1988	2,081,740	78,775	4.4	310.0	507,697	19,500
1989	2,400,591	82,399	4.6	328.9	559,712	19,500
1990	$2,338,749	$ 87,425	6.1%	355.1%	$ 513,942	$ 19,500

Retirement Income (Inflation-Adjusted) is Perpetual
Principal Value Fluctuates Around Original Real Value

*Consumer Price Index

CHART A13-1

Moderate Domestic Model
Maximum Perpetual "Real" Retirement Income
Two-Thirds Adjustment for Inflation (CPI*) Increases

Initial Portfolio: $500,000   Initial Income: $26,500 (5.30% of Original Portfolio)

	The Numbers You See				The Numbers You Feel	
Year	The Portfolio Grows in Nominal $ Even After Paying Out Retiree Distributions	Retiree's Annual Distributions– Increasing Annually with the ⅔ Change in Inflation	⅔ x CPI: Two-Thirds of Annual Inflation Rate %	⅔ x CPI: Two-Thirds of Cumulative Inflation %	This Portfolio Remains Fairly Stable in Real $ (Adjusted for ⅔ Inflation)	Retiree's Annual Distributions in Real $ (Adjusted for ⅔ Inflation)
1960	$ 502,967	$ 26,500	1.0%	1.0%	$ 497,985	$ 26,500
1961	548,014	26,624	0.5	1.5	540,064	26,500
1962	507,466	26,837	0.8	2.3	496,133	26,500
1963	533,137	27,123	1.1	3.4	515,727	26,500
1964	560,874	27,340	0.8	4.2	538,250	26,500
1965	592,366	27,687	1.3	5.5	561,358	26,500
1966	556,045	28,315	2.3	7.9	515,253	26,500
1967	628,129	28,881	2.0	10.1	570,630	26,500
1968	668,683	29,787	3.1	13.5	589,007	26,500
1969	596,152	30,999	4.1	18.1	504,589	26,500
1970	610,743	32,136	3.7	22.5	498,646	26,500
1971	653,942	32,865	2.3	25.3	522,076	26,500
1972	678,257	33,610	2.3	28.1	529,481	26,500
1973	591,029	35,583	5.9	35.6	435,806	26,500
1974	499,986	38,478	8.1	46.7	340,931	26,500
1975	590,797	40,275	4.7	53.5	384,883	26,500
1976	680,501	41,564	3.2	58.4	429,569	26,500
1977	647,030	43,449	4.5	65.6	390,718	26,500
1978	645,007	46,058	6.0	75.5	367,440	26,500
1979	696,482	50,143	8.9	91.1	364,434	26,500
1980	766,211	54,291	8.3	106.9	370,294	26,500
1981	748,890	57,513	5.9	119.2	341,642	26,500
1982	880,774	59,010	2.6	124.9	391,620	26,500
1983	963,833	60,505	2.5	130.6	417,957	26,500
1984	981,285	62,119	2.7	136.8	414,467	26,500
1985	1,161,764	63,694	2.5	142.8	478,566	26,500
1986	1,269,423	64,161	0.7	144.5	519,105	26,500
1987	1,233,763	66,044	2.9	151.7	490,139	26,500
1988	1,320,323	67,983	2.9	159.1	509,571	26,500
1989	1,504,744	70,068	3.1	167.1	563,460	26,500
1990	$ 1,447,861	$ 72,919	4.1%	177.9%	$ 520,963	$ 26,500

Retirement Income (Inflation-Adjusted) is Perpetual
Principal Value Fluctuates Around Original Real Value

*Consumer Price Index

CHART A13-2

Moderate Domestic Model
Worst Case Study* (Retire in 1968)
Maximum Perpetual "Real" Retirement Income
Full Adjustment for Inflation (CPI**) Increases)

Initial Portfolio: $500,000   Initial Income: $17,000 (3.40% of Original Portfolio)

	The Numbers You See				The Numbers You Feel	
Year	The Portfolio Grows in Nominal $ Even After Paying Out Retiree Distributions	Retiree's Annual Distributions– Increasing Annually with the Full Change in Inflation	CPI: Annual Inflation Rate %	CPI: Cumulative Inflation %	This Portfolio Remains Fairly Stable in Real $ (Adjusted for Inflation)	Retiree's Annual Distributions in Real $ (Adjusted for Inflation)
1968	$ 538,193	$ 17,000	4.7%	4.7%	$ 514,033	$ 17,000
1969	485,881	18,037	6.1	11.1	437,389	17,000
1970	504,041	19,029	5.5	17.2	430,082	17,000
1971	546,215	19,676	3.4	21.2	450,743	17,000
1972	573,297	20,345	3.4	25.3	457,534	17,000
1973	506,467	22,135	8.8	36.3	371,507	17,000
1974	435,420	24,836	12.2	53.0	284,663	17,000
1975	521,755	26,574	7.0	63.7	318,791	17,000
1976	608,523	27,850	4.8	71.5	354,777	17,000
1977	586,304	29,744	6.8	83.2	320,058	17,000
1978	592,262	32,421	9.0	99.7	296,616	17,000
1979	647,112	36,733	13.3	126.2	286,042	17,000
1980	719,112	41,288	12.4	154.3	282,800	17,000
1981	709,758	44,962	8.9	176.9	256,310	17,000
1982	841,766	46,716	3.9	187.7	292,571	17,000
1983	928,202	48,491	3.8	198.6	310,803	17,000
1984	952,031	50,430	4.0	210.6	306,521	17,000
1985	1,134,117	52,347	3.8	222.4	351,779	17,000
1986	1,246,438	52,923	1.1	225.9	382,412	17,000
1987	1,218,425	55,251	4.4	240.3	358,063	17,000
1988	1,310,653	57,682	4.4	255.3	368,933	17,000
1989	1,500,107	60,336	4.6	271.6	403,692	17,000
1990	1,449,069	64,016	6.1	294.3	367,538	17,000
1991	1,745,160	66,001	3.1	306.5	429,328	17,000
1992	1,839,355	67,915	2.9	318.3	439,749	17,000
1993	1,984,616	69,748	2.7	329.6	462,003	17,000
1994	1,864,643	71,632	2.7	341.2	422,662	17,000
1995	2,247,639	73,566	2.7	353.1	496,083	17,000
1996	$ 2,411,433	$ 75,993	3.3%	368.0%	$ 515,232	$ 17,000

*1968 was the worst possible year to retire in the Inflation Era (1960-1996). This was the kick-off year for the Super Bowl, the huge 14-year bout of inflation, and (not coincidentally) the worst stock market conditions since the Great Depression (1968-1974).

**Consumer Price Index

CHART A13-3

Moderate Domestic Model
Worst Case Study* (Retire in 1968)
Maximum Perpetual "Real" Retirement Income
Two-Thirds Adjustment for Inflation (CPI**) Increases

Initial Portfolio: $500,000   Initial Income: $24,500 (4.90% of Original Portfolio)

	The Numbers You See		⅔ x CPI: Two-Thirds of Annual Inflation Rate %	⅔ x CPI: Two-Thirds of Cumulative Inflation %	The Numbers You Feel	
Year	The Portfolio Grows in Nominal $ Even After Paying Out Retiree Distributions	Retiree's Annual Distributions– Increasing Annually with the ⅔ Change in Inflation			This Portfolio Remains Fairly Stable in Real $ (Adjusted for ⅔ Inflation)	Retiree's Annual Distributions in Real $ (Adjusted for ⅔ Inflation)
1968	$ 530,724	$ 24,500	3.1%	3.1%	$ 514,592	$ 24,500
1969	471,465	25,497	4.1	7.3	439,262	24,500
1970	481,157	26,432	3.7	11.3	432,429	24,500
1971	513,203	27,032	2.3	13.8	451,001	24,500
1972	530,150	27,645	2.3	16.4	455,563	24,500
1973	459,597	29,267	5.9	23.2	373,040	24,500
1974	386,081	31,649	8.1	33.2	289,788	24,500
1975	453,138	33,127	4.7	39.4	324,949	24,500
1976	518,561	34,187	3.2	43.9	360,328	24,500
1977	489,306	35,738	4.5	50.4	325,248	24,500
1978	483,537	37,883	6.0	59.5	303,211	24,500
1979	517,179	41,244	8.9	73.6	297,882	24,500
1980	563,216	44,655	8.3	88.0	299,617	24,500
1981	543,972	47,306	5.9	99.1	273,164	24,500
1982	632,573	48,536	2.6	104.3	309,603	24,500
1983	684,355	49,766	2.5	109.5	326,667	24,500
1984	688,157	51,094	2.7	115.1	319,945	24,500
1985	805,359	52,389	2.5	120.5	365,180	24,500
1986	870,040	52,774	0.7	122.2	391,636	24,500
1987	834,840	54,322	2.9	128.7	365,077	24,500
1988	881,743	55,917	2.9	135.4	374,594	24,500
1989	992,258	57,632	3.1	142.6	408,996	24,500
1990	940,975	59,977	4.1	152.5	372,694	24,500
1991	1,114,983	61,217	2.1	157.7	432,667	24,500
1992	1,156,237	62,402	1.9	162.7	440,161	24,500
1993	1,227,938	63,525	1.8	167.4	459,187	24,500
1994	1,133,414	64,669	1.8	172.2	416,342	24,500
1995	1,345,136	65,834	1.8	177.1	485,374	24,500
1996	$ 1,421,386	$ 67,283	2.2%	183.2%	$ 501,842	$ 24,500

*1968 was the worst possible year to retire in the Inflation Era (1960-1996). This was the kick-off year for the Super Bowl, the huge 14-year bout of inflation, and (not coincidentally) the worst stock market conditions since the Great Depression (1968-1974).

** Consumer Price Index

Moderate Domestic Model
Maximum 30-Year "Real" Retirement Income
Full Adjustment for Inflation (CPI*) Increases

Initial Portfolio: $500,000   Initial Income: $27,000 (5.40% of Original Portfolio)

	The Numbers You See				The Numbers You Feel	
Year	The Portfolio is Depleted After 30 Years of Paying Increasing Retiree Distributions	Retiree's Annual Distributions– Increasing Annually with the Full Change in Inflation	CPI: Annual Inflation Rate %	CPI: Cumulative Inflation %	The Real Value of this Portfolio is Fairly Stable at First– then Declines Steadily	Retiree's Annual Distributions in Real $ (Adjusted for Inflation)
1960	$ 502,467	$ 27,000	1.5%	1.5%	$ 495,041	$ 27,000
1961	546,878	27,189	0.7	2.2	535,051	27,000
1962	505,680	27,515	1.2	3.4	488,877	27,000
1963	530,332	27,956	1.6	5.1	504,636	27,000
1964	556,829	28,291	1.2	6.4	523,566	27,000
1965	586,753	28,829	1.9	8.4	541,415	27,000
1966	549,013	29,809	3.4	12.1	489,934	27,000
1967	617,999	30,703	3.0	15.4	535,433	27,000
1968	655,059	32,146	4.7	20.8	542,065	27,000
1969	580,266	34,107	6.1	28.2	452,567	27,000
1970	589,765	35,983	5.5	35.3	435,996	27,000
1971	626,010	37,206	3.4	39.9	447,573	27,000
1972	642,989	38,471	3.4	44.6	444,596	27,000
1973	552,172	41,857	8.8	57.3	350,920	27,000
1974	456,101	46,963	12.2	76.5	258,346	27,000
1975	525,430	50,251	7.0	88.9	278,145	27,000
1976	589,511	52,663	4.8	98.0	297,774	27,000
1977	541,911	56,244	6.8	111.4	256,302	27,000
1978	517,487	61,306	9.0	130.5	224,542	27,000
1979	529,556	69,459	13.3	161.1	202,805	27,000
1980	545,779	78,072	12.4	193.5	185,959	27,000
1981	489,388	85,021	8.9	219.6	153,118	27,000
1982	525,797	88,336	3.9	232.1	158,335	27,000
1983	519,808	91,693	3.8	244.7	150,801	27,000
1984	467,361	95,361	4.0	258.5	130,371	27,000
1985	484,669	98,985	3.8	272.1	130,249	27,000
1986	456,276	100,073	1.1	276.2	121,285	27,000
1987	362,721	104,477	4.4	292.8	92,353	27,000
1988	299,082	109,074	4.4	310.0	72,940	27,000
1989	242,638	114,091	4.6	328.9	56,573	27,000
1990	$ 124,174	$ 121,051	6.1%	355.1%	$ 27,287	$ 27,000

Principal is Depleted
Retirement Income (Inflation-Adjusted) Lasts 30 Years

*Consumer Price Index

CHART A13-5

Moderate Domestic Model
Maximum 30-Year "Real" Retirement Income
Two-Thirds Adjustment for Inflation (CPI*) Increases

Initial Portfolio: $500,000   Initial Income: $32,000 (6.40% of Original Portfolio)

	The Numbers You See				The Numbers You Feel	
Year	The Portfolio is Depleted After 30 Years of Paying Increasing Retiree Distributions	Retiree's Annual Distributions– Increasing Annually with the ⅔ Change in Inflation	⅔ x CPI: Two-Thirds of Annual Inflation Rate %	⅔ x CPI: Two-Thirds of Cumulative Inflation %	The Real Value of this Portfolio is Fairly Stable at First– then Declines Steadily	Retiree's Annual Distributions in Real $ (Adjusted for ⅔ Inflation)
1960	$ 497,467	$ 32,000	1.0%	1.0%	$ 492,539	$ 32,000
1961	536,205	32,149	0.5	1.5	528,426	32,000
1962	490,383	32,407	0.8	2.3	479,431	32,000
1963	508,646	32,753	1.1	3.4	492,036	32,000
1964	528,179	33,015	0.8	4.2	506,874	32,000
1965	550,475	33,433	1.3	5.5	521,660	32,000
1966	508,844	34,191	2.3	7.9	471,514	32,000
1967	566,363	34,875	2.0	10.1	514,518	32,000
1968	593,817	35,969	3.1	13.5	523,062	32,000
1969	519,503	37,432	4.1	18.1	439,712	32,000
1970	521,416	38,805	3.7	22.5	425,714	32,000
1971	546,670	39,685	2.3	25.3	436,435	32,000
1972	554,507	40,585	2.3	28.1	432,875	32,000
1973	469,317	42,968	5.9	35.6	346,059	32,000
1974	381,113	46,464	8.1	46.7	259,873	32,000
1975	432,399	48,634	4.7	53.5	281,692	32,000
1976	478,282	50,191	3.2	58.4	301,917	32,000
1977	432,827	52,467	4.5	65.6	261,369	32,000
1978	406,668	55,617	6.0	75.5	231,666	32,000
1979	410,187	60,550	8.9	91.1	214,630	32,000
1980	417,668	65,558	8.3	106.9	201,850	32,000
1981	370,127	69,450	5.9	119.2	168,851	32,000
1982	393,216	71,257	2.6	124.9	174,836	32,000
1983	384,247	73,063	2.5	130.6	166,625	32,000
1984	340,957	75,012	2.7	136.8	144,011	32,000
1985	348,884	76,913	2.5	142.8	143,716	32,000
1986	323,005	77,478	0.7	144.5	132,086	32,000
1987	250,985	79,752	2.9	151.7	99,709	32,000
1988	200,331	82,092	2.9	159.1	77,317	32,000
1989	154,333	84,611	3.1	167.1	57,791	32,000
1990	$ 67,925	$ 88,053	4.1%	177.9%	$ 24,440	$ 32,000

Principal is Depleted
Retirement Income (Inflation-Adjusted) Lasts 30 Years

* Consumer Price Index

CHART A13-6

Moderate Domestic Model
Worst Case Study* (Retire in 1968)
Maximum 30-Year "Real" Retirement Income
Full Adjustment for Inflation (CPI**) Increases)

Initial Portfolio: $500,000   Initial Income: $22,500 (4.50% of Original Portfolio)

	The Numbers You See				The Numbers You Feel	
Year	The Portfolio is Depleted After 30 Years of Paying Increasing Retiree Distributions	Retiree's Annual Distributions– Increasing Annually with the Full Change in Inflation	CPI: Annual Inflation Rate %	CPI: Cumulative Inflation %	The Real Value of this Portfolio is Fairly Stable at First– then Declines Steadily	Retiree's Annual Distributions in Real $ (Adjusted for Inflation)
1968	$ 532,434	$ 22,500	4.7%	4.7%	$ 508,533	$ 22,500
1969	474,370	23,873	6.1	11.1	427,027	22,500
1970	485,182	25,185	5.5	17.2	413,991	22,500
1971	518,343	26,042	3.4	21.2	427,742	22,500
1972	536,064	26,927	3.4	25.3	427,820	22,500
1973	464,572	29,297	8.8	36.3	340,775	22,500
1974	388,838	32,871	12.2	53.0	254,209	22,500
1975	453,958	35,172	7.0	63.7	277,367	22,500
1976	516,229	36,860	4.8	71.5	300,968	22,500
1977	482,581	39,367	6.8	83.2	263,437	22,500
1978	470,498	42,910	9.0	99.7	235,634	22,500
1979	493,721	48,617	13.3	126.2	218,239	22,500
1980	524,423	54,645	12.4	154.3	206,236	22,500
1981	489,626	59,509	8.9	176.9	176,816	22,500
1982	549,697	61,829	3.9	187.7	191,057	22,500
1983	572,101	64,179	3.8	198.6	191,565	22,500
1984	549,449	66,746	4.0	210.6	176,904	22,500
1985	613,630	69,283	3.8	222.4	190,335	22,500
1986	631,046	70,045	1.1	225.9	193,607	22,500
1987	569,587	73,127	4.4	240.3	167,387	22,500
1988	561,002	76,344	4.4	255.3	157,915	22,500
1989	585,525	79,856	4.6	271.6	157,570	22,500
1990	503,055	84,727	6.1	294.3	127,594	22,500
1991	538,376	87,354	3.1	306.5	132,446	22,500
1992	495,259	89,887	2.9	318.3	118,405	22,500
1993	457,382	92,314	2.7	329.6	106,475	22,500
1994	347,754	94,806	2.7	341.2	78,826	22,500
1995	331,605	97,366	2.7	353.1	73,189	22,500
1996	$ 262,203***	$ 105,307	3.3%	368.0%	$ 56,023	$ 22,500

*1968 was the worst possible year to retire in the Inflation Era (1960-1996). This was the kick-off year for the Super Bowl, the huge 14-year bout of inflation, and (not coincidentally) the worst stock market conditions since the Great Depression (1968-1974).

**Consumer Price Index

***Minimum of two years' income remaining.

CHART A13-7

Moderate Domestic Model
Worst Case Study* (Retire in 1968)
Maximum 30-Year "Real" Retirement Income
Two-Thirds Adjustment for Inflation (CPI**) Increases

Initial Portfolio: $500,000   Initial Income: $28,500 (5.70% of Original Portfolio)

Year	The Numbers You See				The Numbers You Feel	
	The Portfolio is Depleted After 30 Years of Paying Increasing Retiree Distributions	*Retiree's Annual Distributions– Increasing Annually with the ⅔ Change in Inflation*	*⅔ x CPI: Two-Thirds of Annual Inflation Rate %*	*⅔ x CPI: Two-Thirds of Cumulative Inflation %*	*The Real Value of this Portfolio is Fairly Stable at First– then Declines Steadily*	*Retiree's Annual Distributions in Real $ (Adjusted for ⅔ Inflation)*
1968	$ 526,598	$ 28,500	3.1%	3.1%	$ 510,592	$ 28,500
1969	463,302	29,660	4.1	7.3	431,657	28,500
1970	467,904	30,748	3.7	11.3	420,518	28,500
1971	493,748	31,445	2.3	13.8	433,904	28,500
1972	504,317	32,158	2.3	16.4	433,364	28,500
1973	430,803	34,046	5.9	23.2	349,669	28,500
1974	354,518	36,816	8.1	33.2	266,098	28,500
1975	407,722	38,535	4.7	39.4	292,381	28,500
1976	457,298	39,769	3.2	43.9	317,758	28,500
1977	421,127	41,572	4.5	50.4	279,928	28,500
1978	404,339	44,068	6.0	59.5	253,548	28,500
1979	418,559	47,977	8.9	73.6	241,079	28,500
1980	439,516	51,945	8.3	88.0	233,812	28,500
1981	405,817	55,029	5.9	99.1	203,787	28,500
1982	451,030	56,461	2.6	104.3	220,749	28,500
1983	464,841	57,892	2.5	109.5	221,885	28,500
1984	441,918	59,436	2.7	115.1	205,461	28,500
1985	489,026	60,943	2.5	120.5	221,743	28,500
1986	498,037	61,390	0.7	122.2	224,184	28,500
1987	444,786	63,191	2.9	128.7	194,505	28,500
1988	433,415	65,046	2.9	135.4	184,129	28,500
1989	447,811	67,042	3.1	142.6	184,582	28,500
1990	380,627	69,769	4.1	152.5	150,756	28,500
1991	403,108	71,212	2.1	157.7	156,425	28,500
1992	366,425	72,590	1.9	162.7	139,492	28,500
1993	333,698	73,897	1.8	167.4	124,786	28,500
1994	248,549	75,228	1.8	172.2	91,301	28,500
1995	230,885	76,582	1.8	177.1	83,312	28,500
1996	$ 175,162***	$ 78,268	2.2%	183.2%	$ 61,844	$ 28,500

*1968 was the worst possible year to retire in the Inflation Era (1960-1996). This was the kick-off year for the Super Bowl, the huge 14-year bout of inflation, and (not coincidentally) the worst stock market conditions since the Great Depression (1968-1974).

**Consumer Price Index

***Minimum of two years' income remaining.

CHART A13-8

Endnotes

[1] <u>Investor's Business Daily</u>, 5/29/96, p.1.

[2] Gary P. Brinson, L. Randolph Hood, and Gilbert L. Beebower, "Determinants of Portfolio Performance," <u>Financial Analysts Journal</u>, July-August, 1986.

[3] Jim Barlow, <u>Houston Chronicle</u>, 11/27/97.

[4] John F. Merrill, <u>Barron's</u>, 9/8/97.

[5] Lowell Bryan and Diana Farrell, <u>The McKinsey Quarterly Report</u>, No. 2, 1996.

[6] "Perspective," <u>Investor's Business Daily</u>, 11/19/97.

[7] <u>Investor's Business Daily</u>, 9/26/96.

[8] Standard & Poor's Statistical Service, "Description of Method Used in Computation."

[9] Jeremy J. Siegel, <u>Stocks for the Long Run</u>, 1994.

[10] Jeremy J. Siegel, <u>Stocks for the Long Run</u>, 1994.

[11] David Roche, economist in London at International Strategy, Ltd., <u>The Wall Street Journal</u>, 11/22/95.

[12] Associated Press release in <u>Houston Chronicle</u>, 5/27/96.

[13] Peter Lynch, <u>Beating the Street</u>, 1993.

[14] Robert G. Hagstrom, Jr., <u>The Warren Buffett Way</u>, 1994.

[15] Ray Dalio, Bridgewater Associates, <u>The Wall Street Journal</u>, 4/9/96.

[16] Charles Carignan, Letter to the Editor, <u>Barron's</u>, 6/3/96.

[17] Gary P. Brinson, L. Randolph Hood, and Gilbert L. Beebower, "Determinants of Portfolio Performance," <u>Financial Analysts Journal</u>, July-August, 1986.

[18] Gary P. Brinson, L. Randolph Hood, and Gilbert L. Beebower, "Determinants of Portfolio Performance," <u>Financial Analysts Journal</u>, July-August, 1986.

[19] John Kenneth Galbraith, <u>The Great Crash 1929</u>, 1954.

[20] <u>Worth</u> magazine, 3/97, p. 125.

[21] Kenneth Volpert, Vanguard Funds, <u>Investor's Business Daily</u>, 1/24/97.

[22] Smart Money, 10/97.

[23] Worth Magazine, December/January 1998, p. 126.

[24] Mark Hulbert, column in Forbes, 7/1/96.

[25] From Longleaf Partners Fund's Shareholder Letter dated 7/8/96.

Bibliography

Bernstein, Peter L. <u>Against the Gods, The Remarkable Story of Risk</u>. New York: John Wiley & Sons, 1996.

Bogle, John C. <u>Bogle on Mutual Funds: New Perspectives for the Intelligent Investor</u>. New York: Irwin Professional Publishing, 1994.

Bryan, Lowell and Farrell, Diana. <u>Market Unbound: Unleashing Global Capitalism</u>. New York: John Wiley & Sons, 1996.

Ellis, Charles D. <u>Investment Policy: How to Win the Loser's Game</u>. Homewood, Illinois: Business One Irwin, 1985.

Ellis, Charles D. and Vertin, James R. <u>Classics II: Another Investor's Anthology</u>. Homewood, Illinois: Dow Jones-Irwin, 1989

Ellis, Charles D. and Vertin, James R. <u>Classics: An Investor's Anthology</u>. Homewood, Illinois: Dow Jones-Irwin, 1989

Fisher, Kenneth L. <u>The Wall Street Waltz</u>. Chicago: Contemporary Books, Inc., 1987.

Galbraith, John Kenneth. <u>The Great Crash 1929</u>. Boston, Massachusetts: Houghton Miffin Co., 1954.

Gibson, Roger C. <u>Asset Allocation</u>. Homewood, Illinois: Business One Irwin, 1990.

Graham, Benjamin. <u>The Intelligent Investor</u>. New York: Harper & Row, 1973.

Hagstrom, Robert G., Jr. <u>The Warren Buffett Way</u>. New York: John Wiley & Sons, 1994.

Hoff, Benjamin. <u>The Tao of Pooh</u>. New York: Penguin Books, 1982.

Ibbotson Associates. <u>Stocks, Bonds, Bills & Inflation 1996 Yearbook</u>. Chicago, Illinois: Ibbotson Associates, 1996.

Ibbotson, Roger G. and Brinson, Gary P. <u>Global Investing</u>. New York: McGraw-Hill, Inc., 1993.

Lederman, Jess and Klein, Robert A. (Editors). <u>Global Asset Allocation</u>. New York: John Wiley & Sons, 1994.

Leuthold, Steven C. <u>The Myths of Inflation and Investing</u>. Chicago: Crain Books, 1980.

Lynch, Peter. <u>Beating the Street</u>. New York: Simon & Schuster, 1993.

Malkiel, Burton G. <u>A Random Walk Down Wall Street</u>. New York: W. W. Norton, 1973, rev. 1991.

O'Higgins, Michael. <u>Beating the Dow</u>. New York: Harper-Perennial, 1992.

O'Shaughnessy, James P. <u>What Works On Wall Street</u>. New York: McGraw-Hill, Inc., 1997.

Rosenberg, Claude N., Jr. <u>Investing with the Best</u>. New York and Toronto: John Wiley & Sons, 1986.

Siegel, Jeremy J. <u>Stocks for the Long Run</u>. Burr Ridge, Illinois: Irwin Professional Publishing, 1994.

<u>The Vanguard Retirement Investing Guide</u>. Chicago: Irwin Professional Publishing, 1995.

Tobias, Andrew. <u>The Only Investment Guide You'll Ever Need</u>. San Diego: Harcourt Brace & Co., 1978, rev. 1996.

Train, John. <u>The Money Masters</u>. New York: Harper & Row, 1985.

Train, John. <u>The New Money Masters</u>. New York: Harper & Row, 1989.

Index